Caring for
CHILDREN

Caring for
CHILDREN

Kate Williams and Ruth Gardner

PITMAN
PUBLISHING

PITMAN PUBLISHING
128 Long Acre, London WC2E 9AN

A Division of Longman Group UK Limited

© Kate Williams and Ruth Gardner 1993

First published in Great Britain 1993
Reprinted 1994

British Library Cataloguing in Publication Data
A catalogue record for this book is available from the British
Library

ISBN 0-273-60088 5

Typeset by Avocet Typesetters, Bicester, Oxon
Printed in England by Clays Ltd, St Ives plc

The
publisher's
policy is to use
paper manufactured
from sustainable forests

Contents

PART 2: CASE STUDIES 59

PART 3: ASSIGNMENTS 109

PART 4: APPENDICES   285

Introduction

How to use this book

The Children Act 1989, in effect since October 1991, has drawn together legislation relating to children previously dispersed through civil, criminal and welfare law into a single cohesive piece of legislation. The effect of this on all people working with children is profound. All providers of services for children – childminders, playgroup supervisors, day nursery staff, providers of specialist services, residential care workers and others – have to meet specific and stringent standards of care.

'Working Together', the guidelines from the Department of Health on the child protection aspects of the Children Act, is an appropriate catchphrase for the changed context for the delivery of quality child care into the 1990s and beyond. All agencies – health, education, police and others – have an explicit duty to work in partnership with each other, and with Local Authority Social Services, who have the lead responsibility. The context of child care itself is also changing as local authorities move towards a 'contract culture' by which providers are expected to specify the precise nature of the services they offer in return for funding in the form of grants and payments.

This book is designed as a core text for tutors and students working with children in this changed context, in initial or in-service training. Its approach is also cohesive and integrated; throughout, specific child care settings are placed in the context of the provisions of the Children Act. Particular activities and wider questions for discussion and debate are designed to promote good practice. With a sound knowledge base as a starting point, activities and assignments are designed to lead to vocational competence in particular areas as well as a broader competence in a multi-disciplinary environment.

The book is relevant to a range of pre-professional courses and training programmes in child care. The mandatory topics in BTEC GNVQ Health and Social Care Level 2 are well resourced, and many activities, as well as the in-depth guide to the Children Act, are appropriate to Level 3. The needs of students of all ages preparing for NVQ accreditation at Levels 1 and 2, are the starting point for many assignments, which are designed to meet the requirements of validating bodies such as City and Guilds. Most assignments and all the Case Studies extend beyond this, and offer material suitable to students working towards NVQ Level 3, such as those taking NNEB courses. The book offers flexibility to the tutor to adapt the material to the needs of students with different levels of experience, whether full or part time, and builds on the approach developed in *A Practical Approach to Caring*.

Part 1: Children in Need provides an up-to-date guide to the Children Act 1989, and shows how the philosophy and practice of child care has changed over the last century. The reader is invited to consider wider issues of policy and practice from a strategic perspective, while gaining a working knowledge of the provisions of this key piece of legislation.

Part 2: Case Studies. These case studies, written from the perspective of different adults responsible for a key area of a child's life, whether as a parent, a playgroup worker, a childminder, residential care worker, invite the reader to respond to the problems and dilemmas faced by people working or living with children day-to-day. While outcomes and activities are realistic and open-ended, the background is set clearly within the context and requirements of the Children Act. The Case Studies reflect many, but by no means all, of the major care settings for children, and the diverse and multicultural nature of our society.

Part 3: Assignments. These assignments – 25 in all – cover those core areas common to all courses in child care, and, through an integrated approach, extend beyond into a number of options areas. Care has been taken to focus the student on practical strategies for working with children; discipline in a group setting; playground bullying; activity programmes, for example.

The assignments vary in difficulty, styles of activity and the degree of support and input the tutor needs to give. The aim is to maintain a balance between classroom-based learning activities, and research activities that take the student out into their own environment. All assignments are resourced so that students can start work on the topic from the text and care has been taken to offer fresh source material.

Within the assignments, there is a balance between a clear knowledge base and the four skill areas that underpin most courses and training programmes:

1 Communications
2 Numeracy
3 Interpersonal skills
4 Problem-solving.

The style of the activities is designed to embrace the range of assessment methods and forms of presentation favoured by the various accreditation bodies, and although it was not felt appropriate to include any particular checklist of competences, the need to demonstrate competence in the workplace is key to all activities. The index is helpful in identifying these; multiple choice, data presentation, group work, letters, order forms, role play, scale drawing, posters etc. The index will also help the tutor to draw up particular work programmes, by identifying relevant or linked activities across a number of assignments.

The book has been written with the needs of three client groups in mind:

- for the **tutor**, a resource providing essential information and an introduction to strategic and professional issues in Part 1; an immediate point of departure for considering the demands of particular care settings, issues and dilemmas in Part 2; flexible and adaptable learning activities in Part 3, and comprehensive indices with integral cross references.
- for the **student**, a structured way of thinking critically about the needs of children and their carers; an accessible information source on the Children Act; a direct and accessible style. *A Practical Approach to Caring* provides complementary guidelines, with a 'How to . . .' reference section and fuller job search skills.
- for the **client**, the child and the family, better quality services, delivered by child care workers who have rehearsed their practical caring skills, and have thought about the implications of what they do and how they do it.

Part 1

CHILDREN IN NEED

Chapter 1

The Children Act 1989

The Children Act 1989 came into effect on 14 October 1991, after a delay to give courts and child care agencies time to prepare for the many changes the new law requires. In fact many of these changes are still under way, and affect everyone with a concern for children – parents, child-care organisations and people caring for children either temporarily or full time. You are likely to be a member of at least one of these groups, so it is worth knowing about the most important messages from the Children Act. The law can seem off-putting, but in fact most of these messages are straightforward.

First, what changes were brought about by the Children Act?

- The Act was based on several years of research, on enquiry reports about particular children's experiences, and on consultation with organisations representing different points of view about children and families. At the end of the day 'it aims to strike a balance between the rights of children to express their views on decisions made about their lives, the rights of parents to exercise their responsibilities towards the child, and the duty of the state to intervene where the child's welfare requires it' (*Guidance & Regulations*, VOLUME 1 (1991), HMSO).
- The Act clearly sets out its principles (basic ideas) and criteria (rules for decisions) about children and families for the first time.
- It also brings together private law (e.g. about divorce) and public law (e.g. about children entering local authority care) and so replaces a variety of previous laws. All these matters are now called family proceedings.

Many official guides and training packs have come with the new legislation, helping people who work with children to adapt their practice to the new law. We are learning that good practice with children and families needs not only a strong legal framework but also:

- clear information for everyone involved on their rights and responsibilities;
- training and preparation in child-care work;
- agencies able and willing to put money into developing new ideas;
- standards for good work with families which are carefully set and then monitored to improve practice.

SELF-CHECK 1 Give in one sentence the meaning of each of these words: rights, responsibilities, principles, criteria, legislation, standards, monitoring, practice.

The following sections consider the principles behind the Act and give some examples from practice and from the Act itself.

1 **Children are best looked after within the family, with support if necessary.**

In practice

- This principle means, for instance, that courts may ask separated parents and relatives such as grandparents to negotiate arrangements about looking after and visiting the children.
- Parents in difficulty have a right to know of services which could help keep the family together, such as day care or respite (temporary) care, and to be involved in decisions.

The Children Act

2 (5) More than one person may have parental responsibility for the same child at the same time.

(For more about parental responsibility *see* p 43.)

17 (1) It shall be the general duty of every local authority:
  (a) to safeguard and promote the welfare of children within their area who are in need; and
  (b) so far as is consistent with that duty, to promote the upbringing of such children by their families, by providing a range and level of services appropriate to those children's needs.

SELF-CHECK 1 The welfare of which children is to be promoted by every local authority, according to s. 17(1) of the Children Act?

2 What do you think 'promote the upbringing of such children by their families' (s. 17(1)) means? How does the Act say local authorities are to do this?

2 **In taking decisions about children, a number of important matters must be taken into account (*see* s. 1(3) below). However, the child's welfare is the paramount consideration, which means that it has the greatest weight.**

In practice

- Where parents have separated they will each want time with their children (contact time) and may not agree as to what is a fair amount for each parent. The welfare principle says that contact must be organised primarily around the needs of children.

- Where a child is likely to have been harmed by a parent, the local authority has to decide whether to remove the child with the welfare principle in mind, as well as the other criteria the court will have to use. The 'no order' criterion in s. 1(5) means that no action should be taken unless it would clearly benefit the child.

The Children Act

1 (1) The child's welfare shall be the court's paramount consideration.
(2) Delay in determining the question is likely to prejudice the welfare of the child.
(3) A court shall have regard in particular to:
  (a) the ascertainable wishes and feelings of the child concerned . . . ;
  (b) his physical, emotional and educational needs;
  (c) the likely effect on him of any change in his circumstances;
  (d) his age, sex, background and any characteristics of his which the court considers relevant;
  (e) any harm which he has suffered or is at risk of suffering;
  (f) how capable each of his parents, and any other person . . . is of meeting his needs;
  (g) the range of powers available to the court under this Act;
(5) A court shall not make the order . . . unless it considers that doing so would be better for the child than making no order at all.

SELF-CHECK

1 Check the meaning of 'ascertainable' in s. 1(3)(a) quoted above. Why do you think this word is put in? How might you ascertain the wishes or feelings of a four year old?

2 Under s. 1(3)(d) what 'other characteristics' of the child do you think might be relevant?

3 Under s. 1(3)(f) what 'other people' might help meet the child's needs if, for example, a parent was very ill?

4 Under s. 1(5) what do you think the 'no order' criterion might have been put in to prevent?

3 Where children are looked after by people other than their parents, special standards must be drawn up.

This is so that children's general welfare and the particular needs of each child are put first when care is provided outside the child's own home.

In practice

- Where children are living in residential homes or with foster carers, regulations apply which set standards. Regular visits by local authority officers must be made.

- Providers of day care such as nurseries, playgroups or childminders must be registered with and inspected by the local authority.
- Local authority officers may also enter public or private nursing homes and independent schools to ensure that a child's welfare is adequately safeguarded and promoted.

The Children Act

22 (3) It shall be the duty of a local authority looking after any child:
   (a) to safeguard and promote his welfare; and
   (b) to make such use of services available for children cared for by their own parents as appears . . . reasonable.

71 (1) Every local authority shall keep a register of:
   (a) persons who act as child minders on domestic premises within the authority's area; and
   (b) persons who provide day care for children under the age of eight on premises (other than domestic premises) within that area.

87 (3) Where accommodation is provided for a child by an independent school within the area of a local authority, the authority shall take such steps as are reasonably practicable to enable them to determine whether the child's welfare is adequately safeguarded and promoted while he is accommodated by the school.

SELF-CHECK

1 List three other services apart from child care where standards are very important. Why do you think standards are important in all these services? Give three ways in which standards can be passed on to workers or staff, and three ways in which practice can be checked to see whether it meets those standards.

2 The local authority is going to inspect a small independent boarding school in your area.
(a) If you were the head, what would you want to know about in advance of this inspection?
(b) If you were the inspector, what would you want to know about the school? How could you find out, first during your visit, and secondly between visits?

4 **Children, parents and other key adults have a right to information and to make their views known about decisions. This includes the right to complain.**

In practice

- Courts must listen to the views of the people mentioned above. A guardian-ad-litem (usually a specialist social worker) can be appointed to represent the child's wishes and interests to the court as well as a solicitor in many cases.

- Parents and people with whom the child has lived have the right to apply to the court to make important decisions. With the court's permission, the child can apply in the same way.
- Local authorities must listen to the views of children, parents and other key adults *before* taking important decisions such as moving the child from his or her parents' home to residential or foster care.
- They should also consult before taking any decisions about a child they are looking after – for instance at case conferences and planning or review meetings.
- Local authorities and voluntary organisations must set up a complaints procedure for children and parents using their services, for foster carers and for other interested persons.

The Children Act

1 (3) Therefore a court shall have regard in particular to:
   (a) The ascertainable wishes and feelings of the child concerned (considered in the light of his age and understanding . . .)

22 (4) Before making any decision with respect to a child whom they are looking after, or proposing to look after, a local authority shall, so far as is reasonably practicable, ascertain the wishes and feelings of:
   (a) the child;
   (b) his parents;
   (c) any person who is not a parent of his but who has parental responsibility for him; and
   (d) any other person whose wishes and feelings the authority consider to be relevant regarding the matter to be decided.

26 (3) Every local authority shall establish a procedure for considering any representations (including any complaint).

SELF-CHECK

1 List two or three times you have had to make a complaint, for example about something you have bought, or had a disagreement, for example where to go for an evening out. How did you make your views known and what was the outcome?

2 List three things that you think make for success in putting your points of view across, and three things that work less well.

ACTIVITY

In a group of two or three, collect as many *guides to services* and *complaints procedures* as you can from local authorities, places of work and libraries. If the guides or complaints procedures are designed for young people, this would be even better.

Take a few of these leaflets each and make some notes as to which are helpful and which less so, and why. Then compare notes, and as a group make a guide or complaints procedure for young people which is as clear and readable as possible, either as a leaflet or as a poster for display.

Chapter 2

Different lives

One hundred years before the Children Act of 1989, the Prevention of Cruelty to Children Act set in motion government legislation to improve the plight of young people in society. Much has improved since 1889, when poverty and attitudes undermined the welfare of children. However, the need for legislation has not lessened; every decade and every century brings with it a need for reform and a range of problems both old and new.

Important child care legislation:

- Prevention of Cruelty to Children 1889
- Children Act 1908
- Children and Young Persons Act 1933
- Children Act 1948
- Children and Young Persons Act 1963
- Children and Young Persons Act 1969
- Children Act 1975
- Child Care Act 1980
- Children and Young Persons (Amendment) Act 1986
- Children Act 1989

Today, as in the nineteenth century, poverty is one of the major factors responsible for the problems faced by families and children in our society.

As it was then

Income and class

A century ago, some of the most striking differences between families were due to income and class. A far larger section of the population survived in very poor conditions.

SELF-CHECK

1 What are the most obvious differences and similarities between the people shown in the photographs overleaf? Look at their faces, dress and background. What do you conclude about their class, income and standard of living?

Courtesy: The Children's Society

Courtesy: The Children's Society

Courtesy: G A Clark ARPS

Health and diet The similarities may be striking but certainly, in the nineteenth century, the amount families could spend on food was less, and as a result their health was poorer.

Milk was often dirty and carried tuberculosis, or else had been adulterated, as had butter, to make it last longer. However, by the early years of the twentieth century, output of dairy foods had increased greatly. After 1900 the practice of boiling milk spread and the Board of Agriculture instituted minimum legal standards for the quality of milk in 1901.

These changes and the availability of potatoes meant that even the poorest families with an income under 20 shillings a week seem to have been eating better. However, the calorie intake for working people was still about one third lower than present standards at about 1,200 to 2,000, and it must be remembered that work hours were often much longer and the work itself gruelling.

Mortality rates, both for mothers in childbirth and for babies, were far higher then. The life expectancy of poorer people was shorter because of poorer diet and health.

> The death rate was high, but was possibly less than we might expect. There are no official figures before the mid-1860s and thereafter the kinds of under-reporting that I have described earlier particularly apply. In 1865, 39 London workhouses reported 2,728 cases of childbirth, with 16 deaths, concentrated in nine of the workhouses. Over all the rate equals 6 per 1,000, or about equal to the reported rate of the British Lying-in Hospital for 1849–61, at 7 per 1,000, but much below the 40 per 1,000 rate for 1857 to 1863 at Queen Charlotte's, the hospital which admitted single women. But the workhouse rate is almost twice the death rate for the outdoor midwifery department of St George's Hospital for 1853–63, at 3.5 per 1,000. The Liverpool Workhouse Hospital had a notably good record from the 1860s. Two-thirds of its intake were single women, and about half were primiparae. In the late 1860s the maternal death rate was about 4 per 1,000, that is below the national average, almost the same as in the 1890s. But Liverpool led the country in having trainee obstetric nurses, fully trained midwives and monthly nurses for post-natal care. The Liverpool figures were probably exceptionally good also because the guardians were unusually generous with orders for outdoor deliveries managed by closely supervised midwives. The workhouse at Brighton, newly built in the 1860s, with similar proportions of single primiparae mothers, and similar generous administration, also claimed exceptionally good results: only one death among 223 confinements between 1862 and 1868.
>
> **Stability and Change in the Maternal Death Rate**
> This survey of the evidence about maternity practices and maternal death rates suggests three general conclusions. First a woman and her infant did best if the birth was managed outside a hospital. Second, mother and child were safest, if the birth was a normal one, with a midwife; and if not, they were in grave danger. Midwives carried less infection with them, doctors brought instruments that in the last resort could save life.

9

Table 1.1: Mean Annual Death Rate per 1000, 1881–90

	'Puerperal fever'	'Accidents'	Total
England and Wales	2.59	2.13	4.73
London	2.44	1.53	3.91
Manchester	3.13	2.06	5.20
North Wales – counties	3.25	3.47	6.73
South-west England – counties	2.05	2.32	4.36

Source: Dr Thursfield, *Lancet*, 7 January 1893, p. 21; *Parliamentary Papers*, 1884–5, vol. XVII, p. lxxiv.

(Source: F. B. Smith *The People's Health 1830–1910*, Weidenfeld & Nicolson, 1990)

SELF-CHECK

1 Make a list of maternal death rates from lowest to highest (a) by region; (b) by specific place of birth. Comment on the differences.

2 Find out the meaning of the following terms given in the passage: obstetric nurse, primiparae, puerperal fever, post-natal infection.

3 What was the safest way to give birth at that time? Why do you think this was so?

4 Why do you think the rates for the workhouse and hospitals admitting single women were so high?

Getting help

At the turn of the century, any help needed by poor families was given only after careful consideration of whether they deserved it and could make use of it.

Towards the turn of the century, chidren whose parents' 'habits of modes of life' were considered to make them 'unfit', could be permanently removed from their families. Adoption was not in use until later in the twentieth century; these children were either 'boarded out' (fostered) with families in this country or overseas – many in Canada and Australia – or else brought up in large children's homes and then apprenticed out. As today, it depended very much on the particular foster family or children's home, and whether carers were supported and supervised, as to how happy or miserable children were.

SELF-CHECK

1 Why do you think single parenthood was thought to be so wrong?

Because of the higher birth and mortality rates, families were likely to be larger (on average, about four children in the late nineteenth century) but many families, particularly poorer ones, had lost at least one child in birth or infancy. It was not uncommon for children to lose their mother while she was still a young woman, and far less common than it is today for children to know their grandparents throughout their childhood.

ACTIVITY

1 How many calories are needed daily by (a) a working man; (b) a pregnant woman?

2 Today the concern is more with the nature of the diet than with ensuring adequate calories. What are the particular dietary needs of (a) a manual labourer; (b) a pregnant mother; (c) a child under 5 years old?

3 Talk to older people in your family — your grandparents or great-grandparents if possible — about the things they did as children, what they wore, their diet, and how they obtained health care or support if someone was out of work for instance. Try to get a clear picture of when this was.

Your parents and grandparents may have lived, or still live, in other countries. Find out what you can about ways of life in the country where they live, paying particular attention to children's lifestyles.

Then compare notes with a friend or another student, and collect research material on your family going back to the turn of the century; this may be difficult but you will almost certainly find some stories, photographs or even family possessions which are from that period. Write a brief account of what you have found out and share this with your partner.

NOTE *There is more on food and diet in Assignments 19 and 20 of* A Practical Approach to Caring *(Pitman 1991) by Kate Williams. Assignment 16 of the present text also covers food for children.*

As it is now

What has changed since then?

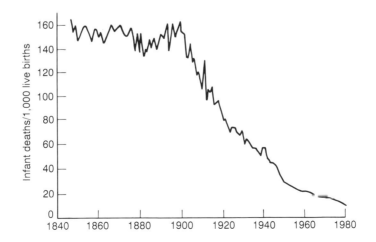

Infant mortality 1846–1981
Source: Figure 5.2 in A H Halsey, *Change in British Society* OUP 1988

11

SELF-CHECK

SELF-CHECK   1   Describe the changes in infant mortality before 1900 and after 1900.

2   What do you think the 'peaks' in the graph might represent?

The mortality rate for women in childbirth has also reduced greatly. The number of children in *all* families (not just better-off ones) became smaller and parents could usually choose the timing of parenthood.

> Working men returning from the first war had to accommodate to wives who had acquired a more independent outlook, had worked and run a home unaided. Literacy, the wireless and cinema opened up new horizons . . . after the second war, hours of work were reduced, holidays lengthened, home-ownership more common, children less ever-present, and men drawn into a more intimate and longer spousehood than their predecessors had ever known.
>
> (Source: A. H. Halsey *Change in British Society*, Oxford University Press, 1988)

SELF-CHECK   1   What does this passage tell you about change in the roles of women and men in family life during this century?

2   What different choices about family life and work have been opened up? List the possible *gains* and *problems* for (a) women; (b) men; (c) children.

Attitudes and judgements

Families take many different forms – this has always been the case. Only now, as the Children Act 1989 asserts, do we regard different kinds of family as of *equal value*:

> Patterns of family life differ according to culture, class and community and these differences should be respected and accepted. There is no one, perfect way to bring up children and care must be taken to avoid judgements and stereotyping.
>
> (Source: *The Care of Children: Principles and Practice*, HMSO, 1990)

However, you will notice that the 'typical' families you see on television and in advertisements are much more similar to one another than those you see out shopping for instance, just as 'typical' models have a similar shape instead of the many different shapes of ordinary women! These 'ideal' images of individuals and families are meant to attract us to the products they are seen to use, by making us feel 'inadequate' unless we possess the same things. But they can also just be depressing.

We also get contradictory messages about families from those in government. On the one hand:

> It is important in a free society to maintain the rich diversity of lifestyles

which is secured by permitting families a large measure of autonomy in the way they bring up their children.

Source: *Review of Child Care Law*, HMSO, 1985)

On the other hand, mothers who leave small children in day care to go out to work – and of course many single parents have no choice – have been severely criticised in recent years. Even *within* the Children Act 1989, certain types of family do not have equal status. For example, if you look at the definition of parental responsibility, unmarried fathers do not have this status legally, although they are still legally obliged to maintain their children, and the mother may not receive state benefit unless they do so. Another example is the guidance on selection of foster parents which states: 'It would be wrong arbitrarily to exclude any particular groups of people from consideration but the chosen way of life of some adults may mean that they would not be able to provide a suitable environment for the care and nurture of a child.'

Here is a summary of research findings on children's development in different kinds of families:

Research findings have shown consistently that children in single-parent families function more adequately than children in two-parent but conflict-ridden families. Again, the sheer number of parents present in the home does not tell us everything about the conditions that promote a child's well-being. It is clearly necessary to take note of the great changes that have taken place in recent decades in traditional family structure and not base action on what is now in some respects an outdated model. This will be a recurrent theme for us, but it is particularly well illustrated by what is one of the more extreme deviations from the norm, namely children reared by lesbian couples. As we saw, there is no evidence that the sex-role development of such children (or, for that matter, other aspects of psychological functioning) is thereby adversely affected. It is true that as long as this type of household is a relatively rare social phenomenon its unconventional status may have indirect consequences for the child by, for instance, being teased or even ostracized by other children. However, this again shows that it is people's attitudes to particular forms of families rather than those forms themselves that are the operative factor.

(Source: H. R. Schaffer, *Making Decisions about Children*, Basil Blackwell, 1990)

SELF-CHECK

1 Look up and add to your list the meaning of the words traditional, deviations, norm, functioning, unconventional, ostracized.

2 Are there modes of life or lifestyles which *you* think would *not* be a suitable environment for a child? What are they? Why do you hold this view? Do you think the government should say what types of family are suitable or not?

3 What kind of families do you think are most damaging to children? Do

13

you think a child from an unconventional family is in as much danger as a child with a potentially violent father?

Despite some internal contradictions, a strong message in the Children Act and supporting documents is that people working with families and children should be aware of any *value judgements* they may carry around. We all have them – they may be the views of our parents which we have never questioned; they may be prejudice or sincere beliefs. Commonly we do not have a rational basis for these judgements, and they are often contradictory, for instance:

'I don't think that children can ever grow up right without a father, do you?'

'I don't think a man should be allowed to bring up girls on his own – it's not natural.'

ACTIVITY

Interview three people of different ages, one a teenager, another a parent of teenagers, and a third, older person. Ask them separately to complete these sentences with examples:

A good daughter is someone who . . . .
A bad daughter is someone who . . . .

A good son is someone who . . . .
A bad son is someone who . . . .

A good father is someone who . . . .
A bad father is someone who . . . .

A good mother is someone who . . . .
A bad mother is someone who . . . .

Then compare the answers and list the differences and similarities. Which answers are most reasonable, do you think, and why? Do some answers reveal strong beliefs or prejudices, and what makes you think so?

We may think that some parents' behaviour is harmful to their children – for instance, many people believe that you should never smack a child. However, the Children Act 1989 says that discipline is the parents' business and the state cannot intervene without strong evidence that harm to the child's health and development has happened or is likely to, and that the parents' care is not 'what it would be reasonable to expect a parent to give'. This is sometimes a difficult borderline to judge.

Movement in families

Not only are children brought up in many different cultures, but individual families change over time. Within a few years a young couple can become a family, or parents may split up and remarry so that several new families with step-brothers and step-sisters may be formed.

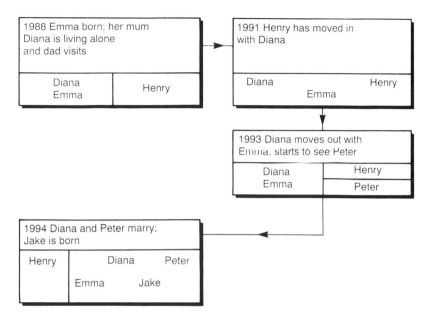

Movement in families

The Children Act 1989 tries to recognise the variety and movement in family patterns in a number of ways. Unmarried parents can reach a formal agreement to share parental responsibility, without going to court. Whenever decisions are made which might lead to a child or children being separated from the family even for a short while, then not only the parents but other relatives and important adults (perhaps, for instance, a neighbour the child has stayed with) *must* be consulted. Where the family members or other carers cannot agree, the court can make orders which set out what is going to happen.

**Children Act 1989
Part II**

Orders with respect to children in family proceedings:

8 (1) In this Act:

‘a contact order’ means an order requiring the person with whom a child lives, or is to live, to allow the child to visit or stay with the person named in the order, or for that person and the child otherwise to have contact with each other;

‘a prohibited steps order’ means an order that no step which could be taken by a parent in meeting his parental responsibilities for a child, and which is of a kind specified in the order, shall be taken by any person without the consent of the court;

15

'a residence order' means an order settling the arrangements to be made as to the person with whom a child is to live; and

'a specific issues order' means an order giving directions for the purpose of determining a specific question which has arisen, or which may arise, in connection with any aspect of parental responsibility for a child.

Certain people have a right to apply for orders – for instance, if the child has lived with them; others, for instance a young person, can ask the court for permission to apply.

Working it out

1   When Diana marries Peter in the scenario above, Emma's father decides that he wants parental responsibility for Emma and a contact order. He doesn't want to remove Emma from her mother, but as he does not get on with Peter, he wants to make sure he will be able to see his daughter. The contact order sets out his visiting contact once a fortnight.

2   Marcus and Dionne are divorced and the children are living with Dionne. Both parents have parental responsibility, and Marcus has contact with his children every other weekend at his mother's address. Dione does not want Marcus to collect the children from school, as he has kept them out late in the past; they have come home over-tired and she has been very anxious. The prohibited steps order tells Marcus that he cannot exercise his parental responsibility in this way. The school has a copy of the order.

3   David's mother, Julia, has admitted to hitting him too hard and bruising him badly. She is very depressed and has not been attending the Family Centre. The local authority has an emergency protection order and has applied to the court for a care order, but Julia's mother wants to look after David until Julia can be treated for her depression. The court agrees and makes a residence order saying that David will live with his grandmother for six months, and a family assistance order instructing the local authority to supply a social worker to the family.

4   Michael and Rose are foster parents who have a residence order with respect to Pamela. They thus share parental responsibility with Pamela's mother and father, who see her from time to time. Pamela is shortly to go to a boarding school and her mother has asked the school to speak first to her about any problems which arise. Rose is unhappy with this and wants the court to make a specific issues order confirming that she is the person who deals with Pamela's education and the school. The order asks the school to send copies of all reports to Pamela's mother, but otherwise to deal with Rose. The school has a copy of the order.

SELF-CHECK I List the various court orders mentioned here and what you think they are for. Use the index to locate other information about courts and court orders.

Chapter 3

Families needing support

As it was then

The economists of the Charity Organization Society had in their journal in the 1870s the equivalent of the modern weeklies' competitions. The 'Difficult Cases' clues were printed one week and readers' solutions the following week. 'CD's' case is typical and 'AGC's' response provides an insight into the COS mentality: not unkind, but involved 'cases' which threatened waste and social dislocation, not human beings in need; contriving 'solutions' which perverted the ostensible aim of the exercise by building fantasies of 'independence' for their producer while imposing control and conformity on the 'object'. The game was to save the case, or at least the case's family, from indiscriminate charity and if possible from pauperism:

> CD, aged 51, is a ropemaker with four children six months to nine years. Wife aged 40, earns 8-10/- a week – washing. Husband's sight has been gradually failing over last four years – finally had to give up work completely eight months ago – medical certificate says optic nerve is failing and there is no hope – He used formerly to belong to his Trade Club – No relatives able to assist – would it be worth the family moving to Hampstead, instead of their present 'low neighbourhood' where more washing is available?

'AGC' gave the fullest answer. The case was a knotty one and 'AGC' was somewhat defeatist:

> it does not seem to me to be a case for a pension. First, it seems to me that unless there are other circumstances of providence and desert besides that of the man having belonged to his trade club, the case should be dealt with by the guardians. The man should enter the infirmary, whence he might be removed to a blind asylum when eligible, at the expense of the rates, and that number of the children which the wife cannot maintain should be taken into the District schools. Ropemakers are not usually of a sufficiently high class to have any fair objection to such a mode of assistance.

(Source: F. B. Smith *The People's Health 1830–1910*, Weidenfeld & Nicolson, 1990)

ACTIVITY

1 Having read the passage do you think CD and his family 'deserve' help? What attitudes would be different today from those in the 1870s when this passage was written?

2 Read the passage describing CD and his family again. What was their situation four years ago? What has changed in the family in those four years and what have the couple done in the way of 'self-help' – what are *they* suggesting as an answer? Write down your answers.

3 Then read the solution put forward by AGC, who visited such families on behalf of the Board of Guardians. What do 'providence' and 'desert' mean? Can you think of anything that would have made this family appear more 'providential' or 'deserving'? What would AGC's solution mean for this man, his wife and his four children?

4 What does the last sentence tell you about AGC's attitude and values and how they affect her or his professional judgements?

5 Write down briefly what this passage tells you about the good and bad aspects of early attempts to provide family support.

There appears to have been little intentional ill-treatment, but workhouse life was pervaded by a painful austerity exemplified in systematic stinting of clothes, food, warmth and affection. The pervasive smell was a mingling of sour potato and stale urine, the prevailing noise a mingling of intermittent groans, oaths and screams from the idiots, the howling of babies, syncopated by the clinking keys carried by the matron and taskmasters. Everybody in the Poplar Workhouse, except the bedridden, had to rise at 5.45 a.m. in summer and 6.45 a.m. in winter. Breakfast was at 6.30 a.m. in summer, 7.30 a.m. in winter. Dinner was at 12 noon and supper at 6 p.m. There was nothing in between. Meat was served to everybody although 'many [could] not masticate it'. Everybody also received 14 ounces of suet each day. There were no vegetables except potatoes and onions. The doctor never remarked on the diet except occasionally to order beer or stout. He did 'not like to inconvenience the cook'. The meal was badly cooked. The tea was always stewed. Friends were permitted to visit on one Monday in every month. The meeting was supervised. The inmates had no flannel underclothes, only cotton, through winter and summer. They had one thin coat each. There were no overcoats in winter.

(Source: F. B. Smith, *The People's Health 1830–1910*, Weidenfeld & Nicolson, 1990)

SELF-CHECK

From this description of the workhouse in 1892:

1 What range of people are living there?

2 What might be some of the reasons why they have to live there?

3 Why do you think that the 'social services' of the day were made to feel like punishment?

Sidney Webb wrote in 1889:

> The 'practical man', oblivious or contemptuous of any theory of the Social Organism or general principles of social organization, has been forced by the necessities of the time, into an ever deepening collectivist channel. Socialism, of course, he still reject and despises. The individualist Town Councillor will walk along the municipal pavement, lit by municipal gas and cleansed by municipal brooms with municipal water, and seeing by the municipal clock in the municipal market that he is too early to meet his children coming from the municipal school hard by the county lunatic asylum and municipal hospital, will use the national telegraph system to tell them not to walk through the municipal park but to come by the municipal tramway, to meet him in the municipal reading room by the municipal art gallery, museum and library, where he intends to consult some of the national publications in order to prepare his next speech in the municipal town hall, in favour of the nationalization of the canals and the increase of the government control over the railway system. 'Socialism, sir', he will say, 'don't waste the time of a practical man by your fantastic absurdities. Self-help sir, individual self-help, that's what's made our city what it is.'
>
> (Source: E. Butterworth and R. Holman, (eds), *Social Welfare in Modern Britain*, Fontana/Collins, 1975)

SELF-CHECK

1 Write a definition of each of the following terms in one sentence. Look them up in a dictionary first if you need to: collectivist, socialism, individualist, municipal, nationalisation, self-help.

2 Divide your page into three columns. On the left, list the municipal services Webb mentions as existing in 1889. In the middle column, say whether they exist now; in the right column enter who owns or provides the service.

3 What is the ordinary person's attitude in 1889 to (a) 'self-help' and (b) socialism, according to Webb? What do you think is Webb's attitude?

4 Write two short paragraphs comparing public services in 1889 with public services today. In one point out the similarities, in the other the differences.

Unless the family enjoyed good health and income, life for children born before the turn of the century was extremely risky. Although without birth control the birth rate was higher, so was the mortality rate in childbirth and infancy, with infectious diseases such as diphtheria still rife.

Before the introduction of antiseptics on a wide scale, doctors and nurses could carry infection from family to family unless their hygiene was excellent. So, even if poor families could afford a doctor, they often felt he would be of little use. As we have seen, poor diet often contributed to ill-health, but parents who found that they simply could not afford to feed their children faced desperate decisions. They might send older children out to beg, steal or borrow; they might, depending on the generosity and the judgements of the local Board of Guardians of the Poor, receive some 'Outdoor Relief' or charity. The Charity Organisation Society was set up in the late nineteenth century so that Guardians and others visiting the poor could plan their work better; these were the first social workers. Without charity, some families might be forced to enter the workhouse. Here men, women and children were separated and performed menial work. The place was synonymous with the loss of health and hope for most poor people.

As it is now

We are used to seeing children on television who are trying to survive without enough food, or in inhumane surroundings, or both; it is difficult for us to realise that children also starved and were worked to death in this country in the last century. We also see contemporary children, on the Children In Need appeal for instance, some of whom desperately need medical treatment or some specialised equipment to ensure a better chance of enjoying and making use of life. In the UK, it is these needs about which politicians and others argue – should the state pay to meet them out of taxation? Should people with needs depend on asking for charity? It is important to remember that children depend almost completely on adults to meet their needs.

ACTIVITY

Working on your own, make a list of a child's physical, emotional and environmental needs in the UK today. Mark them E essential, D desirable or B a bonus. In the next column note the people involved in meeting that need. When you have finished, compare your list with a partner's, and discuss any differences. What could you each do without or not do without, and why?

Most of us, adults and children, are in fact dependent on many people to meet our needs. Whose needs, if any, are not being met in the following situations, and what might help?

- A young mother has split up from her boyfriend. She is crying a lot. Her baby boy is 9 months old and her crying upsets him. He won't sleep so easily and his mum is getting very tired.

- A family who speak little English come to the neighbourhood and the children aged 5 and 7 go to the local playground. Some children want to play with them, but a boy of 12 tells the newcomers to go away and threatens the other children if they don't agree. There is no other play area.
- A young mother wants to take a language course in Switzerland. Her husband is an executive and often abroad. She asks the nanny to come with her and look after the children full time. She sees the children for half an hour after breakfast and kisses them goodnight.

SELF-CHECK   Read the article 'Why the poor are getting poorer' opposite.

1   In what ways does family income affect the needs of children you listed earlier?

2   Taking the income of £90.00 p.w. after housing costs for a family of two adults and two children under 11, cross off the items on your list of needs which could no longer be met.

3   What are the current rates of income support for the four groups of people listed here?

What does the law say?

The Children Act 1989, s. 17, defines *need* so that local authorities know whom they have a legal duty to help:

Part III Local authority support for children and families
Provision of services for children in need, their families and others

17   (1)   It shall be the general duty of every local authority (in addition to the other duties imposed on them by this Part):
    (a)   to safeguard and promote the welfare of children within their area who are in need; and
    (b)   so far as is consistent with that duty, to promote the upbringing of such children by their families, by providing a range and level of services appropriate to those children's needs . . .
    (10)   . . . a child shall be taken to be in need if:
    (a)   he is unlikely to achieve or maintain, or have the opportunity of achieving or maintaining, a reasonable standard of health or development without the provision for him of services by a local authority;
    (b)   his health or development is likely to be significantly impaired, or further impaired, without the provision for him of such services; and
    (c)   he is disabled.
    (11)   . . . 'development' means physical, intellectual, emotional, social or behavioural development; and 'health' means physical or mental health.

WHY THE POOR ARE GETTING POORER

Families, Unemployed people, Young people, Students, Low paid, Old people, Disabled people

FAMILIES 1988–90. Child benefit frozen for three years running to 1980, with a loss of £1.35 per week per child.

1986. Single payments replaced by social fund loans. Repayments deducted at source from weekly benefit. If the loan fund has run dry, or the claimant is considered too poor to repay it, these loans are refused.

1986. Family income supplement (FIS) replaced by family credit (FC). Although more people are entitled to FC than FIS, only half the families entitled to it claimed it in 1988/89. FC rates in some instances are higher than FIS rates but the increase was swallowed up by cuts in housing benefit and mortgage interest payments to people in work. Half a million children lost the right to free school meals when it was introduced.

1986. Income support replaces supplementary benefit, cutting the incomes of 80 per cent of couples with children and 74 per cent of lone parents, according to the CPAG.

1991. Child Support Act which would penalise lone parent families where "parent with care" refuses to co-operate in pursuing other parent for maintenance unless doing so would cause her or her children "harm or undue distress", with the burden of proof on the claimant. For the first six months these lone parents will have £8 a week docked off their benefit and then £4 a week for the next 12 months. The act will be implemented in April 1993.

Local authority cuts and privatisation have meant services in kind to families – nursery places, school meals, public transport, leisure facilities – have all become more expensive. Local authorities are no longer allowed to provide free school meals to any children except those whose parents are receiving income support.

UNEMPLOYED PEOPLE Official unemployment rose from one million in 1979 to three million in 1986 and now stands at 2.5 million. The Unemployment Unit's total, estimated on the pre-1979 basis is 3,609,400. There have been 30 changes in compiling the figures since 1979.

1982. Earnings related supplement to unemployment benefit abolished.

1984. Children's additions for unemployment benefit abolished.

Disqualification period from unemployment benefit if you are "voluntary unemployed", ie you left your job or were dismissed for misconduct, has increased from six weeks to a maximum of six months. During that period your income support personal allowance is cut by 40 per cent, or 20 per cent on certain prescribed hardship grounds.

John Major, as social security minister, cut benefit for mortgage interest payments by 50 per cent for first six months of claim.

1989. Social Security Act requires claimants to show they are "actively seeking work". More than 15,000 claimants were sent warning letters about this in the six months to March 1991, and nearly 2,000 had their benefit suspended. Adjudication officers then allowed the appeals of 1,471 against the decision.

YOUNG PEOPLE Young people aged 16 and 17 barred from receiving income support unless they were on a youth training place. After evidence of widespread youth destitution, government made exceptions for some cases of "immediate severe hardship". The saving to the government of cutting young people's benefit was £88m. The hardship concessions cost £4m.

A comparison of claimants' income with average weekly expenditure for all households

	Weekly income support rate (after housing costs) 1990/91	Average weekly expenditure for all households (excl net weekly housing costs) 1989
Single person under 25	£28.80	£120.81 (man) £102.94 (woman)
Single person over 25 (non pensioner)	£35.70	£120.81 (man) £102.94 (woman)
Couple	£57.60	£163.56
Couple with 2 children under 11	£82.30	£187.06

1. Family Expenditure Survey does not provide separate expenditure figures for those above and below the age of 25. The figures given relate to all non-retired single people.

(Source: F Rickford, 'Poor show', in *Social Work Today*, 6 February 1992)

SELF-CHECK   1   Refer back to your list of 'children's needs'. Which of them do you think would bring a child within this definition?

The local authority also has a duty (Schedule 2) to:

(*a*)   find out about children in need in their area;
(*b*)   publish information about services;
(*c*)   make sure people who might benefit have the information they need;
(*d*)   keep a register of children with disabilities.

ACTIVITY   Look up your local council in the telephone book, and list the major departments. Find out which department provides each of the services you listed as being currently provided by the local authority in your work on the Sidney Webb extract on p 20. You may find it helpful to draw a 'family tree' of local authority services. (An example is given on p 23 of the companion text to this book, *A Practical Approach to Caring* by Kate Williams (1991, Pitman Publishing).)

Below are two tables showing the results of a survey of thirty local authorities. Table 1 shows what they regard as priorities in assessing and meeting need. Table 2 shows which services they are actually providing. Study the tables carefully and, after discussion, answer the questions that follow.

TABLE 1   Priority perceptions of assessment of individual need and general service development

	Regarded as high priority in assessing individual need	Regarded as high priority in general service development
Children at risk of child abuse, neglect	30	27
Children in care	30	26
Children with disabilities	29	28
Children accommodated under s. 20	28	26
Children placed out of borough (independent home/foster carer)	27	27
Young people on remand	24	19
Children and young people who have been in care/accommodated	21	29
Refugee children	18	19
Young people in bed and breakfast	17	19
Young people in the penal system	17	22
Young people at risk of involvement in criminal activity	15	22
Children with special educational needs	15	18
Carers with mental illness	15	12

Children under 8	14	28
Black and ethnic minority families	15	22
Homeless families	14	17
Carers with disabilities	13	14
Families in bed and breakfast	1	19
Children with special health needs	11	14
Families whose gas or electricity has been disconnected	11	10
Adopted children	11	16
Children/families with English as a foreign language	11	17
Private foster children	8	12
Unemployed parents	8	6
One parent families	5	8
Families on income support/family credit	4	8
Children in independent schools	2	8
Children in hospital more than three months	2	9
Children on supervision orders	1	0

It needs to be borne in mind, when reading these figures, that the questionnaire design took as given that the strategy of prioritising laid out in Volume 2 of the *Guidance*, had been accepted by local authorities. However, some authorities may have had a more extensive debate about the approach they should adopt in doing this, and whether indeed, priorities should be set at all.

(Source: *Capitalising on the Act*, Social Services Inspectorate, London, 1992)

TABLE 2   Family support services

Type of service	Number of local authorities providing it
Child protection services	30
Advice/guidance counselling to parents	30
Advice/guidance counselling to children with disabilities and parents	30
Foster care for children looked after	30
Advice and assistance for young people ceasing to be looked after	29
Reviews and representations	29
Help with travel and transport where needed	28
Residential accommodation for children looked after	26
Day nurseries	24
Accommodation for children on remand	24
Residential accommodation for children with disabilities	23
Help to enable child and family to have a holiday	23
Family centres	21
Accommodation for young people ceasing to be looked after	17
Supervised activities	14
Out-of-school care	12
Education for children looked after who are not attending day school	8

The vast majority of departments provided most of the services, with the least amount of provision in the areas of out of school care, and supervised activities. The nearest to 'blanket provision' was in the areas of child protection; advice, guidance, counselling to parents/general; advice, guidance, counselling to children with disabilities and parents; and foster care for children looked after.

(Source: *Capitalising on the Act*, Social Services Inspectorate, London, 1992)

SELF-CHECK   On Table 1:

1   What do you see as the difference between 'High priority in assessing individual need' and 'High priority in general service development'? In what circumstances might one have a high priority and the other not?

2   If you were responsible for setting priorities for assessing an individual's needs for social and health services, which ten circumstances would you place as top priorities and which ten as bottom? Continue your discussion until you reach agreement, and explain your reasons for each one.

3   The paragraph at the foot of this table says that some authorities do not want to put family needs in order of priority in this way. What do you think are the advantages and disadvantages of a priority list for (a) the families; (b) the local authority.

On Tables 1 and 2:

1   Taking each of either your top ten priorities or the top ten in Table 1 in turn, look at Table 2 to see what services are available to each group. Write your client group as a heading and below each list the services available. Finally, comment on the extent to which individuals with needs can be offered a choice of services.

2   Look down both tables, and note which circumstances and services need to be approached by joint work by the relevant agencies: social and health services; social services and housing; social services and education.

3   Find out about (a) family support services and (b) how priorities are decided by the local authority in your area. If you write a letter to the Director of Social Services or the Head of Children's Services, make sure only one copy is sent after consulting your tutor.

In the work you have done on this section, you will have gained an insight into some of the problems experienced by people who work to provide services to children and families in every local authority. The Children Act calls for services 'appropriate to children's needs in the area', but who decides what these needs are? Which needs are greater? How do you measure need? Is it worth spending money on preventative services such as holidays and after-school care, or should the local authority concentrate on acute needs in child care and child protection?

All resources cost money, and this has to come from local taxpayers or central government. In recent years, the ability of local authorities to raise money to cover services they particularly value has been reduced by central government's determination to control and reduce all public spending. So now the discussion has to be more sharply focused on priorities, which means winners and losers – and some very difficult decisions, as you will have discovered.

Local authorities are having to provide these services in the context of very rapid change in their own organisation. Many services have a number of actual or possible providers, and the government is keen to promote a 'mixed economy' of these. Many local authorities are reorganising so that assessment of need and purchase of services is separated from the providers of services. One arm becomes the **purchaser** with the job of looking for – and paying for – the best services at the right price for individuals in need. The other arm is the **provider**, running the services which will compete with services offered by other providers. In day care for young children, for example, nurseries are provided by social services and education departments in the local authority, and by private and voluntary groups.

ACTIVITY

Given the definition of need in the Act, which of the following people might help the local authority to understand the needs of children under 8 living on a particular estate, and in what ways?

Policeman	General practitioner
Children	Social security officer
Housing officer	Nursery nurse
Psychologist	Playgroup leader
Health visitor	Parents
Pensioners	Shopkeepers
School doctor	Hospital specialist
Imam	Priest

Though most people will go to Social Services for help, the Act lays a *corporate* duty on all local authority departments.

Chapter 4

Race, religion and culture

Racial attitudes among children are environmentally induced, not genetically carried. Yasmin Alibhai looks at one day nursery's attempts to show under-fives how to be colour conscious in a positive sense

Not a shade too soon

YOUNG children are considered incapable of racial attitudes. Yet many black parents know better. Many black children suffer identity crises – denying their families, languages and food. Parental efforts to encourage cultural pride are eroded by overwhelming outside forces.

This was recognised in 1952 by the American anthropologist Mary Ellen Goodman who wrote "White over brown is the most comprehensive idea to which our children are exposed. The idea pervades like a creeping fog." The fog has not yet lifted according to Jane Lane, education officer at the Commission for Racial Equality. "In our society, white is seen as the norm. Consequently black is considered something less worthy – seen as a deviation," she says.

Social psychologist David Milner's research into the effects of this shows that "from about three and a half, children can see the differences between black and white people and know that we value them differently, that there is a pecking order, and white is higher than black."

Racial attitudes among children are environmentally induced and not genetically carried, and a recognition of this has led policy makers, including the DHSS, to re-think their under-fives provision. It is, however, those at the sharp end – nursery workers – who are initiating the most dynamic changes. The Aylesbury day nursery in Camberwell is unaplogetically anti-

sexist and anti-racist. When Norma Niccol, officer-in-charge, first arrived from Nottingham, she found a nursery "which parents ran in and out of, totally insensitive to the needs of the mixed community it served, with all the stereotypes of black people, that they mug and steal, reinforced throughout. The parents were being hurt and the children were being damaged."

For Norma and her deputy, Lucy, the anger they felt fuelled them into action. Norma made her office into the parents' room, to give them the status of joint carers. Initially, one parent came. Now it is difficult to distinguish between the parents and the workers.

Next came changes to the "totally white world": they brought in Building Blocks, a Save . the Children's Fund training project to help under-fives workers give equal prominence and value to all cultural identities.

"It's not just the diet of Goldilocks and Cinderella, but books like the Ugly Duckling," says Lucy. "Think of the implications. Children are actually learning that looking a certain way is wrong." Other changes were simple – paints for different skin colours, different musical instruments, foods. That week the children had been to a Chinese restaurant and to Soho. They are encouarged to look at themselves and talk about the way they look and feel.

"All we are doing," says Lucy, "is giving every child, black and white,

a positive self-identity. How can anyone quarrel with that?"

Sue, a white mother with four children whose father is Jamaican, sees dramatic developments in her younger children who attend Aylesbury.

"The two older ones used to say to me: I want to be white like you. My third son is so confident that when someone calls him nigger, he knows that it is that person who is stupid."

Avril Francis and Audrey Bobb, black workers at the nursery also see results, though they understand there is a long way to go. They approve of children talking openly about race and feel it gives black children strength.

"Their defences against insults are bound to be better if they like themselves better." Yet some black parents express suspicion. Lucy has been accused of being a middle class do-gooder. But the waiting list for transfers to the nursery is growing.

There aren't many peaceful times at Aylesbury. Norma and Lucy agonise, argue, and talk endlessly, and fight on. They have created a nursery where they recognise they have the power to influence future generations. A visitor from New Zealand said "This place is streets ahead of most other nurseries. That is the pity. It should be commonplace."

The Aylesbury Day Nursery is at Dawes Street, London SE17 (01-703 6440).

(Taken from *The Guardian*, 24 November 1986)

SELF-CHECK 1 Why did the new officer in charge decide to use materials and activities relevant to different cultures and backgrounds?

2 What changes occurred in this nursery? List any other good ideas you can think of.

3 What were the results of these changes? What benefits and what difficulties do you think arise?

The Children Act 1989

The Children Act means that everyone working with children must look critically at their practice for ways of taking account of children's 'religious persuasion, racial origin and cultural and linguistic background'.

- **Section 3**. Courts must take decisions with several factors in mind including the child's age, sex, background and any characteristics of his which the court considers relevant.

  The court should have very full information as to the child's religion, race and background and how these will influence the decisions to be made.
- **Schedule 2(8)**. Cultural activities should be provided for children in need living with their families, and at family centres.
- **Schedule 2(11)**. Local authorities must have regard to the different racial groups to which children within their area belong when providing day care or recruiting foster parents.
- **Section 74(1), (6)**. A local authority can cancel the registration of a provider of day care if the care is seriously inadequate in meeting the child's needs. In considering this step they must in particular have regard to the child's religious persuasion, racial origin and cultural and linguistic background.
- **Section 22(5)**. When taking any decision about a child they are looking after, or proposing to look after, a local authority must give due consideration to the child's wishes and those of key adults, and to the child's religious persuasion, racial origin and cultural and linguistic background.

  The same duty applies to private and voluntary organisations when they accommodate children.

What does other legislation say?

The Race Relations Act 1976 tells employers what they can and cannot do and is the basis for good services to people who are black and/or from ethnic minorities. Some definitions provided by that Act follow below.

- By **s. 1(1)(A)**, direct discrimination is one person treating another less favourably than he or she treats or would treat another, on racial grounds.
- By **s. 1(1)(B)**, indirect discrimination is where conditions or requirements are imposed which apply equally but will be harder for certain racial groups to comply with and cannot be justified on other than racial grounds.
- By **s. 3(1)**, racial grounds means any of the following: colour, race, nationality (including citizenship) or ethnic or national grounds.
- By **s. 71**, employers are required to make arrangements to eliminate unlawful racial discrimination and to promote equality of opportunity and good relations between persons of different racial groups.
- By **s. 20(1)**, it is unlawful for anyone concerned with the provision of goods, facilities or services to the public to discriminate by refusal or omission or as regards quality, manner or terms of the provision – whether or not there is payment involved.
- In **s. 20(2)**, examples are given – access to and use of any place to which the public or sections of the public have entry, accommodation, transport, local or public authority services.
- By **s. 32 (1)(2)**, an employer is liable for any act done with or without his knowledge or approval by one of his employees in the course of their employment.
- By **s. 5(1)**, employers are permitted to take positive action in recruiting for a job or providing opportunities for promotion, transfer or training for a job, where being from a particular racial group is a genuine occupational qualification for it.

SELF-CHECK

1 Write one sentence to define race, culture and ethnicity and then compare this with a partner's definition, written separately, and with the glossary given below.

2 List examples of:
   (a) direct discrimination;
   (b) indirect discrimination;
   on the basis of colour, race, ethnicity and religious belief.

3 What kinds of behaviour are illegal as a result of the Race Relations Act?

GLOSSARY

RACE

Unacceptable categorisation of peoples in biological terms constructed by white pseudo-scientists* to aid the justification of the systematic oppression of black people and create an ideology of racism. For the sake of practical advantage it is now commonly used to denote black and white people.

RACISM

A belief that black people are inferior to white people in relation to their culture, religion, intellect, beliefs, lifestyles. An ideology developed by white people backed by pseudo-scientists, historians, literary persons, religious and missionary bodies, academics, politicians and media, supporting the belief that physical criteria determines intellectual and other abilities.

BLACK

The word is used here to define people who suffer racism because of their skin colour. In the context of British society, we refer to those of African, Caribbean and South East Asian origin.

MINORITY ETHNIC

Belonging to a cultural, racial or religious group that is numerically smaller than the predominant white protestant majority power base in the United Kingdom. This includes groups visible on the basis of their skin colour, as well as others such as Irish, Jewish, Polish, Turkish and Travelling peoples. Belonging can come either through personal identification with a group or through the allocation by others or individuals to it.

ETHNICITY

Refers to individuals' identification with a group sharing some or all of the following traits: customs, lifestyles, religion, language, nationality. In the context of this society, the 'racial factor' influences individuals' definition of their own ethnicity (such as black/Asian, black/Caribbean). It is important to remember that white people also belong to ethnic groups.

WHITE

People who do not experience racism (that is, as a result of their skin colour).

EUROCENTRIC

Looking at, exclusively valuing and interpreting the world through the eyes and experiences of white Europeans. This includes, for example, the presentation and interpretation of historical events; defining of 'correct' methods of child rearing and organising family life; seeing Europe as the centre of the world.

SAME RACE

This is included because of its common usage to describe the placement of black children with black substitute families. Within this, it is about placing black children with families of the same or similar ethnic background.

*Refs: Jean-Joseph Virey 1774–1847; David Hume 1742–1745; Robert Knox 1850; Linnaeus 1735.

(Source: S. Macdonald, *All Equal Under the Act?*, Race Equality Unit, NISW, 1991)

DISCUSSION POINT

Look at the Glossary (of terms) published by the Race Equality Unit on p 31. Do you agree with each of the definitions listed? If not, how would *you* define the term?

ACTIVITY

1   Study two or three newspapers, TV soaps and magazines for descriptions and images of people of different race, culture and religion. Cut out or note the points you think are positive or negative, which give importance or which trivialise. If you are not sure, try to note down what makes you undecided.

2   You have to write an article of 400–500 words on the subject of your local market. Visit the market and write about all the cultural influences you see there.

3   Taking into account the legal requirements write a list of **DOs** and **DON'Ts** for people working with children. What kinds of behaviour, language, activities should come under the **DON'T** heading? What behaviour, language, activities would you like to see more of under the **DO** heading?

These points are developed in the assignments section later in this book and particularly in Assignments 1, 8, 11 and 14.

Chapter 5

Children with disabilities

As it was then

In the early nineteenth century, disabled people were still often and wrongly seen as 'defectives'. In an age of high industrialisation physical fitness was seen as an essential for employment, while for those who could not find work but were regarded as deserving of help, that help came in the form of incarceration in the Poor House. But the Victorian age was also an age of conscience, and new humanitarian values began to take root which did help to change attitudes.

By the end of the nineteenth century, metropolitan councils such as the London County Council were being set up and opening special schools and institutions for disabled people. Doctors and politicians believed strongly in categorising or grouping abilities and disabilities together. They thought this would make it easier to learn about and treat certain conditions, as well as being cheaper given the large numbers they intended to reach.

These methods had serious drawbacks which are still with us, but it

Boys at St Martin's Orthopaedic Hospital, Pyrford, Surrey, by their gardens
Courtesy: The Children's Society

Disabled girls photographed at the turn of the century
Courtesy: The Children's Society

is difficult for us in the late twentieth century to realise how bad conditions were for anyone without a steady income, before 'public welfare' was organised. For example:

- there was no unemployment or sickness benefit;
- all health care had to be paid for, and poor quality medical treatment could do more harm to a sick person than none at all;
- working people got little or no leave and were often sacked for being off sick or looking after children.

Prior to 'institutionalised' help for children and young people with disabilities, the following were the main choices:

- if the family could support you, you could remain at home;
- if possible you could work at home, e.g. dressmaking;
- or try to obtain suitable work outside, probably without the necessary training;
- if the family could/would not support you and work was impossible, you might have to enter the workhouse hospital or beg on the streets.

SELF-CHECK

1 What are the practical difficulties and drawbacks to any of these options?

2 How might any of these alternatives affect a person's:
   (a) pride;
   (b) self-image;
   (c) physical health;
   (d) mental/emotional health?

As it is now

A lot of writing about children with disabilities emphasises the disability in a negative way, rather than the strengths and abilities children have and how these can be enhanced. The Children Act 1989 defines disability with a whole group of labels:

> 17 (11) . . . a child is disabled if he is blind, deaf or dumb or suffers from a mental disorder of any kind or is substantially or permanently handicapped by illness, injury or congenital deformity or such other disability as may be prescribed.

These are the kind of categories that began to be used widely in the nineteenth century, and they still coincide with other legal definitions of disability, e.g. the Chronically Sick and Disabled Persons Act 1970, which centre on the inability to work as a right to claim state support. Disabilities here are **deficits** or **defects**, and fail to take into account the whole child with **all** her or his abilities and wider needs.

The Children Act 1989 tries to create a balance by including children with disabilities in a wider group of children in need (*see* definition on p 22) which includes **significant or further impairment of health or development**. This means that children with less clear-cut or visible disabilities – for instance a child who is very emotionally withdrawn – can be assisted. Apart from all the services available to children in need, there are also special duties in the Act which relate to 'children with disabilities'.

The Children Act 1989
Specific duties in relation to children with disabilities:
Schedule 2(6)
Every local authority shall provide services designed:
(a) to minimise the effect on disabled children within their area of disabilities; and
(b) to give such children the opportunity to lead lives which are as normal as possible.

Schedule 2(2)
Every local authority shall open and maintain a register of disabled children within their area.

Section 23(8)
Where a local authority provide accommodation for a child whom they are looking after and who is disabled they shall, so far as is reasonably practicable, secure that the accommodation is not unsuitable to his particular needs.

SELF-CHECK

1 List some of the effects which disabilities are likely to have on children.

2 Refer back to the table of family support priorities and services given on p 25 in Chapter 3 and the information you obtained from your local authority. Which services may help to minimise the effects of these disabilities? What could help children with disabilities to join other children and lead lives which are as normal as possible?

3 What do you think are the advantages and disadvantages of a register of children with disabilities?

In Britain, the concept of 'special needs' has been accepted in education assessment and provision, again emphasising the importance of looking at children's strengths as well as weaknesses . . .

In addition to these problems of definition, the language used in the Children Act is regarded as archaic and offensive.

'The language of disability has been created by a largely able-bodied society. Words used in the context of disability tend to be negative . . . We talk about people as being "weak-hearted", "short-sighted", "deaf to reason" . . . Through words like these, people build up a picture of disability as a negative thing, a problem.'

'People with disabilities are campaigning to be accorded the same respect and rights as able-bodied people. To this end they are devising new terms which stress their many strengths rather than focus on their weaknesses. "Differently-abled" is one such term.'

(Source: S. Macdonald, *All Equal Under the Act?*, Race Equality Unit, NISW, 1991)

Some people have challenged what they see as negative terms used by 'able' people who may have a political or professional interest in categorising and 'treating' disabilities. They prefer the term 'special needs', or a distinction between impairment and disability, as follows:

- 'impairment' is the functional limitation within the individual caused by physical, mental or sensory impairment;
- 'disability' is the loss or limitation of opportunities to take part in the normal life of the community on an equal level with others, due to physical and social barriers.

An example of negative and positive ways of looking at disability is given below. This researcher compared two sets of questions relating to the same topics.

The first is based on the official individualised definition of disability and was used in the recent OPCS surveys, while the second is constructed on the basis of a social definition.

What complaint causes your difficulty in holding, gripping or turning things?

Have you attended a special school because of a long-term health problem or disability?

Does your health problem/disability prevent you from going out as often or as far as you would like?

Does your health problem/disability affect your work in any way at present?

These questions effectively reduce the problems that people with impairments face in their daily lives to their own personal inadequacies or functional limitations, and could have been reformulated as follows:

What defects in the design of everyday equipment like jars, bottles and tins causes you difficulty in holding, gripping or turning them?

Have you attended a special school because of your education authority's policy of sending people with your impairment to such places?

What are the environmental constraints which make it difficult for you to get about in your immediate neighbourhood?

Do you have problems at work because of the physical environment or the attitudes of others?

To understand why the first set of questions is intimidating for individual disabled people it is important to know something about the actual research process. In the OPCS surveys, for example, individuals with impairments were visited in their own home by official 'expert' researchers. They were asked a specified sequence of formal questions and there was no opportunity to clarify or discuss their answers.

(Source: C. Barnes, *Disabled People in Britain and Discrimination*, Hurst & Co., London, 1991)

SELF-CHECK

1 How does the first set of questions indicate that disability is a matter of 'personal inadequacies' or limitations?

2 How does the second set of questions use a 'social definition' of disability? What other factors are suggested as contributing to disability?

3 In terms of *what needs to be done*, how do the two sets of questions differ?

Although reservations have been expressed by organisations of disabled people as to the way surveys are set up, official surveys still provide most of our information.

Estimates of numbers of disabled children in Great Britain with different types of disability (thousands, units)

Type of disabilities	In private households	In total population (including establishments)	In communal establishments
	Thousands	*Thousands*	*Units*
Locomotion	99	100	1,240
Reaching and stretching	21	22	584
Dexterity	38	39	685
Seeing	21	22	909
Hearing	65	65	493
Personal care	83	85	1,458
Continence	103	105	1,472
Communication	119	121	2,048
Behaviour	231	237	5,253
Intellectual functioning	94	97	2,907
Consciousness	53	54	844
Eating, drinking, digestion	7	8	265
Disfigurement	18	19	426

(Source: Table 3.9 in M. Bone and H. Meltzer, *The Prevalence of Disability Among Chidlren*, HMSO, 1989)

NOTE *'Units' refer to individual children, so that, for example, there are 1,240 children with disabilities relating to locomotion who are in communal establishments, but there are 99,000 in private households, and so on.*

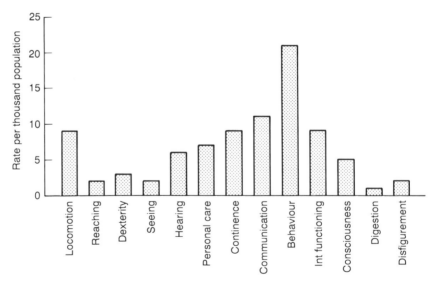

Estimates of prevalence of disability among children in Great Britain by type of disability
Source: Figure 3.3 in M. Bone and H. Meltzer, *The Prevalence of Disability Among Children*, reproduced by kind permission of HMSO. Crown Copyright 1989

SELF-CHECK

1 The children who are in communal establishments are more likely to have certain types of disability. Which are these? Make a list with the most numerous at the top.

2 Make a similar list for children living in private households. What are the most frequent disabilities? What are the similarities in these lists? What are the differences?

3 Can you think of any services which might help children with these disabilities to continue living at home most of the time?

4 What does the term 'prevalence' in the title to the chart mean? List the most common disabilities shown on this chart, again with the highest number at the top.

5 What behaviour might lead a child to be considered as having a 'behavioural disability'? Can you think of any family, social or environmental factors which might contribute?

Read the account, on p 40, of integrated education in a North London school, then answer the questions below.

SELF-CHECK

1 In this article, how are the following terms used: integration; learning difficulties; theoretical; in practice.

2 John Dowd is quoted as recommending integration at an early age. Why?

3 What are the difficulties and advantages of integration mentioned here, (a) by Yragael and (b) by able-bodied students?

NOTE *The issues raised here are explored further in Case study 4 and Assignment 20.*

It's 12.00 at a large North London comprehensive. Lunchtime. A door swings open and Yragael heads the rush down the long corridor to the stairs. But here he must wait, for unlike the other students on their way to the canteen he needs the lift and a friend's help to take him to the ground floor. Yragael lives his life from a wheelchair. He is one of fifteen students with a physical disability at Northumberland Park Community School, which also includes on its roll a number of statemented children with pronounced learning difficulties.

To watch Yragael talking animatedly with his friends, joking and laughing, it's hard to imagine how such a lively and intelligent person could ever have been excluded from what the rest of us would call ordinary life.

Following the Warnock Report of 1978, the 1981 Education Act gave legal support to the practice of integration – the bringing together of those with and without disabilities into mainstream education. On the face of it the Act heralded a new deal for children in this country with special educational needs. The Act, which came into force in 1983, obliged Local Education Authorities (LEAs) to identify and provide free full time education for such children, from, if necessary, the age of two up to 19. In conjunction with parental wishes an LEA could assess the child and then issue a Statement, describing the child's special needs and detailing how and where they should be met. Parents were to be given easier access to this information and the right to challenge it. Thoughtless and demeaning labels were to be discarded, and a single definition 'children with learning difficulties' adopted. This was to cover both children with physical disabilities and those with pronounced learning difficulties. Integrated education was to be pursued, within certain limitations.

Since the implementation of the 1981 Act progress across the country towards integration has been erratic. The Centre for Studies on Integration in Education (CSIE) has highlighted the lack of firm policy commitments by a large number of LEAs, all too often dominated by vague notions of 'as and where appropriate.'

For the able-bodied students who have moved up through the school during that time, integration has had a positive effect on their view of disability, in itself an important reflection of the way that society as a whole regards people with disabilities, and the way in which that view might be changing:

'Before I came here I hadn't seen a disabled person in a wheelchair. At first I felt indifferent, it wasn't pity, I looked at them and I felt guilty.' *Meena, Sixth Form*

'I used to see disabled people outside school, I kept on staring at them, I couldn't take my eyes away. When they looked at me I felt bad, I felt sorry for them. But now I know they're not helpless.' *Curtis, Year 7/First year*

. . . Equally important are links with a local junior school, itself having a number of disabled students, which has created an important sense of continuity between junior and secondary levels. As John Dowd says: 'Younger children do exhibit less discrimination, perhaps because they are better able to articulate their feelings at that age . . . there's more obvious acceptance'. This view is endorsed by many of the able-bodied students at Northumberland Park:

'I think we should integrate with disabled people as early as possible, right from the junior school. It gives you a longer period to learn together.' *Michael, Sixth Form*

'It was this fear of disability that held us back at first . . . it was anxiety, I was scared, very wary, I hadn't encountered many disabled people before. He made me overcome my fears, to know how I should speak to them.' *Carla, Sixth Form*

A few last words . . . from Yragael . . .

'I like this school. It's a lot less protective, so people treat you in a normal sort of way. I always found the special school rather difficult. They were perfectly nice, it's just that they couldn't accept that you were normal, that once you got out of the system you would have to fight for your own independence. There was little acceptance of the fact that you might be able to do what you wanted to do.'

(Source: R Giles, 'Celebrating integration', in *Childright*, May 1992, published by the Children's Legal Centre)

Chapter 6

Children away from home

As it was then

The idea of putting children in large institutions at a distance from their homes is no longer a popular one, although in this country, some parents continue to pay a great deal of money to send their children to expensive boarding schools. A century ago, placing children in institutions which aimed to instil moral values was seen not only as a way of dealing with poverty, but also as a way of intervening in a child's upbringing. The theory was that children could be 'reclaimed' from an 'evil life' in these disciplined institutions.

Below is a description of life in a lodging-house for children in the middle of the nineteenth century. Mayhew's descriptions were first printed as newspaper articles – they were true to life, and as a result so shocking that many people refused to believe them. As you read it, consider the points of comparison and contrast for children and young people at risk on the streets today.

> Boys have boastfully carried on loud conversations and from distant parts of the room, of their triumphs over the virtue of girls and girls have laughed at and encouraged the recital. Three, four, five, six and even more boys and girls have been packed, head and feet into one small bed; some of them perhaps never met before. On such occasions any clothing seems often enough to be regarded as merely an encumbrance. Sometimes there are loud quarrels . . . at others, there is an amicable interchange of partners. In these haunts of low iniquity, or rather in the room into which the children are put, there are seldom persons above twenty. The younger lodgers in such places live by thieving and pocket picking or by prostitution. The charge for a nights lodging is generally 2d, but smaller children have often been admitted for 1d. If a boy or girl resort to one of these dens at night without the means of defraying the charge for accommodation, the 'mot of the ken' (mistress of the house) will pack them off, telling them plainly that it will be no use their returning until they have stolen something worth 2d.

(Source: J. Canning (ed.), *The Illustrated Mayhew's London*, Guild Publishing, 1986. Originally H. Mayhew (1861–2 *London Labour & the London Poor*, Griffin, Bohn & Co.)

SELF-CHECK   I   Who do you think these young people were? List six reasons why children might have ended up in a lodging house in the nineteenth century. Give six reasons why children might run away from their homes today.

2 What dangers are faced by children who run away from home today? Are there any new risks to health?

Towards the end of the nineteenth century large locally-governed councils started to be formed and to build homes for destitute children. Some were also run by religious groups, and, as well as these, individuals such as Dr Barnardo, Revd Stephenson and Edward Rudolf also set up children's charities which still exist as Barnardos, National Children's Homes and the Children's Society (originally the Waifs and Strays Society). The titles alone tell you what they set out to do – rescue children and give them a 'new start'. Most of them had a Christian basis and a primary concern was saving souls – they were often called 'missions to the poor'. Some workers tried very hard to support entire families and keep them together, but far more commonly the parents were seen as a waste of time and resources, and the children were separated from them as well as siblings from each other.

As the general public became more aware of poverty and need, and children's rights gained some ground, so this solution seemed more attractive and gained legal backing.

- Between 1867 and 1906, Dr Barnardo's sent 18,645 children overseas, most never to see their families again.
- In 1888 the NSPCC gained legal powers to remove children from their homes.
- In 1899 the Guardians of the Poor were given legal powers to remove parental rights where a parent had been deemed 'unfit'; this could include disability, mental deficiency, living in the workhouse, or being of 'vicious habits or mode of life'.

SELF-CHECK What do you think 'vicious habits or mode of life' meant in 1899? List some of the behaviour the writer might have been referring to. How strongly do you think we disapprove of this behaviour in parents now? What kind of help is available now?

As it is now

The Children Act 1989 emphasises that the best place for children to be brought up is within their own families. Different people have different views about what a 'good upbringing' is, even within the same class, culture and religious – or non-religious – background. But those with the power to do so, in particular the police, social services and NSPCC, should not intervene in family life on the basis of these judgements, but only where there is clearly harm, or the possibility of harm, to children (*see* p 4).

To reinforce this view of the family, the idea of 'parental rights' (which in some circumstances could be taken away) has gone. Instead the law now talks of parental responsibility. (*See also* Case study 6 and Assignment 22.)

When children are accommodated by a local authority, their parents' responsibilities for care and control are exercised in part by foster carers or residential workers. This task has been likened to the child's being 'in trust' to the local authority, since it is their duty to ensure the child comes to no harm while away from home. Unfortunately children in this position are very vulnerable to abuses of power. They arc sometimes isolated and confused, and some may already have suffered abuse and lack all confidence to stand up for themselves.

There have recently been enquiries into what was known as 'pin-down' control of children in Staffordshire, and abuse of both children and staff by a head of home, Frank Beck, in Leicestershire. The reports showed that in these cases residential managers were capable of persuading their seniors that they had helpful ways of coping with children with behavioural or emotional problems. Children were actually damaged even more, either by inappropriate punishment such as long periods of isolation, or by sexual abuse and threats.

Over the past twenty years there has been a number of reports recommending greater attention to and investment in residential care. Two of the latest are *Children in the Public Care* (HMSO, 1991) and *Choosing with Care* (HMSO, 1992). They call (among other things) for tighter checking of references and police records before appointment of staff, and more rigorous supervision and planning of staff development and training on an individual basis.

The Children Act regulations also have to be translated into standards for practice. This includes children having as much contact as possible with their friends and relatives, private access to a telephone and information about a complaints procedure that works. Young people's knowledge about their personal rights and the ways they can protect themselves are very important elements in dealing with bad practice. Staff members who become aware of such practice also have a duty to confront this and talk to a senior officer or if necessary an outside agency such as ChildLine, the NSPCC or the Police.

What does the law say?

The Children Act 1989

Section 3 (1) In this Act parental responsibility means all the rights, duties, powers, responsibilities and authority which by law a parent or a child has in relation to the child and his property.

Parental responsiblity can be shared:

Section 2 (1) Where a child's father and mother were married to each other at the time of his birth, they shall each have parental responsibility for the child.
(2) Where a child's father and mother were not married to each other at the time of his birth,
(a) the mother shall have parental responsibility for the child;
(b) the father shall not have parental responsibility for the child, unless he acquires it in accordance with the provisions of this Act.

Other circumstances where parental responsibility can be shared are if a person, such as a separated father or grandparent, holds a **residence order** so that the child lives with that person for all or part of the time (*see* p 16), or if the child is on a **care order**, when the local authority will share parental responsibility with one or both parents.

If you are looking after someone else's children – as, for example, a nursery nurse, a childminder, a hospital nurse, babysitter, residential carer, teacher – you need to know:

- Who has parental responsibility?

Parents or others with parental responsibility can arrange for someone else to meet part of their responsibility – for instance by collecting a child from nursery or school. So the carer also needs to know:

- Who else is sharing or meeting part of a parent's responsibilities, and in what ways?

DISCUSSION POINT   Why do you think this is important?

In an emergency, a carer can act on her or his own initiative:

The Children Act 1989
Section 3 (5) A person who:
(a) does not have parental responsibility for a particular child; but
(b) has care of the child;
may (subject to the provisions of this Act) do what is reasonable in all the circumstances of the case for the purpose of safeguarding or promoting the child's welfare.

SELF-CHECK   1   Imagine you are looking after your friend's baby daughter aged 9 months for the evening. Think of three situations in which you might have to take a decision on behalf of your friend about the baby's welfare.

2   How could you prepare yourself beforehand, in order to be as certain as possible that you are doing as the baby's mother would wish?

When a local authority has been involved in arrangements for a child to be cared for away from home, even for a few hours, then that local authority has special duties towards the child. This includes the following:

- **Day care.** In a crèche, day nursery, playgroups or with childminders.
- **Respite care.** This is when a foster carer or community (residential) home cares for the child, usually for a short period at a time; it is also called 'short-term accommodation' and is arranged with parents on a voluntary basis, sometimes with relatives. Young people over 16 can seek short-term accommodation directly.
- **Children in care.** This is where the local authority has gone to court for a care order, usually against the parent's wishes. The local authority may place the child with relatives, with foster-carers or in a community (or residential) home until she or he is 18 years or the court ends the order.

The diagrams overleaf show changes in the way children in care have been looked after, between 1980 and 1990. The term **in care** then covered **all** children looked after by local authorities whether by court order or voluntary agreement. This was before the Children Act 1989 became effective.

SELF-CHECK

I   Look at the graph 'Children in care 1980–1990'. What has happened to the overall number of children in care in this decade, to the number of children in residential care, and in foster care? Can you think what some of the reasons for these changes are?

2   Look at the pie chart 'Type of accommodation'. List any changes that you have not already noted in the numbers of children in all types of accommodation. Has there been a change in 'other placements'? Which carers do you think this includes?

3   Draw an extension to the graph taking it up to 1995, and continue the lines as you think they might look over the next few years.

4   Draw another pie chart for 1995. If all the changes you have noted take place, what might it look like?

Children whose parents have come to a voluntary agreement and children in care are '**looked after**' by local authorities. Some voluntary organisations also **accommodate** children, for instance children who have run away from home, or have left local authority care. In all these circumstances, the voluntary organisations have special duties, and both central government and local authorities will arrange for inspections to make sure the duties are carried out.

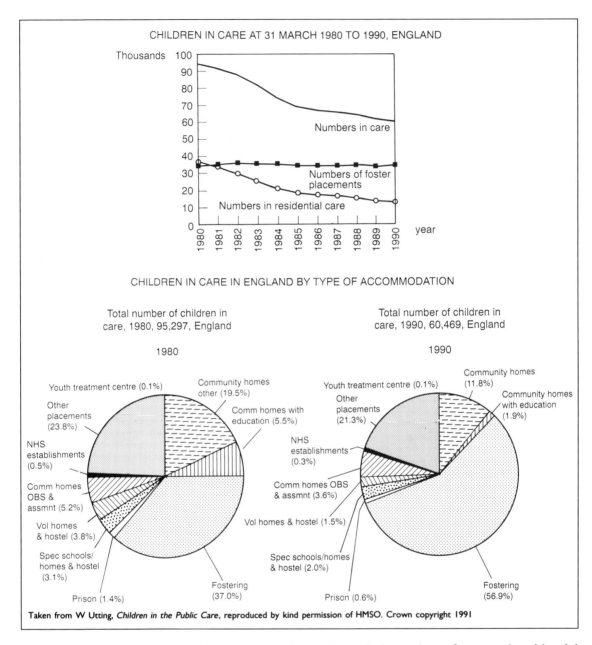

CHILDREN IN CARE AT 31 MARCH 1980 TO 1990, ENGLAND

Numbers in care

Numbers of foster placements

Numbers in residential care

CHILDREN IN CARE IN ENGLAND BY TYPE OF ACCOMMODATION

Total number of children in care, 1980, 95,297, England

1980

Total number of children in care, 1990, 60,469, England

1990

Taken from W Utting, *Children in the Public Care*, reproduced by kind permission of HMSO. Crown copyright 1991

In addition there are detailed **regulations** about foster and residential care; even when a child stays for just a day or two, they still apply. Here are some examples:

Children's Homes Regulations 1991
- In each home there must be a sufficient number of wash basins, baths and showers with hot and cold running water and lavatories, for the number of children accommodated.
- In each home there must be facilities for the child to meet privately with a parent, relative, friend or other visitor.

- Certain measures shall **not** be used in a children's home, including: any form of corporal punishment, deprivation of food, drink or sleep, or restriction of visits, telephone calls or post from parents, relatives or other visitors.
- Certain offences must be declared by people who want to work in children's homes, and may mean that they cannot be employed there.

The Foster Placement (Children) Regulations 1991

- The child must be visited regularly in the foster home by a local authority officer, and if appropriate he or she must arrange to see the child alone.
- Foster parents must give information about their health, accommodation, religion and cultural background and capacity to care for a child of a particular racial/ethnic origin, culture or linguistic background; their past and present employment, occupation, standard of living and leisure activities; and their criminal record and that of any other adult member of the household.

SELF-CHECK

1 What do you think these regulations are intended to **prevent**?

2 What are they intended to **promote**?

Chapter 7

Children at risk of harm

As it was then

Letter to *The Times*, 26 May 1884
'I have visited the shelter in Liverpool opened by the Society for the Prevention of Cruelty to Children. During the first six months there have been 211 cases involving the welfare of no less than 378 children. Of these, there were 50 cases of violence, 106 of cruel neglect, 210 of begging, vagrancy and exposure and 12 of immorality.'

Letter to *The Times*, 30 June 1884
'First when we see young children exposed to bitter weather in the streets for begging purposes, or find them covered with sores or eaten up by vermin . . . dying a lingering death through cruel neglect, there is as yet neither law nor charity to appeal to.'

(Source: *A Short History*, NSPCC, 1991)

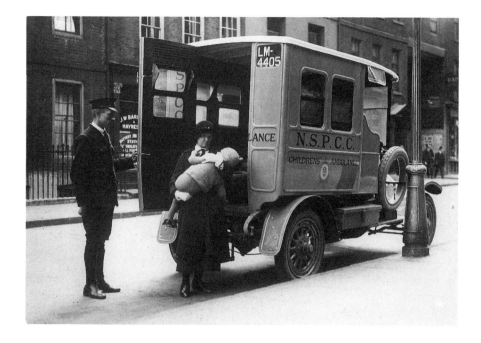

An NSPCC ambulance
Reproduced by kind permission of the NSPCC

The Roots of the Problem

The years of the late 19th century were precarious ones for children. Legally, the child was the property of its parents and whatever the circumstances of its existence, the law was powerless to intervene.

Appalling social conditions and attitudes meant that many children were subject to cruel and neglectful treatment from drunken, uncaring parents. They were put to work long hours or left to beg in the streets, often starving and without proper medical help. The practice of 'baby farming' and insuring the lives of infants commonly led to their murder for financial gain.

In 1881, George Staite, the vicar of Ashton-Hayes in Cheshire was so disturbed by what he saw around him that he wrote to the Liverpool Mercury asking readers to consider that *'whilst we have a Society for the Prevention of Cruelty to Animals, can we not do something to prevent cruelty to children?'*

The tide of opinion about parental rights was so strong that even Lord Shaftesbury, a leading reformer of the day, to whom Staite turned for advice could only reply, *'The evils you state are enormous and indisputable, but they are of so private, internal and domestic a character as to be beyond the reach of legislation and the subject indeed, would not, I think, be entertained in either House of Parliament'*.

The year 1889 saw the fruition of five years of effort to convince Parliament of the need for sensible, humane laws to improve the lot of

A young child suffering from starvation and photographed before her successful treatment. Could this happen today, and if so, under what circumstances?
Reproduced by kind permission of the NSPCC

49

children. On July 13th, the first Act of Parliament for the Prevention of Cruelty to Children was passed and a jubilant Waugh was able to send a telegram to his wife saying 'Bill at last law of land'.

The Bill, which became known as the 'Children's Charter', made it possible for the police to arrest anyone ill-treating a child and for them to obtain a warrant to enter a home if there was reasonable suspicion that a child was in danger. It also laid down guidelines about the employment of children and outlawed begging in the streets.

Five years later in 1894, the practical effect of the Bill could be evaluated and, with the Society's help, amendments were incorporated to extend its scope. Now children were allowed to give evidence in court, mental cruelty was recognised and it became unlawful not to call a doctor to a sick child.

When an Act of Parliament in October 1904 gave the NSPCC 'authorised person' status i.e. the right to remove children from the home without the police but with the consent of a Justice of the Peace, the bedrock of child protection legislation was clearly in place.

Important Child Care Legislation
Prevention of Cruelty to Children Act, 1889
Children Act, 1908
Children and Young Persons Act, 1933
Children Act, 1948
Children and Young Persons Act, 1963
Children and Young Persons Act, 1969
Children Act, 1975
Child Care Act, 1980
Children and Young Persons (Amendment) Act, 1986
Children Act, 1989

(Source: NSPCC information leaflet, 1991)

SELF-CHECK

1 Go through the passages above and list the threats from which children were unprotected in the late nineteenth century before the NSPCC created refuges and campaigned for legislation. Write a sentence or two to describe what they were.

2 List as many aims as you can of the early legislation.

3 Alongside 'cruelty', 'appalling social conditions' are also mentioned. Does any of the early legislation affect the conditions under which many parents also suffered? From legislation described in Chapter 3, Families needing support, when does it appear that the living standards of whole families began to have some protection by law?

From then to now

Since the late nineteenth century there have been many pieces of child care legislation. All of them have preserved the special role of the National Society for Prevention of Cruelty to Children, but have also demanded that **local authorities** take on similar duties to protect children if and when they are at risk. Over the years a range of descriptions has been used for damage caused to children deliberately – cruelty, baby battering, abuse, non-accidental injury, significant harm. Although sexual and emotional abuse were also known of a century ago, it is only in the past ten years or so that they have been acknowledged and debated widely, and fuller statistics collected.

ACTIVITY

Over the next two weeks make a collection of newspaper and magazine cuttings and take notes from news bulletins, about incidents involving child abuse occurring now. What are the similarities between abuse now and 100 years ago, and what are the differences, do you think? Write a brief account of what you have found out.

As it is now

What is harm?

Our knowledge of the various kinds of harm which children may suffer has increased enormously in the last 20–30 years. Behaviour which in 1960 was known as 'baby battering syndrome' plus 'child neglect' is now known to have a number of different aspects; some are:

- physical abuse;
- sexual abuse;
- emotional abuse;
- failure to thrive;
- neglect.

Look carefully at the table on p 53 showing reasons for registration. The information comes from areas which altogether include some 10% of the children living in England and Wales. (Since October 1991, Government figures have not included 'grave concern'.)

SELF-CHECK

1   What have been the changes in the numbers of children registered in these areas between 1989 and 1990? List these changes. Which are the greatest and which the smallest changes?

2   If numbers of children registered were similar throughout the population, what would the figures for England and Wales look like for 1989/90?

WHAT IS CHILD ABUSE?

CHILD ABUSE IS

Making a child feel unwanted, ugly, worthless, guilty, unloved

Being physically violent to a child

Exploiting a child sexually

Failing to provide the things needed for a child to grow

Child abuse is not usually one single incident but part of a pattern of behaviour; it takes place over a period of time and its effects add up. Child abuse can isolate and damage a child physically and emotionally. The longer the abuse continues the more difficult it is to stop and the more serious is the effect on the child.

Children are often bewildered by the fact that the person hurting them can be a parent, relative, friend or neighbour, a man or woman. They are confused because the same person should be loving and protecting them. The result is they have no one to turn to, or don't want to tell because they are afraid. They may have been threatened into silence. They are often terrified of the thought that the entire family will be destroyed.

Abusers come from all social, economic, ethnic, racial and religious groups. It is not fully understood why people abuse children, but it is necessary to try and understand abusers in order to protect children at risk. Abusers may be confused by their actions. They may not like what they do but don't know how to cope with their feelings. They may have had very poor experiences as children themselves and in some cases are little older than the children they are abusing. Whilst not all abused children grow up to be abusing adults, some of them do repeat their experiences with their own children. Sometimes the cycle of abuse can be broken by dealing with the abuser, but there are also ways of teaching children how to protect themselves.

© *KIDSCAPE, 82 Brook Street, London W1Y 1YG*

Source: *Who would hurt a child?* BBC Childwatch, 1986

Family factors

At the time of registration 35% of the children were living with both their natural parents. Nationally some 73% (3) of children from similar social classes are living with both their natural parents.

The atypical parental situation of the registered children was reflected in the stress factors recorded as affecting the family at the time of the abuse. The most frequently recorded factor (39%) was relationship problems between the child's caretakers. Violence between them was also recorded for 25% of the cases. Inability to respond to the maturational needs of the child was recorded for 27% and debts for 26% of the registered cases.

Discord between the caretakers was also ranked highest amongst the stress factors judged to have precipitated the abuse. This was followed by 'inability to respond to the maturational needs of the child', 'heavy drinking' and 'authoritarian control'. The pattern of stress factors also varied by the type of abuse. Discord between the child's caretakers was recorded most often for the injured, sexual and emotional abuse and grave concern cases. Debts was recorded most frequently for the neglect cases and 'inability to respond to the maturational needs of the child' for the failure to thrive cases.

Discord was also rated as the most severe stress affecting the sexually abused children's families and 'inability to respond to the maturational needs of the child' was the most severe for those children who failed to thrive.

(Source: S. J. Creighton *Child Abuse in 1990*, NSPCC Research Briefing, 1991)

Number of registered children by reason for registration 1989 and 1990

	1989	(%)	1990	(%)
Physical abuse	973	(28)	932	(28)
Fatal and serious injuries	94		109	
Moderate injuries	879		823	
Sexual abuse	620	(18)	496	(15)
Neglect	273	(8)	248	(7)
Emotional abuse	114	(3)	75	(2)
Failure to thrive	45	(1)	28	(1)
Physical and sexual abuse	24	(1)	21	(1)
Neglect and physical abuse	33	(1)	47	(1)
Neglect and sexual abuse	12		8	
Neglect, physical and sexual abuse	14		5	
Total abused	2108	(60)	1860	(55)
Grave concern	1384	(40)	1495	(45)
Accidental injuries	0		0	
Total registered	3492	(100)	3355	(100)
Rate per 1000 under 5s**			4.64	
Rate per 1000 under 15s**			3.42	
Rate per 1000 under17s**			3.20	

* Comparable data base to 1990.
** OPCS Population Estimates 1989 (1).

(Adapted from S. J. Creighton, *Child Abuse in 1990*, NSPCC Research Briefing, 1991)

SELF-CHECK 1 Read the information above about stress factors.

2 List the family and stress factors and any organisations you know which can help parents and children in these kinds of difficulties. Begin to keep an address book of these organisations.

We must also consider environmental harm to children caused by conditions which may be beyond parents' direct control. These might include:

• pollution of air and water by chemicals;

- harmful additives to food;
- poor housing (damp, infested);
- neighbourhoods which are dangerous to children (as regards play areas, traffic controls, dogs, etc.).

Too often the debate about authority and discipline focuses on the parent–child relationship, divorcing it from any wider context – of extended family, friends, neighbourhood and culture. But even the most superficial discussion with a parent reveals the external influences which impinge at every point on the relationship with their child. From nursery school on, children are progressively more influenced by their peer group. Does peer group pressure, the television children watch and their immediate environment reinforce or contradict the way the parent is trying to bring them up? By moving to the country or suburbs and sending their children to private schools, wealthy parents can select some of those outside influences. That task is more difficult for a parent who can't choose where to live.

Chris lives in the same tower block as Edna. He is a single father bringing up his two-year-old daughter, Lisa. He describes the pressure of a materialistic consumer culture on parents. 'It makes parents feel bad when they can't buy toys for their children. Kids go through fads with clothing and toys and parents feel guilty if they can't give the kids the same as other kids have. Kids are so spiteful to other kids who don't have the right clothes.'

It's a matter of great pride to Chris that 'if Lisa needs something, she will get it. She's got a Wendy house, a slide, and boxes and boxes of toys. I'll go without to provide for her.'

But one thing Chris cannot give Lisa is a garden, and he feels it keenly: 'I'd love a garden for Lisa, but I can't let her out of the flat. The parks are covered in dog shit, so the only place for kids to play is on the deck walkways where the dogs have urinated. On the stairways you see silver paper everywhere – it's been chased for skeg (heroin). It's not the right place to bring up a child. It's a hard area; one of the first things your kid learns to do is fight. Children on this estate can't be children because they are too restricted. I'm always telling Lisa not to do something – either because it's dangerous or because neighbours will complain about the noise.'

Such an environment makes the task of being a good parent immeasurably harder.

(Source: M. Bunting, *The Guardian*, 17 September 1991)

SELF-CHECK   What kind of environmental hazards to children are mentioned here? Who do you think can or should take action to improve things? As you collect information about harm to children, don't forget harm caused by environmental problems, as opposed to harm from within the family. Which do you think gets most attention from the media?

The Children
Act 1989

Section 31(9) says that 'harm' means ill-treatment or the impairment of health or development; 'development' means physical, intellectual, emotional, social or behavioural development; 'health' means physical or mental health; and 'ill treatment' includes sexual abuse and forms of ill-treatment which are not physical.

What needs to be done?

The flowchart on p 56 shows some of the stages to be followed when a child is suspected of having been harmed.

NOTE *Child abuse is considered further in Assignment 7 later in this book.*

Legal duties under the Children Act 1989

By Schedule 2(4)(1) local authorities have a duty to 'take reasonable steps, through the provision of services under Part III of this Act, to prevent children within their area' suffering ill-treatment or neglect. These services can be provided by any part of the local authority – housing, leisure or environmental services, education, social services.

Schedule 2(4) also imposes a duty on a local authority to give information about children at risk of harm to another authority if the child moves home.

There is no legal requirement on individuals to inform the local authority of a child at risk, but once the local authority knows of such a child, they must by Section 47(1):

> make such enquiries as they consider necessary to enable them to decide whether they should take any action to safeguard or promote the child's welfare.

Where the local authority or NSPCC thinks that the child is 'suffering or likely to suffer significant harm', they can apply to a court for various orders. They must give evidence of the harm they are concerned about. The court orders are:

- **Child assessment order** (s. 43): under which the child can be seen and assessed.
- **Emergency protection order** (s. 44): under which the child can be kept in, or removed to, a particular place (e.g. a hospital or children's home). An individual can also apply for this order.
- **A care or supervision order** (s. 31): under a care order the local authority can decide where the child is to live until he or she is 18 years old, and make most other major decisions (e.g. with regard to education). Under a supervision order the young person can be required

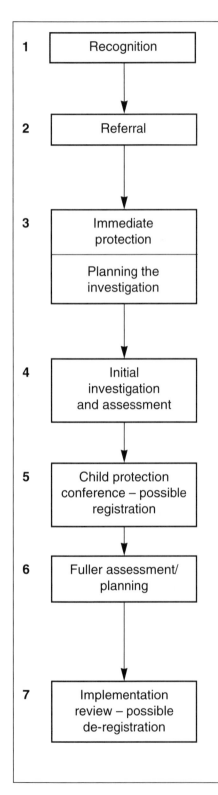

1 Recognition

For instance, see checklist for possible signs of sexual abuse

2 Referral

If the child is old enough the need to get help should be discussed with her/him. Childline, the NSPCC and Social Services all have experience in this field of work, and many voluntary organisations offer support through groups or advice centres.

3 Immediate protection

Planning the investigation

If the abuse is continuing there may need to be action to protect the child.

Sometimes the abuser will leave the home. **Strategy discussions** are held to co-ordinate action between the people involved, for example police and social workers. At this stage an Emergency Protection Order may be needed.

4 Initial investigation and assessment

- Establish the facts.
- Decide if there are grounds for concern.
- Identify sources and levels of risk.
- Decide protective action in relation to the child and others, e.g. siblings.
- **Continue strategy discussions**.

5 Child protection conference – possible registration

The conference shares concerns about the level of risk to a child and recommends action, including registering the child's name. Many authorities now invite parents to all or part of these meetings.

6 Fuller assessment/ planning

Contributions are invited from all relevant agencies to cover social, medical and development factors. A social worker may undertake the assessment, drawing on information from those who know her or him, to make a written plan.

7 Implementation review – possible de-registration

The plan may include:

- Working with the parents and children separately or together;
- support for the family at a family centre, with day care etc.;
- regular weight, health checks for the child;
- reports on the child's progress.

Although the following signs do not necessarily indicate that a child has been sexually abused they may help adults recognise that something is wrong. The possibility of sexual abuse should be investigated if a child shows a number of these symptoms, or any one of them to a marked degree:

- personality changes such as becoming insecure or clinging
- regressing to younger behaviour patterns such as thumb sucking or bringing out discarded cuddly toys
- sudden loss of appetite or compulsive eating
- being isolated or withdrawn
- inability to concentrate
- lack of trust in a familiar adult, such as not wanting to be alone

with a babysitter or childminder
- starting to wet themselves again, day or night
- having nightmares, being unable to sleep
- being overly affectionate and knowledgeable in a sexual way inappropriate to the child's age
- medical problems such as chronic itching or a pain in the genitals

It is important to note that it is normal and natural for children to want to explore their own bodies and sometimes those of their own age group. This 'playing doctor' activity is part of growing up and should generally not be cause for concern.

© KIDSCAPE, 82 Brook Street, London W1Y 1YG

Source: *Who would hurt a child?* BBC Childwatch, 1986

to attend certain activities and the supervisor must **'advise or befriend'** him or her.

- The court can also make one or more of the orders described in s. 8, if this would be better for the child. (Section 8 orders are listed in Chapter 2, p 15.)

In all these cases, the local authority must allow parents to have reasonable contact with their children, and include parents and children so far as possible in decisions.

A child can refuse any treatment or medical examination if the doctor considers her or him to be mature enough to understand the situation.

SELF-CHECK

1 List the ways in which the Children Act 1989 protects children from harm. (Refer back to Chapter 3 if you need to.) Does the Children Act suggest ways in which families under stress can be helped to stay together, and if so, what are they?

2 If a friend with a small child told you that he or she was frightened of hurting the child, what could you suggest they might do? How would you feel yourself?

ACTIVITY

Draft a letter to your local authority or go to your local social services office and ask for information on their child protection procedure and support services for parents in difficulty with their children where harm is a possibility. Show the draft to your tutor before sending the letter. Tell them that you want this for study on a course. Do you think the services offered are helpful or not, and why?

One of the key changes that the Children Act is designed to bring about, along with the recommendations of recent inquiries into the running of children's homes and the placement of children with foster parents, is that the professionals must work together to protect and further the child's needs and interests. This means that agencies must work together – social workers (who are usually the key workers with children), teachers, health visitors, nursing and medical staff, and the police. These professionals need to develop the skills and procedures to generate good information to share. They need to work with others in their workplace and agency to encourage the sharing of information, impressions, concerns and anxieties that people in day-to-day contact with the child may have but, as recent reports show, have often not felt able to express. This enables good monitoring to take place, which in turn helps to keep the interests of the child where they should be – at the heart of every child care setting.

Everybody who works with children is important and their observations and views are important. The case studies and assignments that follow aim to demonstrate this. In these you are invited to share the experiences and perspectives of the only people who can deliver good quality care to children – those who look after children day by day as childminders, in family centres, at playgroups, at school in the dinner queues and in the playground as much as in the classroom, in play schemes and in residential care. The Children Act and the detailed specifications and guidelines for good practice that this compendium of legislation contains are all directed at creating a framework within which the care and best interests of each child are placed at the centre of all arrangements for the care of children.

Part 2

CASE STUDIES

Case Study 1

Lena's children

Lena started childminding when her eldest child, Kerry, now 12, was a toddler, and she has minded children more or less ever since. Ercan (Kanny), named after her Turkish Cypriot father, is now nearly 8 and Michael (5) started in reception last September. At this time, Laura, who she had minded since she was a toddler, also started school full time with Michael, and Lena had vacancies. While she was re-registering as a childminder (under the Children Act) she was approached by the Social Services, and asked if she would take Kylie James, 9 months old, whose young mother, Brenda, was under stress and needed support in looking after Kylie.

Lena has always been a popular childminder, and mums who heard about her by word of mouth would approach her at school or get her number from a friend of a friend – she had rarely had to advertise. But at the time Millie, the childminding adviser, asked her about taking Kylie, she had no firm arrangements. There just did not seem to be the work around. Whenever somebody lost their job, childminders were hard hit, as the parent at home took over the child care. Her husband, Kriss, a draughtsman, had worries about his job too. His firm is up for sale.

She had a meeting with Millie and then with Mary Davis, Brenda's social worker/care manager and met Brenda James and Kylie before deciding she would look after her. Her heart went out to Brenda, who under her black clothes and white make-up she felt was a nice girl who had got herself into a terrible state. She seemed so much more frail and vulnerable than Kerry, who was only 12 . . . So she agreed, and talked through what she would offer. It was a different approach to what she was used to, but it made Lena realise just how much she did know about children and youngsters. Mary Davies asked her views on what would work, and seemed to value her experience.

They drew up a written agreement, shown opposite, and sent a copy to Lena with Brenda's agreement.

Background report on Kylie (James) age 9 months (d.o.b. 25.4.9—)

1   Kylie's mother, Brenda, is 19 years old (d.o.b. 16.06.7—). She has recently been rehoused permanently (June 199—) after two years in bed and breakfast accommodation with her boyfriend, Ibrahim Osman, who is Turkish Cypriot.

2   Unfortunately, their relationship was under great stress and eventually Ibrahim moved back in with his family. Brenda says that she looks forward to seeing Ibrahim but when she does they argue bitterly, and this always upsets Kylie. The arguments seem to centre on why they split up – Brenda thinks there is another woman and Ibrahim says no, but he cannot stand her jealousy.

3   Brenda is also suffering from what appears to be an eating disorder – the social worker has noticed weight loss over the past six months but tests indicate no physical illness. Brenda currently weighs under 7½ stone, she is 5'9" tall and if this weight loss continues her GP will consider in-patient treatment.

4   Currently Kylie is thriving and putting on weight normally, although there were concerns about her weight in the early months. Brenda is always anxious about her health and reports spending nights awake looking at her in case she has stopped breathing, as well as calling out the GP locum on several occasions.

5   Kylie is now showing anxiety (tears, screaming) when apart from Brenda. We have assessed Kylie is at no direct risk, but in need since her development is clearly threatened by her mother's current frailty and anxiety.

Ms James and the social worker have therefore made an agreement about the need for a childminding place as follows:

PURPOSE OF PLACE

(*a*)   to maintain Kylie's good progress;
(*b*)   to help Kylie separate from Brenda for a few hours each day;
(*c*)   to help Brenda separate safely from Kylie; and
(*d*)   concentrate on her own needs, e.g.

 • outings, exercise with friends
 • enjoying food more
 • less lonely and depressed.

DURATION

 • Six months, to begin with a meeting between Brenda, Kylie and Lena, an outing together *then* a slow increase in Kylie's time with Lena.
 • To review with Brenda and Lena after two weeks and then at three months. It is envisaged that Brenda will bring Kylie to Lena at 9.30, and collect her at 1.30.

BRENDA TO:

- Supply Lena with any special toys and list of foods Kylie likes or must not have.
- May phone Lena each day at 11 a.m. to reassure herself.
- Not be more than 20 minutes early or late for collection; if she is delayed to call Lena.

LENA TO:

- Make a note of Kylie's attendance, weight gain and any observations on her sleep pattern/eating/play/separation from and return to Brenda.
- Send a weekly account to Mary Davis for agreement and payment.
- Tell Brenda directly of any worries, and also phone social worker if it is something major or cannot be sorted out with Brenda (i.e. would affect the outcome of this plan).

MARY DAVIS (SOCIAL WORKER) TO:

- Ensure prompt payment to Lena.
- Offer support to Brenda in dealing with her anorexia.
- Arrange review meetings, or any interim meetings which are necessary.

AGREED .... parent

.... childminder

.... social worker

DATE ....

As luck would have it, Lena has since been approached by several parents, asking her to look after their children. She has started to look after Jamie aged 3, three days a week, collecting him from playgroup at 12.00. It fits in well with taking Kylie out, and she used to look after his brother, Sam. On Mondays and Fridays, Lena hands Jamie over to his mother, Jean, at school at 3.30 p.m. when she picks up Sam (now 6) and Chris (9). On Wednesdays, Jean works late, and Jamie and his brothers go back to Lena's until 6.30 p.m.

Laura's mum has now started work full time, and has asked Lena if she would look after Laura again, collecting her from school at 3.30 and looking after her till 5.00 or 5.30 at the latest. They could make alternative arrangements for one day if this would help. She has been asked to look after Simone (18 months) two days a week 9.30 a.m.–5.30 p.m. Jamie has made a friend at playgroup – David, and David's mum wanted to know if Lena would collect him from playgroup on the days she collects Jamie, and look after him till 3.30 on those days.

A neighbour, Fran, would like her to look after Liam (just 2) one day a week 9.30 a.m.–4.30 Fran works from home and has not got much work at present, but when she is busy, she will want Liam looked after for up to four days, hopefully not later than 4.30 but until Liam's bedtime (6.30) and the occasional Saturday morning when she is really pushed. This would not be more than for three weeks every three months.

While it's nice to be in demand, Lena realises she will have to sit down and think through what she can taken on, and what she wants to take on. After school is a busy time with her own kids. Kerry needs some peace and quiet for homework and sometimes a bit of help, and Michael comes home with a little reading book every night, and is full of enthusiasm. She is keen to respond to this, as reading was (and still is) quite a struggle with Kanny. But then, Laura and Sam are almost part of the family . . .

She's pleased with the arrangement with Kylie and she can see the improvement in her. She's eating well and playing with her food, giggling as she squelches her hands in it. Lena was careful to start Kylie off only on the foods Brenda said she liked, but when she started showing an interest in Jamie's dinner, Lena tried out new foods with her, and so far so good. Brenda has taken to coming in at lunchtime. She only picks herself, but she cuts up Jamie's food and helps him, and pulls funny faces at Kylie in between mouthfuls. Lena sends them on their way at 1.30 though – by then she has the rest of the day to think about.

ACTIVITY 1: Kylie's week

1   Lena has agreed to keep careful records of Kylie's attendance, progress and activities. Lena decides to do this by devising and filling in a chart, one for each week. Draw up a chart for Lena with all the headings she will need.

2   **Discussion point:** Brenda faints at Lena's flat one day when she comes to collect Kylie. When she comes to, she is tearful and says she has not been eating – she knows this makes Ibrahim worry about her, and she wants him back. She asks Lena not to tell anyone, especially not Mary Davis. What should Lena do?

ACTIVITY 2: Kylie's progress

1   Kylie's development has been delayed in some ways. Find out about the stages of development you would expect in a 9 month old. Summarise your findings under the headings: movement; handling things; seeing, hearing and talking; social behaviour and play. Refer to the developmental charts in Assignment 6 and Appendix 1.

2   Suggest one game or activity Lena might do with Kylie to promote her development in each of these areas. This is not a question about toys as such, more about offering activities and experiences, styles of talking and interaction with a young child.

| **ACTIVITY 3: How many children?** | The Children Act gives a standard recommended ratio for children per childminder: |

 1:3 children aged under 5
 1:6 children aged between 5 and 7
 1:6 children aged under 8 of whom no more than three are under 5.

These ratios include the childminder's own children. Local authorities will probably add requirements of their own. For example, they often stipulate that no more than one child should be under 12 months, as in the checklist in Case Study 3. Assume that this is so here.

1 Phone or write to the childminding adviser and ask to be sent details of their registration process. If you have this information before you start this activity, use these details for the tasks below.

2 (a) Lena has to make some decisions about which children she will take on. Draw up a weekly schedule, and write in the children Lena is already looking after, not forgetting her own, noting days and times.

 (b) Lena charges £2.50 per hour per part-time child. What times and days could Lena offer the parents of the other children she has been asked to take on? Make sure Lena stays within the limits set down by law, or as required by your local authority.

 (c) In small groups identify the other factors that you think would influence Lena's decision to accept – or not – the children she has been asked to care for. Remember she has financial worries herself, but her reputation as a good childminder depends on her offering good child care. When will Lena do her shopping, cooking and cleaning? Does she need any free time in her week?

| **ACTIVITY 4: So you want to be a childminder?** | All childminders must be registered. Under the Children Act it is illegal not to be, and local authorities may use their powers to prosecute illegal minders. The childminding adviser will want to be satisfied that the childminder is a 'fit person' under the Act and that everyone else living in the household is also a 'fit person' as defined in the extract below. |

Fit person

7.32 Section 71(7) and (8) define two categories of fit person. Where the person is proposing to look after children age under 8 the social services department of the local authority has to be satisfied that he is 'fit' – i.e. suitable – to do this. The local authority has to satisfy itself that other people living or working on the premises are 'fit to be in the proximity of children aged under 8'. The local authority should have regard to these points when considering whether someone is fit to look after children aged under 8:

- previous experience of looking after or working with young children or people with disabilities or the elderly;

- qualification and/or training in a relevant field such as child care, early years education, health visiting, nursing or other caring activities;
- ability to provide warm and consistent care;
- knowledge of and attitude to multi-cultural issues and people of different racial origins;
- commitment and knowledge to treat all children as individuals and with equal concern;
- physical health;
- mental stability, integrity and flexibility;
- known involvement in criminal cases involving abuse to children.

With persons living or working on the premises the points are:

- previous records;
- known involvement in criminal cases involving abuse to children.

Local authorities should use the above list as a basis for deciding on the fitness of an applicant for registration. Persons applying for registration should know what factors are being considered when their fitness is being assessed.

(Source: Taken from *Children Act 1989 Guidance and Regulations Vol. 2 Family Support, Daycare and Educational Provision for Young Children*, HMSO, 1991)

In groups decide how you would set about deciding whether someone was a 'fit person'. Would you use a questionnaire type form? If so, what questions would you include? Would you observe? Would you visit announced? Unannounced? Would you require childminders to attend a course?

1   After your discussion, draw up your procedure for assessing the suitability of people applying for registration as childminders. Write this up.

2   Compare the procedure you drew up with the procedure used by your local authority, noting similarities and differences.

Local authorities see the registration process as an opportunity not only to guarantee the legal minimum to parents, childminders and children, but also to develop good practice in the care of children in their areas. This means that they will want to explore and promote positive attitudes to children, their behaviour and development in people caring for children. A Code of Good Practice will incorporate the guiding principles of the Children Act, and often include specific points which the local authority particularly wishes to stress. Pre-registration courses, care with pet foods, public liability insurance, outside playspace or taking children out, and policy on smoking are examples of these.

The principles of the Children Act are:

- children's welfare and development are paramount;
- children should be treated and respected as individuals whose needs (including special educational needs) should be catered for;

- parents' responsibility for their children should be recognised and respected;
- the values deriving from different backgrounds racial, cultural, religious and linguistic – should be recognised and respected;
- parents are generally the first educators of their children; this should be reflected in the relationships with other carers and providers;
- parents should have easy access to information about services in their area and be able to make informed choices.

(Taken from Children Act 1989 Guidance and Regulations Vol. 2 Family Support, Day care and Educational Provision for Young Children, HMSO, 1991)

3 Suggest at least one 'Good Practice' point you would want to promote to further the objective of each of these six principles.

ACTIVITY 5: How safe is your home?

If you were to become a childminder, would you have to make changes to your home to make it safe?

Shown opposite is a checklist used by a childminding adviser on registration visits.

1 Go round your own home ticking the features that already meet the safety requirements, and make a note of any changes you would have to make.

2 Where these changes would cost money, cost them.

CHILDMINDING: CODE OF GOOD PRACTICE
SAFETY REQUIREMENTS & RECOMMENDATIONS

IMPORTANT: Equipment must be manufactured to the relevant BSI standard

☐ Fireguards should be secured to the wall.

☐ Stairgates to be securely fixed where used, and particularly to prevent children gaining access to the kitchen whilst meals are being prepared.

☐ Safety catches should be fitted to windows, balcony doors, etc. Keys should be kept safely at hand in case of fire.

☐ Medicines and tablets to be kept locked inside a medicine cabinet out of reach of children.

☐ Poisonous substances, bleaches, matches, etc. must be stored out of reach of children.

☐ Pet food should be kept in hygienic containers and not accessible to young children.

☐ Oil stoves or portable gas heaters should not be kept in rooms in which minded children are present and should, in any event, be fitted with a safety device and be regularly inspected and maintained. Gas cylinders must not be stored on the premises.

☐ There should be no electrical appliances in the bathroom, except those worked by a pull-cord switch.

☐ Lower power points should be covered.

☐ Low windows should be securely bolted.

☐ Garden equipment and poisonous chemicals should be locked away before children are allowed access to the garden.

☐ Saucepan handles should be kept turned away from the edge of the cooker, and guards used where recommended. Children should be supervised at all times whilst in the kitchen.

☐ Flex from electric kettles should be short and beyond the reach of children.

☐ Highly polished floors should be avoided, and slippery rugs secured with a 'gripping' device.

☐ Tablecloths should not hang down from tables.

☐ Large areas of glass should be shatter-proof or covered with safety film.

☐ Open staircases should be made safe.

☐ Garage doors should be kept locked.

☐ Cellar doors should be kept locked.

☐ Worn areas of carpeting which constitute a safety hazard must be removed/replaced.

☐ Long leads and multi-point adapters should not be used and never overloaded.

☐ Smoke alarms should be installed.

☐ Where there are double-glazed, sealed units without casements, alternative exits should be provided.

☐ Ponds should be covered or fenced.

☐ Car safety requirements should be adhered to.

☐ Children should not be able to gain access to roads unsupervised.

☐ External door grilles, where fitted, must be kept unlocked at all times when children are present.

☐ It is recommended that fire extinguishers/blankets should be fitted.

☐ Fire evacuation plans should be made and practised with the children.

**ACTIVITY 6:
Partnership
with parents**

'You need to feel good about yourself and the parents if you are to feel good about the child. And money comes into this. If you overprice yourself, you are restricting the kids who can come to you. If you underprice yourself, you undervalue yourself, and this rubs off in your care for the child.'

(Donna, childminder)

Many of the problems that can arise between parents and childminder can be avoided by having a straightforward contract.

1   What would you look for in a childminder? Working in pairs, list the points you would look for in a person who would look after your child. Identify any negatives – points that you would have serious reservations about.

2   In pairs, design a form to be used as the basis of an agreement between parents and childminder. Consider whether any of the 'Good Practice' points above or your own criteria, are suitable for inclusion. Make sure you include on it:

   (a) **essential details** (as specified in Assignment 13, Task 3);
   (b) **fees and conditions**: basic agreed hours and rates; unsocial hours/weekends; holidays (minder, child, parents); retainers; sickness (minder, child); period of notice (minder to parent, parent to minder);
   (c) **emergencies**;
   (d) **who supplies what**.

3   Compare your form with the one used by your local authority or the National Childminding Association's model contract. Make any changes you wish to make to either, and decide on a final version. Type it out and print several copies.

4   Working in pairs, take it in turns to be Lena and the parents whose children she is already looking after, plus those you decided in Activity 3 she would take on. Complete one form for each child.

Case Study 2

The Simons family

Julia Simons is 19 years old and has two children, David aged 3½ years and Pete aged 18 months. They have just moved into a family flat at the Congreve Family Centre. The centre is large and provides a wide range of services – play activities and play therapy for children, family therapy, and residential facilities for two families. A number of groups for children under 10 and for adults are held at the centre. The centre manager is Anjana Matthews. Julia and her family moved in today from bed and breakfast accommodation. She has repeatedly left and returned to her husband Mark, aged 20, following arguments and eruptions of violence in which each threatens the other with knives, chairs – whatever comes to hand – and shouts abuse.

Neither parent has ever deliberately hurt the children but they have to sit out these scenes. Pete usually ends up crying and unable to sleep, and David tries to hide under the bed. Julia has frequently gone to the police alleging assault and then refused to follow this up because she and Mark have made up and are trying to get back together. However, last night, Sunday 1 November, Julia alleges that Mark threatened her with a breadknife when she was holding the baby. He had been drinking and she was afraid that this time the baby might be hurt. The hotel manager called the police who in turn called the emergency social worker.

ACTIVITY 1: Harm

1 The local authority has applied (Monday 2 November) for an Emergency Protection Order on the basis that 'there is reasonable cause to suspect that the child is suffering or likely to suffer significant harm'.

Look back in Part 1, to the definition of 'harm' in s. 31 on p 55 and the local authority's duties. What *evidence* do you think the local authority will present in order to obtain the order, and what powers would the order give to the local authority?

NOTE *An EPO would not affect parental responsibility – who holds this at the moment? (See Part 1, p 44.)*

2 What other actions, apart from moving the mother and children to a centre and seeking an order, might have been considered to protect these children and keep the family together?

Using the Centre

Julia and Mark were informed that they could challenge the Emergency Protection Order within 72 hours (by Thursday 5 November) but neither has done so. They have each been informed that the local authority will seek an Interim Care Order on the same grounds as before. The plans the authority intend to put to the court are:

- to investigate and assess the possibility of the family living together without risk of harm to the child(ren);
- to allow the mother reasonable contact with the children with support and assistance as appropriate from the local authority;
- to allow the father reasonable contact with the children under supervision.

The plans have had to be thought out quickly by a senior social worker and council solicitor, because the hearing is just eight days after the original order was made (Tuesday 10 November). The family centre will be responsible for much of the assessment, and for supervising contact between the children and Mark.

ACTIVITY 2: What about the family?

Set out a diary from 1 November to 10 November. Imagine you are Julia and write in your entries – where you are, what has happened and what your thoughts might be. Write in a different colour where Mark might be, and what his thoughts might be. What changes have happened for David and Pete? Exchange your 'diary' with a partner's. Discuss your entries, and how the changes could affect a 3½ year old and an 18 month old child. Then consider who *else* might be interested in, and concerned to know, what has happened? How could you check these possibilities?

David and Pete

The health visitor has provided this report to the family centre:

'David appears to be a healthy 3½ year old who is reaching his milestones. His mother visits the health centre regularly and he has had immunisations and height and weight checks. All normal – some slowing of weight gain recently, but he has had a bad cold and should catch up. Mother also reports him as difficult to feed his meals, but eager to stuff with crisps and sweets in between. He has a few words and likes to explore – we sometimes find he has climbed into a cupboard.

Pete is a very placid baby who, again, is developing normally. I would like to see him receive a little more stimulation – he tends to be wakeful at night times so mother is only too keen to put him down at other times.'

ACTIVITY 3:
Making an
assessment

You are a day-care worker at the family centre who has been asked to provide information to the social worker concerning:

- the children's current functioning and likely future needs;
- any health or developmental concerns;
- any indications about each child's relationship with his mother and father.

Other family centre workers will also be involved, but your perspective is important as someone who spends time with the children, and is present at some of the meetings they have (twice a week for two hours) with their father.

Using the assessment chart on p 72 as a guide, in twos or threes list the questions you need to be able to answer under each heading, and the ways in which you might find the answers, e.g. discussions (who with?), activities (what kind, with whom?) and observations (when, how?).

Do this for each child separately, making a large chart.

Nanny Simons

It is Thursday 12 November and the family centre holds a staff meeting. The information that is shared about the Simons family includes the following:

- An Interim Care Order was granted on the 10th, lasting 21 days. The local authority has to return to court on Tuesday 1 December.
- Julia and Mark have tried to reconcile but ended up having a fierce argument. This started in front of the children, but they were able to control themselves until the children were in the playroom. In the end Mark voluntarily left the family centre. Each parent is considering divorce and the possibility of applying for a Residence Order so that one or the other could be the full-time carer for David and Pete.
- Mrs Anne Simons, Julia's mother, came to court on the 10th with her solicitor. She is very annoyed with the local authority for not contacting her at the time of the Emergency Protection Order, and she wants to be considered as an alternative future carer for the children. She too is considering applying for a Residence Order (*see* Part 1, pp 15–6 for more information on these orders). A Contact Order has been made for two 2-hour visits per week to the children by their grandmother.

Some other staff are surprised by this news. Julia has not talked about her mother a great deal, and seemed to suggest that her mother lived a long way away, which is not the case. You, as the Day Care Worker, now remember and mention that David has talked about 'Nanny Simons' occasionally.

What I know (facts)	Home routine and environment	Relationships	Opinions	Assessment
David age 3½ (dob)				
Where he has lived, who with, number of moves	What has the routine been up to now?	Who is important to David and how is this shown?	Other views to take into account	Future needs re: • care • contact with other key people
Important people	What resources/play/possessions have been available?	Describe David's responses to: • Julia • Mark • other key adults		• environment • resources/support and the basis for this assessment
Health history (weight/height)	What is different now and how has David responded to the changes?	when they are together – at the beginning, middle and end of the session		(facts/written report/opinion)
Likes/dislikes				
Food/play		How does each parent behave (and other key adults)		
Sleep pattern				
Any unexplained or worrying behaviour				
Pete age 18 m (dob)				

ACTIVITY 4: Getting in touch

1 The family centre worker who knows the Simons family best is off sick for the rest of the week. You are asked to draft a letter to Mrs Simons, explaining briefly what the family centre is and how it is involved with her grandchildren, and inviting her in for a meeting. The social worker has offered a number of times when she can be present as well.

Draft this letter, with the following headings as a guide:

(a) What the Congreve Family Centre provides
(b) Why the centre is working with Julia, Mark, David and Pete
(c) Why the centre workers would like to meet Mrs Simons
(d) Possible times

2 You are also asked to discuss Mrs Simons' interest in the children with Julia, tell her about the invitation that is to be sent to her mother, and find out whether Julia wants to meet her mother at the centre or not. In order to prepare, you set out the thoughts you have at the moment. Try to answer these questions as fully as you can.

(a) How might Mrs Simons' interest help to 'protect and safeguard the welfare' of the children? What are the possible advantages and disadvantages?
(b) What do we need to know about Mrs Simons to answer these questions more fully?
(c) What might Julia's views be? The possible reasons for her quietness about her mother? What do I need to ask Julia?

Staying contact

It is now 4 January and a second Interim Care Order was made on 22 December. A great deal has happened. The children's grandmother, Anne Simons, has visited regularly. Julia has agreed that since she and her husband cannot decide about their relationship, the children should stay with her mother. Mark is not so certain. David and Pete have visited their grandmother's home with Julia and the social worker for a few hours last week (Christmas Eve) and you are asked to take the children with Julia for their first overnight stay with their granny, and collect them the next day. ('Staying contact' means an overnight visit by children to a parent or relative they do not usually live with.)

ACTIVITY 5: Getting ready to stay

Discuss in twos or threes how best to help Julia prepare David and Pete for this overnight stay, both in terms of explaining to David what is going to happen and in terms of the things the children and their grandmother need to have. What would you need to check for an overnight stay which would not have applied to the earlier daytime visit? What arrangements should be made in case one of the children just can't cope and becomes distressed, and for the children's return to their mother?

Planning for the future

On 26 January a Residence Order was made to Mrs Anne Simons. Julia and Mark both have contact orders – Julia visits her mother once a week for the night, and Mark, who is working part time, has the children for one day a week and one day every other weekend. Mrs Simons has given up her job as a shop assistant, but now receives family allowance. The relationship between Mark and Julia is still very stormy – they cannot stay together without arguments, though these are less violent now. Julia sometimes brings David and Pete – who is now a very sturdy 21 month old infant – to the family centre and wants to talk about preparing to apply to the court for the children's return to her. Mrs Simons would not oppose if she thought this was in the children's best interests.

ACTIVITY 6: What has to be done?

1   Using the worksheet on rehabilitation illustrated below as a guide, consider in groups of two or three what Julia *and* others would need to be able to tell the court in order to make it clear that the children's welfare would be safeguarded and promoted by their return to her care. (**Note:** 'Rehabilitation from care' is of course not the same as children returning to a parent from care in the extended family – but many of the decisions to be made will be the same.) What other people would need to be involved?

2   If you were representing the *children's* interests, how would you find out what the *advantages* and *disadvantages* of returning to Julia might be for David and Pete? Use any of the tools and questions set out in this case study.

Worksheet: Rehabilitation

This worksheet is designed to be used by anyone involved in planning a child's rehabilitation. It can be used by individuals in their work, or by all the planning group in reviews or other planning meetings.

Part 1: Planning the rehabilitation

1 **Name of child**
Date of birth
Placement
Date of admission to care
Legal status

Reason for admission to care

2 **The planning group**
Name all those concerned with the planning for this child.

---

3 **The start of the plan**
When was the plan for rehabilitation first made?
Has it always been the plan since then?
If not, what other plans have been made?

4 **Views of all concerned**
What is the attitude of each of the following towards the proposed plan?
(a) the child
(b) the birth parent(s)
(c) the carers
(d) the social worker
(e) the team leader
(f) doctors/health visitor
(g) teachers
(h) psychiatrist/psychologist
(i) child's peer group
(j) others
Who is motivated to try and make the plan succeed?
Who is opposed to the plan?

5 **Assessment of present situation**
(a) What changes have taken place since admission to care?
(b) What are the child's priority needs?
(c) What are the strengths and resources of the birth family and how far will these meet the child's needs?
(d) What are the priority needs of the parents and other family members, and in what ways will these prevent them from meeting the child's needs?
(e) What has been the effect on the child and family of the admission to care?

6 **Changes needed in order that the child's needs can be met at home**
List any changes required in the following:
(a) practical aspects of child care
(b) supervision of safety of child
(c) family's attitude to the child
(d) family's lifestyle
(e) the physical environment
(f) the support available to the family
(g) the child's ability to cope
(h) other

7 **Potential for change**
What is the potential for change in
(a) the child?
(b) the parent(s)?
(c) other family members?
(d) the environment?
(e) the support structure?

8 **Objectives for rehabilitation**
(a) What is the aim of work with the family as a group?
(b) What is the aim of work with the child?
(c) What is the aim of individual work with members of the family?
(d) What are the goals for environmental change?
(e) What is the agreed time-scale within which the child should return home?
Are there any difficulties envisaged in keeping to this timetable?

9 **Resources**
What resources are required?
(a) People:
who needs to be involved if the required changes are to take place?
what particular knowledge and skills will be required?
(b) Money and materials:
what are the financial implications of the plan?
what other material resources are required?

10 **Decision making:**
There is much detailed decision making involved in the carrying out of a plan for rehabilitation. What are the arrangements for decision making in this case?

11 **Contingency plans**
What are the expected difficulties in carrying out the plan?
What contingency plans should be made in case these difficulties do prove severe enough to prevent the plan from being carried out?

▶

12 Tasks

Who will be responsible for working out with the family the necessary tasks to be achieved?

Will there be a form of written agreement and if so, who will be party to it?

What will be the criteria for successful completion of these tasks?

Who will monitor the progress of the family and others involved?

13 Review and evaluation

When will the plan next be reviewed and by whom?

If rehabilitation is to stand a good chance of success certain criteria must be met.

How far are these criteria met?
What are the implications for the planned rehabilitation?
(If it is clear that rehabilitation will not or should not take place, the planning will move to consideration of long-term alternatives.)

Part 1 completed by _____

Date _____

(Source: M. Bryer, *Planning in Childcare* (BAAF 1988))

Case Study 3

Manor Court Playgroup

Manor Court Playgroup takes place in a hut behind a block of flats, in an inner city area. It takes children from about 2½ to 4, for a morning session, 9.30 a.m. to 12.00. It has an enclosed tarmac outdoor area, with a low wall and high fencing around it. It is a popular playgroup – some parents visit several playgroups before deciding they want their child to go to Manor Court. Others come because it is the nearest. Some have to be turned away because they did not get their child's name down soon enough.

The children come from all sections of the local community, which includes a large postwar estate, well-to-do owner-occupied housing, small shops and restaurants in a busy main road. The ethnic and social background of the area and its children is about as mixed as you can get; while many children of Afro-Caribbean and Irish origin have British born parents, other children have had little experience of English when they start. Families of the children speak a variety of languages at home – Greek, Turkish, Urdu and other European and African languages. Children have a variety of carers – unemployment has brought more dads to the playgroup, and minders and grandparents bring their children as well as mums.

Roisin, the playgroup leader, had been in quite a flap about the process of registration under the Children Act. She has run the playgroup for years. Other workers have come and gone, but she has kept it going and it is very much her playgroup. If the inspector had found things wrong she would have felt that it was her personal failure . . . It didn't help that at the time Charlene, the other playworker, had left, and the only way they could keep going was by having a regular rota of parents while they recruited a new worker.

Roisin has a strong and supportive Irish network herself, and many of the regulars, parents with several children and childminders who have looked after a succession of children over the years, are part of this network. Roisin minds children after playgroup, not regularly, but to help out particular parents she knows when their arrangements come unstuck. It works for the mums, as their children are looked after by a loved and familiar figure, and it helps Roisin, struggling on low and part-time pay to support three teenage kids on her own. Her eldest daughter is doing well – she will be taking her A levels in the summer, and Roisin is

77

enormously pleased for her. Her son, Adam, is a worry. He has been unhappy at school and is set to leave without any exams. Rather than pressurise him, she has decided to let him be, and go along with his casual truanting in the hope that he will make a new start at college in September.

It had been a difficult period with Charlene. Roisin had been pleased when Charlene was appointed. Charlene was younger, and also a single mum with two young children. It had started off well. Charlene was very keen and had a lot of bright new ideas for activities which Roisin welcomed. She had a strong presence, was very busy in the playgroup, talked to the children, and was very structured in what she did. But their differences soon became apparent. For Roisin the playgroup was a community centre. Parents at a low ebb could stay for a cup of tea and she had always parent helpers – some were marvellous, some needed help themselves. Charlene did not get involved in relationships with parents, partly, she said, because she thought there was too much gossiping, and the children were just being left to get on with it, and partly because she felt that black children and parents were underrepresented in the playgroup – too many children came from outside the immediate neighbourhood.

Roisin accepted that at that moment this was probably true; the local authority had cut their subsidy so that all parents had to pay £1.50 a morning. Previously children nominated by Social Services had not had to pay and others on Income Support had paid £1 a week. So she took children from the waiting list – which was always long. Roisin felt personally got at by Charlene's observations but felt that over a longer period, Charlene would see that the playgroup took a changing group of children from across the board in the area.

After a while, Roisin felt that Charlene needed to think about her priorities in her play work with children. Charlene was very keen on the children producing attractive artwork to take home, and, although she talked with the children while she did it, she directed too much energy at precise painting and sticking. At the end of the morning they would all leave with a mask with two streamers hanging off, or a nature collage, a loo-roll snowman or whatever. The parents loved it, and Charlene was pleased, but Roisin felt that the children's confidence in what they could do themselves was being eroded. When she spoke to Charlene about this, she exploded – the first of several disagreements.

A playgroup is a small world. Roisin was aware that her own feelings of frustration were being picked up by parents. Hazel, who cleaned the playgroup, was less discreet in her criticisms and complained openly about Charlene's lateness on Mondays and her days off for the doctor and Lord knows what, and how the playgroup was running out of money through having to pay for cover. There was some truth in this, and Roisin was worried about the ever-escalating insurance premiums; the playgroup suffered from vandalism. Children and young people from the neighbouring estate climbed in in the evenings. Graffiti, litter, condoms, evidence of glue sniffing and even syringes had been found in the mornings. Mondays in the summer are particularly bad; the playground cleaning rota of parents consists of three on a Monday morning and one every other day.

Then Charlene left.

**ACTIVITY 1:
What are the
problems?**

1   What are Roisin's problems? Write her name in the middle of a sheet of paper, and draw a line out to the problems she is experiencing.

2   What are the playgroup's problems? Draw these in the same way.

3   What went wrong with the working relationship between Roisin and Charlene?

    Divide your page into three vertical columns. List the problems as you think Charlene might have seen them in the left column. List the problems as Roisin would have seen them on the right. Can you make any suggestions about how they might have been approached constructively? Enter these in the middle.

4   Take each of the playgroup's problems you identified. After discussion, under each suggest a step or steps to take to help. Identify who you think should or could take the initiative.

**ACTIVITY 2:
Registration**

Overleaf is a diagram showing the process in registering a daycare setting, such as a playgroup. Redraw the diagram to show the checks which would have been carried out on:

● Roisin herself;
● Hazel;
● the playgroup premises.

**ACTIVITY 3:
How many
children? How
much space?**

Manor Court used to have up to 20 children, but on any particular day several would be away. Most children are 3; generally, they would start at about 2½, and go on to nursery sometime after 4. At any one time there would be about six under 3s. There are the two paid playworkers, and a regular parents' rota, in addition to the parents who stay to help on a casual basis or for a short period of time.

Your task here is to work out what, if any, changes will have to be made to the playgroup or the numbers of children following registration.

1   A sketch of the playgroup building and playground, not to scale but with accurate measurements, appears on p 81. Copy the sketch, and enlarge it to scale, using squared paper. Work out the area of the playgroup's floorspace.

2   See also the 'Standards checklist' summarising the requirements for registration on p 82.

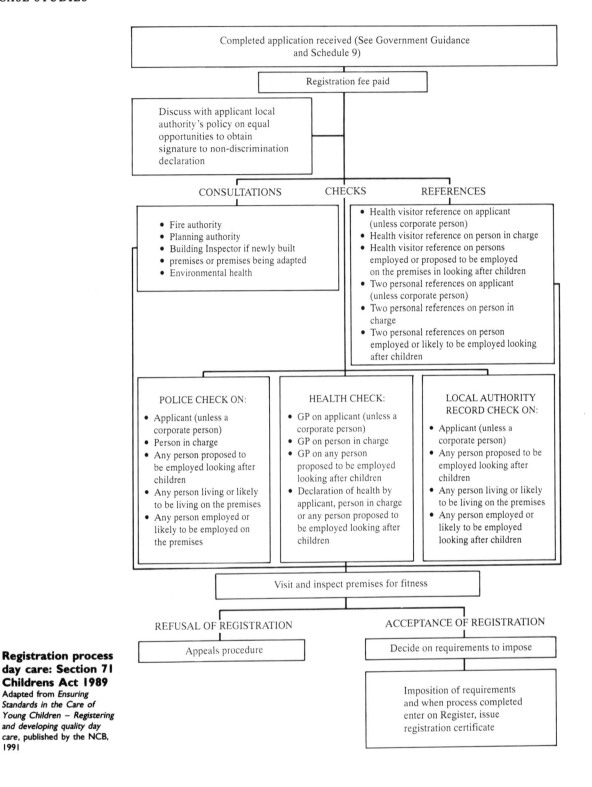

Completed application received (See Government Guidance and Schedule 9)

Registration fee paid

Discuss with applicant local authority's policy on equal opportunities to obtain signature to non-discrimination declaration

CONSULTATIONS   CHECKS   REFERENCES

- Fire authority
- Planning authority
- Building Inspector if newly built
- premises or premises being adapted
- Environmental health

- Health visitor reference on applicant (unless corporate person)
- Health visitor reference on person in charge
- Health visitor reference on persons employed or proposed to be employed on the premises in looking after children
- Two personal references on applicant (unless corporate person)
- Two personal references on person in charge
- Two personal references on person employed or likely to be employed looking after children

POLICE CHECK ON:

- Applicant (unless a corporate person)
- Person in charge
- Any person proposed to be employed looking after children
- Any person living or likely to be living on the premises
- Any person employed or likely to be employed on the premises

HEALTH CHECK:

- GP on applicant (unless a corporate person)
- GP on person in charge
- GP on any person proposed to be employed looking after children
- Declaration of health by applicant, person in charge or any person proposed to be employed looking after children

LOCAL AUTHORITY RECORD CHECK ON:

- Applicant (unless a corporate person)
- Any person proposed to be employed looking after children
- Any person living or likely to be living on the premises
- Any person employed or likely to be employed looking after children

Visit and inspect premises for fitness

REFUSAL OF REGISTRATION   ACCEPTANCE OF REGISTRATION

Appeals procedure

Decide on requirements to impose

Imposition of requirements and when process completed enter on Register, issue registration certificate

Registration process day care: Section 71 Childrens Act 1989
Adapted from *Ensuring Standards in the Care of Young Children – Registering and developing quality day care*, published by the NCB, 1991

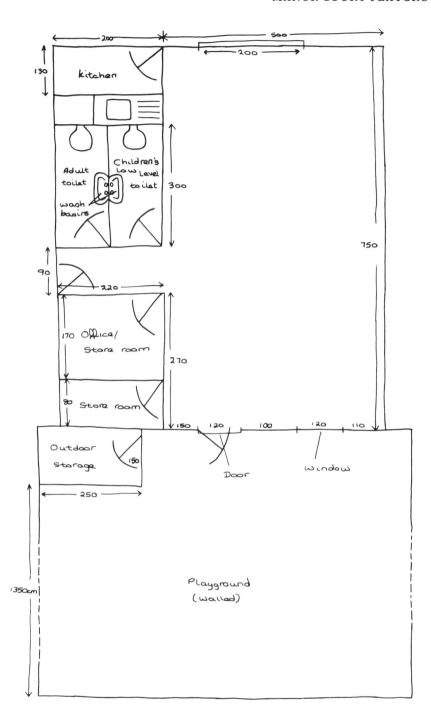

**Manor Court
Playgroup**

81

Standards checklist

Before submitting your application form and fee, the applicant may find it useful to check whether they are able to meet the following basic standards. The check list is a guide and other standards will apply, particularly for afterschool and holiday provision.

Please also check to see that you meet the **Assessment of Fitness** and can comply with the **Equal opportunities** and **child care policies**.

Staffing	**Full day care** (non domestic)	**Sessional day care**	**Childminding**
Ratios	Nurseries for over 20 children Manager is supernumerary 1 worker: 8 children (3–5 years) 1 worker: 4 children (2–3 years)	As per full day care	Minders may care for only 1 child under 1 year. 1 Minder: 3 children under 5 years.
and	1 worker: 3 children (under 2 years)		1 Minder + assistant: 6 children under 5 years.
Qualifications/ experience	*Managers* Qualification + 5 years experience	PPA Foundation Course	1 Minder: 6 children 5–8 years.
	Nursery Workers 50% qualified + 6 months experience Cook Food Hygiene Certificate		Additionally 2 children 5–8 years. Pre-Registration Training Course. Aged 18–65 years
Premises			
Floor space	3.7 sq metres per child under 2 years 2.8 sq metres per child under 2–3 years 2.3 sq metres per child under 3–5 years	As per full day care	Acceptable domestic premises
Lavatories/ wash basins	1 lavatory/wash basin: 10 children	1 lavatory/wash basin: 10 children	Acceptable domestic premises.
Rooms	Office, staff facilities. Storage. Food preparation. Playrooms. Separate facilities for under 2s.	Office, staff facilities. Storage. Food preparation. Playrooms.	Acceptable domestic premises.
Outdoor play	Immediate access	Arrangements for regular outings	Arrangements for regular outings.
Equipment			
Standard essentials	All new equipment must meet British Standard/European (CE), Lion Mark (BS 5665) and non-toxic. Telephone. Fire Safety. First Aid. Multi-racial.	As per full day care	As per full day care
Records	Child's personal record. Outings attendance. Accidents. Food. Medicine. Management Committee. Others on premises.	As per full day care	As per full day care. Additionally parental contract

Insurance	Employer's liability. Public liability. Buildings, Contents and equipment. All risks. Money and personal effects.	As per full day care	Public liability insurance
Fire precautions	Fire alarm. Smoke detectors. Fire exits. Regular drills. Advice from Health and Safety Officer.	As per full day care	As per full day care
Planning permission	Contact Planning Service	Contact Planning Service	Not applicable

(Adapted from *Children Act 1989*, published by the London Borough of Camden)

(a)   What is the playgroup's position in relation to the number and ages of children it can accommodate?

(b)   What is the position with regard to toilets/wash basins?

(c)   What about staffing ratios?

ACTIVITY 4: What do children learn in playgroup?

The PPA suggests that each playgroup session should include the opportunity to develop the following skills:

- a balance of large and small muscle activities to develop physical skills;
- a variety of interaction with adults and other children to develop social and language skills;
- a variety of challenging experiences to develop intellectual ability;
- a range of natural materials to develop creative skills;
- varied opportunities for imaginative play and exploration to encourage personal and emotional development.

(Source: *Guidelines for Good Practice for Sessional Playgroups for 3–5 Year Olds*, p 49, published by the PPA)

1   Compare the PPA's summary of the skills a child should be able to develop in a playgroup with the diagram in Task 1, Assignment 9. Consider the different ways in which the skills are described.

2   The PPA also offers the following quick reference guide to activities and the skills they develop.

PLAY ACTIVITIES FOR TWO TO FIVE YEAR OLDS		
Play which:		
Stimulates children's imagination and creativity	stories, paint, wet sand, dressing up, domestic and adventure play, collage and junk modelling	building blocks, music, pencils & crayons, small scale play (eg dolls, cars, trains, animals), construction materials, cutting & sticking
Enriches language development	talking, asking questions, listening, recalling experiences	conversation, discussion about home and everyday life

83

Forms the basis of mathematical understanding	dry sand, water, building blocks, wood, sorting and matching	construction materials, puzzles, describing, comparing, explaining, classifying
Enables children to come to terms with aspects of their own lives and to express their feelings	domestic play, paint, stories, conversation, music, multi-cultural books, pictures, dressing up clothes	wet & dry sand, water, dough, pencils & crayons, puppets
Encourages the development of manipulative skills	dough, clay, wood, pencils & crayons, cutting & sticking	small scale play, puzzles, cooking, posting, sorting, printing, threading, wet & dry sand, water, construction materials
Offers the chance to explore and enjoy natural materials	water, clay, wet & dry sand, wood	earth, leaves, fabrics, corks, shells, stones
Develops muscular strength and co-ordination	opportunities to build, climb and balance	running, skipping, pushing & pulling, jumping, woodwork, rolling, hopping, throwing, crawling
Establishes the use of symbols and patterns which form the basis of reading and writing	paint, books, stories, pencils & crayons, beads & pegboards	pictures, posters, puzzles, written names, imaginative play
Helps children to respect and enjoy the companionship of other children and of adults	conversation, imaginative and adventure play	things to share (eg climbing frame, road layout, home corner) joint activities (eg singing, outings, stories) sharing jokes
Creates habits of listening and concentrating	songs, rhymes, stories, conversation, individually & in small groups	music, games, water, telephone, play with sound
Extends children's understanding of science and the world around them	books, water, problem solving, investigation, discussion	magnets, lenses, mirrors, wood, living & growing things, cooking, experiments, outings, visitors
Responds to children's need to explore through their senses	fingerpaint, dough, water, dry sand, sounds	wet sand, music, cooking, wood, cutting & sticking, collage and junk modelling

ACTIVITIES IN THE CENTRE COLUMN ARE ESPECIALLY IMPORTANT BECAUSE THEY ARE OPEN ENDED AND CAN EXTEND CHILDREN'S DEVELOPMENT IN A WIDE VARIETY OF WAYS.

(Source: *Guidelines for Good Practice for Sessional Playgroups for 3–5 Year Olds*, pp 58–9, published by the PPA)

Take four varied suggestions from the central panel, link each with related ideas from the right-hand column where possible, and see how many skill areas can be developed from each. Draw a diagram like the one on p 171 for each one. Write the activity in the circle at the centre of the page and add as much detail as you can to the play possibilities under each heading.

ACTIVITY 5:
A tarmac
rectangle

Look back to the text and to your scale drawing for details of the playground. What simple, safe, long-term and (hopefully) vandal-proof improvements can you suggest to make this a more interesting space to play and learn in?

Discuss your suggestions in small groups. When you have agreed proposals, draw them in on your plan. Agree whether you should then cost them.

Case Study 4

A normal life?

Part 1, Chapter 5 gives details of the requirement placed by the Children Act 1989 on local authorities to provide services to 'minimise the effect on disabled children within their area of disabilities' and 'to give such children the opportunity to lead lives which are as normal as possible'.

This case study considers, through the voices of parents of children with disabilities and a few professionals, the obstacles and pathways to a normal life. Many of the extracts are drawn from or based on the newsletter of the CD Family Support Group, a group of parents of children with a range of disabilities in North London. The author is grateful to these parents for allowing their experiences to be brought to a wider audience in this way. I am aware that to these families the picture that emerges from these extracts offers only a fleeting glimpse of their needs. I hope that to those of us considering the help we have to offer, the experiences of these families will make us better helpers.

Following the article below by Diane Crutcher of the USA Down's Syndrome Congress, parents' accounts of aspects of life with their children are quoted in ordinary text typeface and names have been changed; parents' comments on their needs and the responses of service organisers are shown in italics, and items from a list of what this group of parents want from services are given in bold.

When you are going to have a baby, it is like you are planning a vacation in Italy, you are all excited – you get a whole bunch of guide books and you learn a few phrases in Italian so you can get around. When it comes time, you pack your bags and head for the airport for Italy. Only when you land and the stewardess says 'Welcome to Holland' you look at one another in disbelief and shock and say: 'Holland? What are you talking about? I booked for Italy!'

Then they explain there has been a change of plan and you have landed in Holland where you have to stay. 'But I don't know anything about Holland! I don't want to stay!' But you do – you go out and buy some new guide books. You learn some new phrases, and you meet people you never knew existed. The important thing is that you are not in a filthy, plague-infested slum full of pestilence and famine. You are simply in a different place than you planned. It is slower paced than Italy and less flashy than Italy, but after you have been there a while and you have a chance to catch your breath, you begin to discover that Holland has windmills, Holland has tulips, Holland even has Rembrandts!

Of course, everyone else you know is busy coming and going to Italy. They are all bragging about what a great time they had there, and for the rest of your life you will say 'Yes. That's where I was going. That's what I planned!' The pain of that will never, ever go away. You have to accept that pain because the loss of that dream, the loss of that plan, is a very, very significant loss. But if you spend your life mourning the fact that you did not get to Italy, you will never be free to enjoy the very special, the very lovely things about Holland.

(Source: Diane Crutcher, Executive Director, USA Down's Syndrome Congress, in Down's Syndrome Association newsletter, Spring 1991)

The early months

'I am writing this primarily as a guide for parents of newly-diagnosed children, perhaps as a guide or some sort of comfort. I think that the main bit of advice I can give from my own experience is 'never distrust your gut feelings'. If you do, it destroys you. It's like you believe something is white, somebody tells you it is black and you end up believing them. For example, Zoe always had sparkly eyes. I take this as a positive thing but the doctors didn't seem to. This is because they don't want to be responsible for giving you false hopes.'

(Clare)

- **Support from day 1.**
- **Diagnosis from birth or as early as possible.**
- **Honesty about diagnosis.**
- **A named contact to give information, support and coordinate services.**
- **Information parents can understand.**
- **Another parent to talk to.**
- **If initial contacts are refused – follow up please!**

The early years

Karl – a crack at describing the effects of autism

'Our son, Karl, is nearly five years old. He is tall, well built, blond and handsome. He is often happy and sometimes loving. He has terrible rages but rarely cries. He likes to have his back tickled. He loves Thomas the Tank Engine, cereal packets and cartoon characters. He is original, idiosyncratic and totally unpredictable. He is autistic.

Autism is a profound, perplexing and complex disability. It is, primarily, a disorder which affects social and communication skills. Large books have been written on autism, its causes and effects. We live daily with our son's autism and it has completely changed our lives and our expectations from life. Our lives are very different to those who do not live with autism, for we are bounded on all sides by its severe restrictions.

87

The simple mechanics of living are a mystery to Karl; he does not understand them, although he is beginning to. He does not realise that food has to be cooked before it can be eaten, that a drink doesn't materialise out of thin air, that if he has lost one of his precious toy trains we will not instantly know which one and where it is. He doesn't understand what holidays are, nor Christmas, nor birthdays. He doesn't understand that we feel pain, both physical and emotional. He doesn't understand what danger is or where it lies. His lack of understanding is staggering in its range and it affects him profoundly. He copes with this strange world by insisting that it stay as changeless as possible.

His obsession with inanimate objects, like toy trains and cereal packets, reflects this. He spends many hours lining them up in straight lines, always in the same order, always by pushing them past his face at close proximity while lying on the floor. A careless foot or loss of an engine can lead to terrible rages. Changes of any sort can lead to terrible rages; the inexplicable change from term time to holidays, the change from a familiar park to a strange one, a day out with his family, the careless moving of a biscuit tin from one place in the kitchen to another. Life is fraught with fear for Karl and fear turns to anger.

His anger is terrible. He kicks, hits, throws things with deadly accuracy, spits, bites. He vents his anger on his parents and, most distressingly on his eight year old sister. We remove him until he calms down, a process that can take up to an hour. Unfortunately, Karl is oblivious to the constraints of socially acceptable behaviour and these rages are as likely to occur outside the house as in, at which time we are subjected to the condemnation of the public, who see no deeper than an ordinary looking child behaving in a socially unacceptable way. We have grown inured and immune to public opinion. It is the violence itself that causes us pain, both physical and emotional. The fact that Karl himself is unaware that he is hurting us does little to lessen the distress of his aggression.

Our Karl has, over the last eighteen months, started to acquire language. He has started to understand some important words like 'wait!' He has started to sign and speak, although his pronunciation takes a fair amount of imaginative interpretation. Karl has had to learn that which comes naturally to other children. He has had to learn to give and to receive love. He now not only tolerates but enjoys a cuddle and back tickle. He has learned to put his arms around my neck in a loose semblance of an embrace. He has also learnt that I am Mummy and can offer some solace in a frightening world.'

(Maggie)

'I like to think I'm strong and tough and although I'm sometimes unable to cope, it usually only takes half an hour of solitude to crawl back into the realms of coping again. But recently I collapsed. I've never done it before and it's been a frightening experience. The reason? Stress and exhaustion. Stress knocks out the immune system and for the last nine months I've succumbed to stress and suffered endless small infections (flu, tummy bugs, colds, etc.) and Liam just knocks me out, like so many disabled children, he is an exhausting child, not just tiring, exhausting.

I've assessed what the local council has to offer and it's considerably more caring than many councils. There is Home Help, Family Link, Care Attendant scheme and early part-time schooling. But we have found that these services are limited through lack of funding, that they become available almost too late and that they do not address the fundamental issue of the realistic help that is needed. I, like everyone else, have coped unaided through the first couple of years when the physical stress is great and so is the emotional stress of coming to terms with the child's disability and I was already exhausted. Now I have the very real added fear of what will happen if one day I can't get out of bed . . .'

- **Help in a crisis need for a break.**
- **Help when parent is ill or needs a break.**
- **Peripatetic houseparents.**
- **Holiday play schemes.**
- **Support at home or when going out.**
- **Support to enable parents to work.**
- **Quantity of services as judged appropriate by the parents.**
- **Integrated activities.**
- **A key person to coordinate services.**

'Well, when I first phoned (the Social Services) I'd heard about the Attendance Allowance and I thought she'd give me some advice on that but she didn't, she talked about everything else but that . . .'

- **Professionals to be better trained, to work together, and communicate with users.**
- **Be better informed.**
- **If they don't know, refer to someone who does.**
- **A link person between services.**
- **Continuity.**
- **Treat users as equals – with honesty.**

'It's always a case of, if you ask then you receive . . . Instead of waiting for a parent to ask a specific question, and giving him an answer, for God's sake give him the information first . . .'

'Belonging to the group has helped me to get access to the following services: orange badge scheme for car parking; child's car seat (much more complicated . . .); polite notice (small sign fixed on wall requesting parking access outside our house – via Occupational Therapy); plastic mattress cover for child's bed (also via OT); car tax exemption (very complicated . . .); Family Fund (a small grant to help with outings – extremely welcome); horse riding lessons (very successful); Family Link (last but definitely not least – essential for keeping sane and keeping going).'

- **Information book outlining all services – updated annually.**
- **Interpreters and translaters.**
- **Welfare rights information.**
- **Borough Helpline.**
- **Immediate access to experts when needed.**

And so to school

The 1981 Education Act incorporating the recommendations of the 1978 Warnock Report was seen as a watershed in education for children with disabilities. Under this Act a child with a disability is entitled to a Statement of Special Educational Needs detailing how those needs will be met and supported. Mainstream education must be provided if it can be provided – and the Children Act 1989 supports this in the stress it lays upon a disabled child's right to 'the opportunity to lead as normal a life as possible'. The child as a whole must be considered, not just the difficulties – so the curriculum, peer group, closeness to home must all be taken into account.

Current practice is affected by other considerations – cutbacks in funding and resources, delays and resistance. Some parents, staff and children take the view that the benefits brought about by the expertise of the teachers and resources of a special school outweigh the disadvantages of a segregated or special education. This is particularly so where the disorder or difficulty the child has is rare or highly specific, and there are few centres of expertise in the country. Other parents and staff are committed to having their children educated in mainstream schools, with the level of support detailed in the statement. Below are some comments from people involved in the statementing process.

'Perhaps you can help me! I have a child who I feel needs to be statemented but the educational psychologist is blocking the process saying we should try a bit longer to resolve the problem without resorting to the statement . . .'
(Primary head)

'It is a long and complicated procedure which appears to have been designed to put you off initiating it because the resources necessary to implement the legislation are not available . . .' (Primary head)

'He's going to live in the community so it is important that he is really known by his peers and appreciated for who he is rather than known by a label.'
(Parent of child with Down's Syndrome)

'The experience in hospital (a hospital school) on the whole was a positive one. I left nearly two years later, with a much improved skin condition, a lot of confidence, and a lot of optimism about the future.'
(Former student at a special school)

'Special school was recommended for his physical needs but he didn't get much physio . . . Now he's with normal children, he's really doing well.'
(Parent of child injured in car accident)

- **Wider range of health options.**
- **More occupational therapy, speech therapy, physiotherapy.**
- **Offer alternatives such as homeopathy and osteopathy.**
- **Increased choice and improved education services.**

- **Improve the statementing process.**
- **Offer options of integration and alternative education.**

Below are some extracts about a special school, Bishopswood, and its three partner mainstream schools.

> Bishopwood School, for pupils aged 2–16 with developmental delay or severe learning difficulties, has its own budget, governing body, headteacher, staff, a pupil roll of 46, but no school building. Classes for all our pupils, whatever the nature or degree of their learning difficulties, are within mainstream partner schools.
>
> Each Bishopswood class has its own room with a teacher and assistant. This provides a secure base from which pupils move for shared educational and social experiences in the mainstream, as appropriate for each individual . . . Our pupils have a range of difficulties similar to those found in any small special school. We have a number of pupils with profound and multiple difficulties and several who are withdrawn and have difficulty establishing relationships.
>
> Rubbing along with more able children, year after year, undoubtedly increases motivation to learn in some areas, encourages social awareness and enriches the individual child. However, we are more cautious about teaching reading, writing and number skills in a fully integrated setting. Our experience has shown that provided there is a well-resourced, supported and committed school, full-time integration is most successful when children have good language (four word level), an outward personality, and when copying other children is their most useful learning strategy. Children on the Bishopswood roll often do not have these advantages and also need specialist resources, small groups and a high staff ratio to meet their learning needs . . .
>
> (From *Bishopswood Good Practice Transferred*, published 1992 by the Centre for Studies on Integration in Education (CSIE), 415 Edgware Road, London NW2 6NB. Tel. 081-452 8642)

And into the community

> 'Real integration means investment in these children and an awareness of their various difficulties and differences. Children with physical problems need special equipment and carefully thought out play programmes. How is my daughter to be integrated when all she can do is lie on the floor because no one has thought to provide a standing frame to put her on a level and equal footing with her peers?'
>
> (Parent of child with cerebral palsy, after accepting an invitation to go to an 'integrated' Opportunity Group morning at an Under Fives Centre)

Sports news is bad news this month. Community Action Sport has been axed, and all the sports centres we use except one are to close.
FRIDAY NIGHT TRAMPOLINING: will cease as the sports centre is closing.

MULTISPORTS CLUB: can no longer meet at the sports centre but we have sponsorship if a new base can be found.

SWIMMING CLUB: This is building up, but please do come along to show that there is a real need. If we get enough regulars we may be able to ask for some instruction for our children . . .

(Based on extract from parents group newsletter)

- **Better preparation for adulthood.**
- **Training in dependence skills.**
- **A range of residential options.**
- **Support workers in the community especially geared towards 18–30 age group.**
- **Improved further education and access.**

**ACTIVITY 1:
What's the
problem?**

1 Draw a diagram to show the problems the parents in these extracts are experiencing. Take a blank sheet of paper and write 'Parent and child' in the centre. Draw a line out to each problem you identify.

2 Review your web of problems. What would you say is the cause of each problem? Mark these in a different colour.

3 Group the causes of the problems you have identified under headings. Aim for three or four headings only. For clarity, you may need to copy out your list under each heading.

4 On a separate sheet of paper consider the needs of a sibling – younger or older – of a child with disabilities. Write 'Brother/Sister' in the centre of the page and draw lines out to needs you identify.

From the parents' point of view, mark in, using a different colour, where these needs are hard to deliver.

Write a paragraph summarising your discussion and thinking on the impact of a child with disabilities on the family.

**ACTIVITY 2:
What next?**

1 Identify the groups of problems that could be helped if resources allowed.

2 Refer to Table 1 in Chapter 3, Part 1 (p 24). How high a priority are children with disabilities in terms of response to individual need and in service development in the social service departments in this survey?

3 How high a priority are they in your area? What services are available in your area to meet the needs you identified above?

**ACTIVITY 3:
A daft idea?**

Extract 1

'I recently spoke to a mum in our group who had not had a decent night's sleep for six months, and the day I spoke to her she had had no sleep at all the night before. No respite care was available and she was refused home help. This led me to wonder whether we shouldn't be thinking of a total shake up of the system. Work out how much all these social workers, service managers, 'line' managers (whatever that is – certainly nothing to do with my laundry), clerks, secretaries, PAs, desks, telephone lines, paper, office space, etc. cost. Get rid of them all and divide the money between all families needing services and pay them all a weekly tax-free allowance graded according to the severity of the need. With this, we could purchase whatever services we wanted . . .'

Extract 2

'I encountered people from Hampshire Centre for Independent Living, a number of whom had moved out of residential care and into the community. They had done this by persuading the social services to give each person a grant to employ their own care support, proving it to be a more cost-effective option than institutional care.' Simon Brisenden employed 'a team of three care-helpers who are financed by my disability benefits and a grant from Hampshire County Council.'

(Simon Brisenden, in Richard Reiser and Micheline Mason, Disability Equality in the Classroom: A Human Rights Issue, available from 78 Mildmay Grove, London N1 4PJ)

1 Is the suggestion in Extract 1 a daft idea? This is a topic that merits serious and structured discussion. You should prepare for this by researching arguments and evidence for and against this view. It is a suitable topic for a formal debate. (For guidance on formal debates see *A Practical Approach to Caring* by Kate Williams (Pitman Publishing, 1991), p 234.)

2 Simon Brisenden (Extract 2) goes on to say: 'The role of carer should not be to control but to facilitate. I define this as being the necessary interventions enabling the decisions of the individual to be carried out. Anything more than this is an infringement of a person's liberty.'
   (a) What are the implications of this view for someone employed as a care-helper?
   (b) How does this view affect the type and style of care that might be delivered to a child with disabilities and the family by:
   ● a home help;
   ● a peripatetic houseparent/home-based respite care?

ACTIVITY 4: Research

Follow up one issue about children with disabilities. Agree your topic with your tutor, research it and present your findings to the group within an agreed time limit. Possible topics are:

● What is the impact of the Children Act on services for children with disabilities in your area?
● The statementing process.
● The relationship between specialist (segregated/alternative) and mainstream educational provision for children with special needs in your area.
● More detail on a particular disability or learning difficulty and the effect on a child's development.

ACTIVITY 5:
Carry on caring
The lack of information about what services and benefits are available to children with disabilities and their families is a recurring theme. Find out about these in your area and compile a handbook with this information. This is a big topic. You may decide to divide the work between the group. Include information on:

- cash benefits;
- benefits in kind (e.g. leisure passes, parking concessions, equipment);
- social services;
- education services;
- health services;
- leisure and casual play opportunities;
- voluntary and self-help groups.

When you have compiled it, discuss ways of bringing it to the attention of service providers and service users.

Case Study 5

Diana and Joseph Lewis

'Hey, Mrs D, it's me.' Dorothy Douglas winked at Joseph, took his bowl back from him, added a second wedge of chocolate pudding, flooded it with chocolate sauce, and handed it back. He beamed at her and made his way back to the table where the others were well through their single portions . . . He knew he was a favourite with Mrs D. 'You just like my boy at your age,' she would say. 'You got hollow legs?'

As Dorothy left the school when the kitchens closed, she saw Joseph walking very slowly down the corridor. 'What you doing here?' she asked. 'Nothing,' he said. 'I can see that,' she said, 'nice boy like you should be learning, not doing nothing in the boys' toilets.' She laughed and cuffed him gently on the shoulder. 'Go on,' she said as she walked away. He smiled – a little smile, not like the smiles that once lit up his face.

Diana Lewis is in the first year juniors. Like Joseph at her age, she is a bright, outgoing child, and is particularly good at reading and writing stories. She sits with a group of able children including her friends Zoe and Gabriella. She has been to each of their houses for tea – twice – and asks her mum if they can come back to her home. They can't. Mary Lewis works, full time for the last six months, after her husband left the family, and Diana goes to the play centre after school. So as she lines up with the other children to be escorted to the play centre at a neighbouring primary school, she sees her friends going off together, to the park, to dance classes, to each other's homes for tea. Diana isn't a best friend any more, just a friend.

Mary Lewis works as an accounts clerk at a building society. It was a long hard slog to get this job – at 40, she knows her age counted against her. She says as little as possible about her difficulties as a single parent. She knows she is lucky to have a job at all. Shortly after she started, a nearby branch was closed, making staff redundant. The staff at her branch were all asked if they wanted to take redundancy, as they were redeploying people from the other branch.

She had not intended to work full time like this when she went back to college to train in bookkeeping and accounts; her plan was to handle the business side of Michael's electrician business. Just as she qualified, he left her to live with Jean. It was a bitter blow in every way. At 30,

Jean was younger, black, attractive and tough, and knew just what she wanted – Michael. She felt bitter about Michael too – she'd built her life around him and his business. Her mother's told-you-so attitude was unbearable. She had never accepted her black son-in-law, and warned that he'd leave her for one of his own colour, leaving her with 'half-caste' kids. Mary'd proved her wrong all these years – Michael had been a good husband and father, and they'd been very happy – until now.

Then there were the children. Joseph had proved very responsible in some ways, taking Diana to school, locking up the house. But after school was another matter, and now the summer holidays were coming up. Mary had always collected her children from school, or been there when Joseph got home, sometimes early, sometimes later when he'd been to football or computer club. Now Joseph has his own key, and she has no idea what he does on his way home. Not football for sure, as Terry, the football club manager, rang one morning when she'd been at home waiting for the gas man, to ask if Joseph had given up football and what a shame since he wanted him in the team. Then Joseph talked bitterly about Leon – the team's star player – picking on him, keeping him out of his team when he picked players, calling him 'whitey'. Mary is becoming seriously worried about Joseph; at parents' evening his teachers confirmed that his work had gone downhill. His form tutor, Mr Payne, seemed particularly concerned – Joseph seems isolated, is often late in the mornings and sometimes misses lessons.

Michael Lewis had also gone to the parents' evening, and left deeply worried about Joseph. The teachers seemed surprised to see him separately – they had not known that he did not live with Joseph. Michael had known nothing of Mary's concerns – she did not speak to him. When he calls for the children on Saturdays, Joseph answers the door. He now takes them to the lock-up garage where he keeps his van and tools, partly because he has nowhere else to go, partly because he hoped to rekindle the relaxed and happy times he had spent there with Joe in the past. He could see it was not satisfactory, but alternatives had not worked. He tried taking them to Jean's, but they'd sat around awkwardly. He'd tried taking Jean's kids with Joseph to the park to play football, but Joseph lost few opportunities to kick and shove Winford, and Diana was bored. He'd like to take them to stay with his parents for the weekend in Birmingham, but although Mary had been very fond of his dad, there is no way she will let them stay overnight.

Michael has reached the point when he feels he has drawn a blank with Mary. He urgently wants to talk to her about Joseph, and to discuss the summer holidays. The children had always spent a week with his parents in Birmingham, and had a great time, but Mary isn't going to agree to this now. He'd like to take them away, with Jean and her children, but Mary will not see him, let alone discuss this and the wider questions of his contact with the children. He has made an appointment to see a solicitor next week.

Jean Fraser is happier than she has ever been in her life. Michael is mature, practical around the flat, good with the kids, and shows a real interest in making sure Winford, now 12, does his homework – which she'd never managed to do. She'd never stood for any nonsense from her kids, but Winford had been giving her a lot of lip. Not to Michael though.

She'd done a bit of childminding when her kids were at home – mostly helping out friends – but now has a job as a receptionist and, as she's been there a while, she now has the hours she wants. She gets home at 4.15, and is usually there soon after Gary, 9, who has been coming home on his own for nearly two years, gets in. So that just leaves the problem of school holidays. In the past the boys had always gone to holiday play schemes, but this year Michael is talking about them all going on a proper holiday for two weeks at least. She wouldn't mind Joseph and Diana coming too although it would be easier if they didn't. Joseph and Winford don't get on, and Diana is younger, and wouldn't want to do the same things as the boys. She thinks Mary is behaving stupidly – turning down the offer of Michael taking the kids off. She has used playschemes for years and her kids are none the worse for it.

ACTIVITY 1:
Understanding
relationships

1 Draw a family tree diagram to show the relationships of all the members of the Lewis and Fraser families mentioned in the text. Sketch it in rough first. When you copy it out, take a whole side of paper and add in basic information about each person – (approximate) age, race, occupation and working hours.

2 Draw a diagram to show family and social relationships from the point of view of first Joseph, then Diana Lewis. You may wish to work with a partner.
   (a) For each diagram take a whole side of paper. Put the child's name in the middle of the page and around the edge put the names of all the other people (adult and child) and organisations mentioned in the text with whom the child has contact.
   (b) Draw a red line linking Joseph/Diana to people and organisations you think they feel positive about. Draw a blue line to those you think they feel negative about. You may find you use both colours for some links.

3 Putting it into words. Can you explain, in one or two sentences, why Joseph and Diana feel as they do about each person you have shown on your diagram? Keep your presentation simple, e.g. 'Joseph feels positive about ... because ...', 'Joseph has mixed feelings about ... because ...'

4 Write a paragraph about (a) Diana, (b) Joseph, describing how you think

they have been affected by their parents' separation. You can go beyond the text and add in thoughts of your own.

ACTIVITY 2: From the adults' point of view

Both Mary and Michael Lewis have their worries and concerns. What are they? What can they do about them?

1 Give yourself the heading 'Mary Lewis's concerns'. Divide your page into two columns. On the left, list Mary's concerns. On the right, make a list of your ideas for dealing with her problems. Work with a partner.

2 Do the same for Michael Lewis.

3 Discuss your suggestions with another pair. In your small group, agree a written action plan.

4 What do you think are the obstacles to your action plan?

5 The first Michael Lewis knew about Joseph's problems at school was at the parents' evening. Look back at your diagram in Activity 1, Task 1 and see if you can identify any adults in touch with Joseph who had a sense that all was not well with him. Could these people have communicated their concerns to anyone who could help?

ACTIVITY 3: The legal framework

NOTE *Part 1 provides much of the information you need for this activity. See particularly Chapter 2 pp 11–16 and Chapter 6, pp 42–4.*

1 Michael has made a decision — that he must see a solicitor. Put yourself in the position of the solicitor as he considers Michael's options with him.
   (a) What is 'parental responsibility'?
   (b) Who has parental responsibility for Joseph and Diana?
   (c) Suggest ways in which people with parental responsibility who do not live together could share information and come to important decisions about the children. Consider *direct* and *indirect* communication.
   (d) List the consequences for Diana and Joseph of their parents not communicating. If this hostility continues, what other effects might there be on the children?

2 (a) Find out what the following are, and when they are used: contact order; residence order; conciliation service.
   (b) Extend your research to find out more about conciliation services in your area. Start points are the Citizen's Advice Bureau, Relate, the local court. What do these services offer? Who is assisted?

3 Below are the options Michael's solicitor put to him:
   • Reach an agreement with Mary out of court. What would this be?
   • Have either Joseph or Diana or both live with him and Jean permanently, if they want to.

- Have his contact with the children agreed in court. What should this be?
- Have his mother's contact with the children agreed in court.
  - (a) With a partner discuss which, if you were Michael, you would want, and which you think he should realistically go for.
  - (b) Describe how he should go about this legally, and identify the Order(s) he should seek.
  - (c) Set out the **advantages** and **disadvantages** of each option for each of the following: Joseph; Diana; Mary; Michael; Jean; Jean's children.

4   The Children Act states that arrangements over children must 'safeguard and promote the children's welfare'. Which arrangement do you think best achieves this?

5   Write a short report, suitable for use in court, in which you set out, clearly and simply, the arrangements you think would be in the children's best interests. Explain your reasons.

ACTIVITY 4: School holiday options

What are the options for the children of working parents in the school holidays?

1   Devise a simple questionnaire to find out what the members of your group did as children during half terms and holidays, when they were the age of any two of the children mentioned in the case study. If your group includes parents of school age children, find out what they do with their children in the holidays. (For advice on how to draw up a questionnaire and write a report, see *A Practical Approach to Caring* by Kate Williams (Pitman Publishing, 1991).)
  - (a) Decide exactly what you want to find out. This is your 'Terms of reference'.
  - (b) Consider the wording of your questions carefully. Remember 'nothing' will not do as an answer – a parent at home is 'provision'!

2   Present your findings as a short report. Include a bar chart, showing the options used by members of your group.

ACTIVITY 5: What's on offer?

1   Find out what is available to children (i) in the school holidays, (ii) after school, in your area.
  - (a) Pool ideas on the sources of information.
  - (b) Write or phone for details where appropriate.

2   Present your findings in a simple, attractive leaflet, suitable for children and parents in your area. You may wish to include the following:

- a map showing locations, bus routes, etc.;
- details of type of provision, age group it suits, etc.;
- costs;
- how to join/enrol.

Case Study 6

Adrian Costello

'Why I'm at 121 Brooke Road'

Hello, I'm Adrian Costello and I'm 15 years old. I've got two sisters: Roxanne, she's 12 and we get on okay, and Angie who's 6 (they're all at 26 Glebe Court, Hattingdene Road). She can be okay too but most of the time she is a pest. She broke my CDs and I swiped her and that's one reason why mum went to Social Services. My mum's called Angela too, she's about 30-something. We've had some good times. I remember we went to Whipsnade Zoo once on a green bus – Mum, Roxanne and me – and I saw a polar bear live. It was great. My mum takes too many tablets and she says it's my fault she gets upset and has to take them so that's another reason I'm here.

The rest of my family is my nan who lives the other side of town – she's called Ada Mills. She had to retire early from the factory because she can't see well and if it weren't for that I could have lived with her now – but I'd probably move all her things by mistake and she needs to know where everything is. Then there's Uncle Ken and Aunty Shelley; they live in Kent and I've got six cousins there. Oh, there's my dad, he might be anywhere but he's probably in St Lucia. You can fly to Barbados and get a boat there, and I'd like to see it because that's where all the other half of my family come from. I know their names – Garvin, that's my dad, and Uncle Lee and Uncle Mervyn and gran and all of them. My dad's an electrician.

I came here to 121 Brooke Road six weeks ago. I was in voluntary care twice when I was small and mum couldn't cope. I'm not proud of what happened at this time – we had a row at home, well we'd had a lot of rows about Angie because I say she's destructive and mum says I'm jealous, but this time Angela – mum – hit me and I kicked her and then I went out and stayed out. And that night I tried some crack, you burn it and sniff it, I'd never done it before, and when I got in I collapsed and was really sick and mum called the night duty social services and the police. I went to out-patients and then the police put me here on an Emergency Protection Order I think it was, but since that ran out, I'm just 'looked after' by Social Services – it's like the other times but it's got a different name now. I think they said it's section twenty-something of the Children Act 1989.

I've read my reports because they have what's called an Open Files Policy. That means you can see anything that's written just about you, and where the people that wrote it agree. There's nothing I can't see in my file. Most of what's there I agree with but I don't like the way they say some of it.

It says under 'background' that I'm 'mixed race Afro-Caribbean/White' and my complexion is 'dark olive brown' and it makes me sound like a can of paint. I think I should have a chance to say about my background and what I look like. There's an awful lot more about what's bad about my family than what is good. It says my mum and Garvin never got on from when Roxanne was born but I can remember some good times when we were all together. It says I was 'hyperactive from an infant' and had 'poor co-ordination in primary school' and once I even had a fit – not a serious one; I just collapsed and was sick afterwards, I don't remember it. In fact I loved school, the teacher was great back then. It says I 'have good cognitive skills' which means I can read and write and my maths is pretty good – I add up all mum's shopping when we're out together. But I've missed quite a lot of school because mum got so depressed last year and when I went back my friends had all made new friends.

What do I want out of staying here? Well I'm glad it's only for assessment for three months and I think I should be back at home with my mum and sisters because that is more normal. I don't mind your idea about meeting each week with mum and Roxanne and Angie because then we could find a way to get on better. I know mum misses me because she wrote and said so and I miss her. I don't want to think about what if I can't go home because I don't think there is anywhere else. I don't want to live in a children's home and I don't want to live with foster parents because I couldn't be their real son and I don't think any of my family can have me.

Writing this has made me feel very upset inside but it has also helped me sort out my ideas and I would like to send it to my mum. I would also like to try to get into a new school where I could start again with my education because if I can write this I should be able to cope if they will give me some extra help to catch up – but I would like to visit first. I want to thank Eddie my key worker for helping me talk through all this so I could write it down.

I don't like Brooke Road as a building because it's too big and noisy and I'm a vegetarian and the vegetables are overcooked. But I like the staff and the Open Files Policy and you get information about the place before you arrive. You can phone out, they give you a phone card to keep and they treat you with respect.

Signed: Adrian Costello

What follows was written down by Eddie on behalf of Angela Costello.

I do miss Adrian and want him home but it is very difficult for me. He gets temper tantrums – not often but they scare me and the girls. He seems to get angry a lot with Angie who's only six. I can't have him hitting her and he knows it. I sometimes wonder if he shouldn't see a doctor. He is just like his father. My own health isn't good. I was told that I might need a hysterectomy and they took a lot of tests a couple of months ago, but I still don't know what will happen. Until that's sorted out perhaps Adrian should stay here – they seem nice enough and he's talking about school which makes a change. I'd like some home help but I don't expect I'll get any.

Signed: Angela Costello

ACTIVITY 1:
Adrian's family

Draw a plan and fill in all the members of Adrian's family who have been mentioned. It can either be a family tree or a diagram with Adrian in the middle and his family round about. Use coloured lines to show who you think is important to Adrian, and (in different colours) where there is a difficult relationship, or you are unsure. You may have to use more than one colour in some cases.

ACTIVITY 2:
A referral

Imagine that you were the night duty officer who was called in by Adrian's mother. You have to write a first referral for the Head of Home at 121 Brooke Road from what Adrian told you, which is much the same as he later wrote down for Eddie. Below are the headings on the referral form. Using the headings, on a separate sheet fill in as much as possible, indicating by question marks where you need to find out more.

1   Referring agency

2   Social worker

3   Client name

     Home address

4   Age

5   Religion

6   Cultural background

7   Family details (list names, relationships and address where known)

8   Legal status

9   Previous placements (dates, placement and reasons where possible)

10   Family background and reasons for not living at home

11   Envisaged contact/any restrictions on contact

12   Young person:

    12.1   Description: build/height/weight
                             hair/eye colour/complexion
                             name and address of current GP

    12.2   Details of any harm which has occurred or is apprehended in relation to this young person, including self-harm

    12.3   Education: school address/contact name
                             level of attainment/educational needs

    12.4   Health: date of most recent examination
                        details of any accidents/injuries/treatment

13 Any other relevant information

14 Sources for above information

Signed: . . . .

ACTIVITY 3: Research and development

1 Now look at the question marks and gaps in this report. Indicate where you need to go and who you need to speak to, to fill in these details. Where you think it is important to get more than one point of view, say so and give the reasons why.

2 Does this format make it clear what is fact and what is opinion? Does it contain all the information you think is relevant? Does it allow the various people involved to include their different points of view about what has happened?

3 With a partner, re-design the referral form to include the information called for and to take into acount any of these points or any others you think would be helpful. Remember not to make it too long!

Making a plan

Responsibilities and rights

Under the Children Act, the local authority has certain legal duties to Adrian and his family including the following:

Section 22(3)
- to safeguard and promote Adrian's welfare;
- to make use of local services;
- to consult Adrian, his parents and other key people before taking major decisions;
- to take into account these people's views;
- to take into account Adrian's religion, racial origin, cultural and linguistic background.

Section 23(6)
(6)   to enable him to live with a parent, relative or friend if possible;
(7)   to enable him to live near to his home if possible.

Schedule 2
(15/16)   to promote contact between Adrian and his parents, relatives and friends, including travelling costs where necessary.

Under the Arrangements for Placement Regulations, the local authority has a duty to make a *written plan* for Adrian. This plan should take account of all the above points, plus Adrian's health history and needs, his educational history and needs, and what aspects of parental responsibility for Adrian's day-to-day care have been delegated by his mother to the carers at 121 Brooke Road.

Under the Review of Children's Cases Regulations, the local authority must review this plan within four weeks of Adrian's beginning to be looked after, then within three months of the first review, and then within six months for each subsequent review.

The local authority must consult Adrian, his parents and other key people; at the review meeting the local authority should consider the plan and all its elements, what changes if any are needed, and make certain that decisions are implemented.

Under the Representations and Complaints Regulations, Adrian and his parents or other key persons have a right to complain to the local authority if they think that duties have not been complied with. Information about the procedure should be made available. If Adrian's complaint cannot be sorted out locally, the local authority's complaints officer should arrange for it to be investigated and an independent person should talk to Adrian. If their recommendations still do not satisfy him, he can ask for a panel hearing. The local authority's response after this is the last stage, but Adrian could contact an outside agency, and he should have this information as well.

Preparing for the first planning meeting at 121 Brooke Road

ACTIVITY 4: Role playing

This activity will take at least four people. One of you will put Adrian's point of view, one of you his mum's. A third person will be the residential social worker who is new to the job, and a fourth will be this person's manager (a senior RSW or the Head of the Home). If you have an extra person he or she can act as observer.

1   You are enacting, very briefly, a meeting *to find out everyone's views about what should happen* and to find out any common ground or differences, *before* the first planning meeting.

2   Adrian has already thought and written his views about this, and he has been told about the local authority's legal duties.

3   Adrian's mother has not yet had a chance to say what she wants to happen, and she is not very certain as yet.

4   The residential social worker wants to involve Adrian's mother in the plan, and find out what would help to restore Adrian to his family.

5   The manager is responsible for making sure that people are as much at ease as possible, that the aim of the meeting is achieved, that a written note is kept in preparation for the planning meeting and to keep time.

He or she may need to remind people that this meeting is about different points of views, not at this stage to make decisions.

The observer should note what he or she thinks contributes to a successful meeting, what the difficulties seem to be, and what might help to overcome them.

6   Give yourselves five minutes alone, so that you can each consider what you know about the situation and prepare what you want to say; you may want a written note.

7   Then spend ten minutes enacting the meeting.

8   Afterwards, spend five minutes each saying two things which went well, and two things which did not go well for you in your role and what would have helped you. Finally each say which part you have taken and give your real name, this gets you 'out of the role'.

9   Then change parts and try the activity again for another ten minutes. Afterwards, again each person should say two things which went well for the person you were playing, what didn't go so well, and what would have helped. Finish by saying what part you took in this second half, what your real name is and what you hope to have for dinner tonight! This helps to get you 'out of role'.

Plan and review

ACTIVITY 5: The plan

In twos or threes, write a plan for Adrian's stay at 121 Brooke Road. It should include:

- overall aim of the stay;
- areas of need;
- areas of strength;
- short-term objectives;
- day-to-day guidelines;
- brief background.

Take into account all that you know from previous activities, including what you imagined that Adrian's and his mother's points of view might be, plus the points of view of anyone else you think is important to the plan.

ACTIVITY 6: The review

Imagine this plan was agreed at the first planning meeting a week after Adrian came to 121 Brooke Road. It is now three weeks later and the review meeting is due. Adrian has been away from home for nearly a month but he has visited his home after school and for two weekends. Here are two different scenarios for the review:

Scenario One

Adrian has made himself popular at 121 Brooke Road and Eddie, his key worker, thinks a definite date should be set for him to return home or he will settle in and the move will become more difficult.

There is now some uncertainty as to where Adrian may go as his father, Garvin Costello, who is staying with relatives in Liverpool, has written to say he would like to attend the review and that Adrian could return to St Lucia and stay with gran for a while. Mrs Costello does not agree and thinks that so long as Adrian can keep on good terms with his sisters and out of trouble, he should come home to her.

Scenario Two

Mrs Costello's depression has become worse over the past two weeks and her doctor thinks she should have a short period – about three weeks – in hospital for physical and psychiatric assessment and treatment. Adrian's two sisters can go to their uncle and aunt in Kent but they cannot take Adrian as well.

This has made Adrian upset as he fears he may not have a home to return to if his mother is ill. His behaviour has become worse and he is missing school some days.

1   In twos or threes take each scenario in turn and write up on a large sheet of paper the changes that might have to be made to your plan for Adrian and the possible options, under each of the headings listed in Activity 5.

2   In a different colour, note down who you need to talk to before the review and the questions you need to ask, in order to know if these changes and options are realistic.

3   Separate out the factual information you need from certain people, and the wishes, feelings or opinions you need to find out about.

4   Finally decide who will need to do what before the review meeting in order to have the information you need to make a further plan.

5   Looking back at the regulations, remind yourself what other matters must be considered in plans and reviews.

6   Write an outline for the review meeting on the basis of one of the scenarios:

Main aim of the review meeting:

Other aims in order of priority:

Who needs to be present:

Who could be interviewed separately, or provide a report:

Matters to cover at the meeting:

Best place and time for the meeting:

Who needs to be sent this information:

Signed: . . . . Reviewing Officer

ACTIVITY 7:
A debate

A debate is a structured argument. Two or three people put the case **for**, and the same number argue **against**, a definite statement such as:

'Residential care does more harm than good'
or
'Residential care is a good option and deserves more resources'

Once everyone has put their cases, the audience votes.

There is also a 'balloon debate' where the two teams are in imaginary balloons. After each presentation the audience votes for them to stay in the balloon if the argument was a good one, or for a speaker to 'jump out'. The team with the most people still on board at the end is the 'winner'.

The activity can either be on a small scale, with a group of 10–12 students, or organised as an event with an audience of 30 or more, refreshments and a small charge to be donated to charity. You could have a small debate then see if you would like to hold a bigger one.

First you need to decide on a strong and clear statement about residential care which will be the basis for much argument, for and against. Then, two or three people need to be willing to stand up and put the case to the audience – however small or large this is to be. You don't have to agree or disagree with the statement – the purpose is to put together a strong argument whatever your personal views are.

Each speaker can choose another person to help them research, and should prepare a six minute speech, using the strongest evidence they can find. Sources might include:

- the views of young people you know;
- books about residential care;
- newspaper articles;
- debates in Parliament (*Children and Parliament* published by the National Children's Bureau gives up-to-date information).

Six minutes will use up about ten pages of text, or you may prefer to make notes and speak from them. Your researcher can remind you of other points as you talk.

When everyone has spoken, the audience can join in and make their own points for and against. The chairperson needs to be very firm and make sure everyone knows the 'rules' – *not* speaking for too long and *not* getting angry *or* using offensive language.

When people vote you will need at least two people to count who have not been involved in the debate. There could be a small prize for the winners and a consolation prize for the losers.

Part 3

ASSIGNMENTS

Assignment 1

Movement and change

The population of the UK is made up of the many different groups of people who have made the UK their home. People over the years have come for a variety of reasons – Vikings to establish and protect trade routes; Normans to expand a power base; many Jewish people to escape persecution; and an expanding economy in postwar UK brought many people from the West Indies and Ireland.

The process continues today. Movement and change has never been easy for the families and individuals concerned, but it is likely to affect all of us more now than ever before. The upheavals caused by political change in Eastern Europe and conflicts around the world are bringing new groups of people to the country, and as the Single European Market becomes a reality, we have to start thinking about mainland Europe as a place in which to live and work. In this assignment you are asked to find out about other countries from which families have come to the UK.

TASK 1:
Touchdown

1 (a) One inner London primary school has children who have themselves come with their families from the following countries: Turkey (mainland), Turkish Kurdistan, Turkish Cyprus, Bangladesh, Pakistan, India, Angola, Poland, Somalia, Ethiopia (Tigre), Jamaica, Ireland, Zimbabwe.

(b) In addition, children who were born in the UK have one or more parents who were born in the following countries: Brazil, Canada, the Caribbean (Grenada, Anguilla, St Lucia, St Vincent, Barbados as well as Jamaica), New Zealand, Nigeria, Ghana, Cyprus (Greek and Turkish), Hong Kong, Italy, France, Germany, Kenya (Asian), Guyana, Australia, Vietnam, Finland, South Africa, Mauritius, USA.

On a blank map of the world (traced from an atlas), mark in these countries. Use a different colour for the countries in groups (a) than for (b).

2 Choose one country from group (a) and one from group (b) to research. Draw up an outline of the areas to cover, and agree them with your tutor. Here are some suggestions:

• Draw a large-scale map of the country or region. Mark on major towns, cities, mountains, rivers, plains, etc.

- Find out about the way of life. Do most people live in the country or in towns and cities? What are the houses like? How do most people earn a living? Do people wear particular clothes? If so, why?
- What are the main languages and religions of the country? How does religion affect day-to-day life?
- What sort of work do women do? Does the work require childcare? How are children looked after?
- What education is available to children?
- In many cases, recent events will have led to pressure on people to leave the country. Find out about these. Newspaper and TV news reports may be helpful.

TASK 2: First hand experience

The task here is to interview someone who has moved from one country to another to gain an insight into the upheaval involved. First ask for their agreement in principle, then work out no more than ten leading questions. If you want to use a tape recorder, be sure to ask permission. People may be sensitive to questions on some topics – be ready to move on. Below are suggestions for your first five questions:

1 Why did you move?

2 What were the most striking differences between the country you moved from and the UK?

3 Can you describe your first month in the UK?

4 How easy/difficult did you find the move?

5 What did you gain and lose from the move?

Write up your interview in the form of an article suitable for publication in a magazine series on migration. Introduce your interviewee, and make decisions about where you want to record their comments word for word, and where you, as author, take over the narrative.

TASK 3: Many tongues

1 Overleaf are figures showing the languages spoken at home by children at an inner London primary school.

    Present this information in graphic form. Give thought to how best to show the **detail** of the language diversity of the children as well as an **overview** of the language and cultural origins of the children in the school.

2 Find out how language support is offered in schools to children who need it. Points to cover:

- funding from central government (Home Office);
- funding from Local Education Authorities (LEAs);

English (UK)	143
English (Caribbean)	67
Kurdish	12
Turkish	19
Greek	3
Gujurati*	17
Urdu*	7
Bengali*	5
Punjabi*	5
Hindi*	3
Cantonese	3
French (incl. Mauritian)	4
Yoruba	7
Farsi	3
W.I. Creole (or Patwa)	3
Portugese	2
Polish	2
Shona	2
German	3

* Many children speak more than one of these languages. Only the main one is shown.

- how much time a language support teacher has per child who needs help;
- how schools organise support;
- the sort of strategies, materials and methods teachers use with children.

Work with a partner or in small groups. This will enable you to divide up the tasks.

3 Devise a simple activity designed to help a child develop language skills in English. Before you start, you need to be clear about the age and circumstances of the child (newly arrived in the country? no English spoken at home? fluent spoken English? differences of dialect?).

This task may not be appropriate at this point in your course. You may be able to work on it during an observation or visit to a school or nursery.

TASK 4: The world's harvest

At a school's harvest festival, children brought the following: tinned peaches, rice pudding, spaghetti hoops, baked beans, tuna fish, sweetcorn, pineapple, olive oil, soya oil, pasta, rice, lentils, haricot beans, drinking chocolate, tea, coffee, peanut butter, chocolate biscuits, strawberry jam, cornflakes, rice crispies, sugar, Garibaldi biscuits ('squashed flies'), oranges, apples, bananas, pears, tomatoes, potatoes, cucumber.

The head teacher directed each child to place each gift on one of two tables. Table A was for foods that had been grown in the UK, or made from food produced in the UK. Table B was for foods grown in or made from foods produced in other countries.

1 Working with a partner, divide this list of foods into two, corresponding to tables A and B.

2 Report back to the whole group on what you found and suggest reasons for this.

3 On a blank map of the world traced from an atlas, mark the country each item is likely to have come from. To do this you will probably have to visit a supermarket. Most items will have the country of origin on the tln or package, or on a label on the shelf. Where you have 'Produced in the UK', use the list of ingredients to identify the main ingredients, and suggest likely countries of origin.

4 Write a paragraph, 'Where our food comes from'.

TASK 5: Recipe book

1 Find out an everyday family recipe in *either* the country of origin of one of the food items above, *or* from one of the countries in Task 1 above.

Include ingredients, preparation, cooking and serving. Set this out in an easy-to-follow way. Include guidance on where any unusual items can be bought in your area, and an approximate costing for the meal.

You may find that restaurants are a useful source of information.

2 Collate the recipes the group collects and present them in an attractive booklet form, with an appropriate title.

TASK 6: Religion

1 Overleaf is a chart showing the main celebrations of some of the main religions of the world. Choose one religion to study. Write a brief description of the major beliefs of this religion, and find out some details about three or four of the major religious festivals. Describe what is being celebrated, how it is celebrated, and how a school or nursery in the UK might mark the day.

2 On p 115 is a table with some details about the major religious festivals in April.

Choose another month and research the major festivals in that month. Draw up a schedule like the April one, and include brief suggestions on how each festival is celebrated, and how a school or nursery might mark the occasion.

This task should be planned carefully – if the group can cover all the major religions in **1**, then by sharing your information, you should have the material for **2**. Collate your results.

1992

	BUDDHIST	CHINESE	CHRISTIAN	HINDU	JEWISH	MUSLIM	RASTAFARIN	SIKH
JAN.			1 Circumcision of Jesus; 6 Epiphany	14 Makar Sankranti/ Lohri	31 Night of the Journey and Ascension			12 Birthday of Guru Gobind Singh
FEB.	15 Parinirvana	4 Yuan Tan; 19 Teng Chich	2 Candlemas	8 Vasanta Panchami/ Saraswati Puja	20 Tu B'Shevat	19 Lailat-Ul-Bara'h		
MARCH			1 St David's Day; 3 Shrove Tuesday; 4 Ash Wednesday; 17 St Patrick's Day; 19 St Joseph; 25 The Annunciation of the Blessed Virgin Mary	2 Mahashivratri; 6 Birthday of Sri Ramakrishna; 18 Holi	19 Purim	4 Ramadan; 30 Lailat-Ul-Qadr		
APRIL		4 Ch'ing Ming	16 Maundy Thursday; 17 Good Friday; 18 Holy Saturday; 19 Easter Day; 23 St George's Day; 26 Easter Day/ Pascha	4 Chaitra/ Varsha Pratipada; 12 Rama Navami	18-25 Passover/ Pesach; 30 Yom Hashoah	3 Eid-Ul-Fitr		13 Baisakhi
MAY	16 Vaisakha Puja/Wesak		28 Ascension Day		7 Yom Ha'atzma'ut; 21 Lag B'Omer			
JUNE	15 Poson/ Dhamma Vijaya	5 Dragon Boat Festival	7 Pentecost/ Whitsuntide; 14 Trinity Sunday; 18 Corpus Christi		7-8 Shavuot	10 Eid-Ul-Adha		4 Martyrdom of Guru Arjan Dev
JULY	15 Asala			3 Ratha Yatra		1 Al Hijra; 9 Ashura	23 Birthday of Haile Selassie I	
AUG.			6 Transfiguration of the Blessed Virgin Mary; 15 Assumption of the Blessed Virgin Mary	16 Raksha Bandhan; 22 Janamashtami	8 Tisha B'Av			
SEPT.			8 Birth of the Blessed Virgin Mary; 29 St Michael and All Angels' Day; * Harvest Festival	1 Ganesh Chaturthi; 27- Navaratri/ 6 Oct Durga Puja/ Desserah	28-29 Rosh Hashana	21 Birthday of Muhammad	11 Ethiopian New Year's Day	
OCT.	* Kathina Day	4 Chung Yuan		25-29 Divali (Deepavali)	7 Yom Kippur; 12-20 Sukkot; 20 Simkhat Torah			25-29 Divali (Deepavali)
NOV.			1 All Saints' Day; 2 All Souls' Day; 29 Advent Sunday; 30 St Andrew's Day		20-27 Hanukah		2 Anniversary of the crowning of Haile Selassie I	10 Birthday of Guru Nanak; 29 Martyrdom of Guru Tegh Bahadur
DEC.	8 Bodhi Day		8 Immaculate Conception the Blessed Virgin Mary; 24 Christmas Eve; 25 Christmas Day					31 Birthday of Guru Gobind Singh

Religious festivals

Festivals for April

3rd Eid-ul-Fitr is the Muslim Festival which marks the end of the fast of Ramadan. There are celebratory meals, and presents for the children. Giving to charity is also an important aspect of this festival, to ensure that even the most needy can join in the festivities.

12th Rama Navami is the birthday of Rama. Hindus make cradles to hold images of the baby who is the hero of the *Ramayana*.

12th On Palm Sunday, the first day of Holy Week, Christian Churches commemorate the arrival of Jesus in Jerusalem.

16th Maundy Thursday reminds Christians of the Last Supper and the institution there of the Eucharist. As a reminder of the activities of the Last Supper, a feet-washing ceremony is carried out in many churches. 'Maundy money', specially minted, is distributed by the Queen.

17th Good Friday commemorates the day of the Crucifixion, the most solemn day of the Christian year.

18th– 25th Pesach, the Jewish Passover, recalls the Exodus of the Israelites from Egypt after the Angel of Death had passed over their first-born and destroyed only the children of their oppressors. As a reminder that the Israelites, in their haste to escape from Egypt, baked flat loaves without waiting for dough to rise, the Jews eat unleavened bread.

19th Easter Day, one of the most joyous in the Christian calendar, celebrates the Resurrection of Christ. Easter eggs are not Christian in origin but have been integrated into Christian celebrations as symbolic of new life.

30th At Yom Hashoah the victims of the Nazi holocaust are remembered with memorial candles and special services.

The dates and information are taken from the Shap Calendar of Religious Festivals, available with other information from: Alan Brown, Shap Working Party, The National Society's RE Centre, 23 Kensington Square, London W8 4HN

Assignment 2

Changing families

**TASK 1:
What's in a
picture?**

Look at the pictures opposite. If the group has a number of copies of this book, it would be a good idea to spread them out around the room with each book open on a different page of pictures. Like this you will gain an overview of the group's choices.

1   Write your name on two stickers. Stick one on the two pictures you like best.

Take it in turns to explain to the group why you chose the pictures you did, and what you like about them. Wait until each person has spoken before having a whole group discussion.

2   **Note to tutor:** Make two copies of the list of adjectives below (or more for a larger group). Cut them up and ask participants to pick six at random. You will need Blu Tack or something similar.

scruffy	modern	dirty
tired	happy	exhausted
sad	celebrating	lonely
caring	bored	loving
angry	hatred	bitter
loathing	embarrassed	busy
awkward	involved	rich
strong	poor	weak
disadvantaged	hurried	fortunate
unhurried	lucky	optimistic
proud	pessimistic	united
religious	moral	immoral
traditional	struggling	odd

Ask the group members to attach each adjective to the picture they think best illustrates it.

In a whole group discussion, take each picture in turn and discuss the choices of adjectives that it has attracted. Did some have only positive ones? some only negative? some mixed? What evidence is there in the picture to support the choice of each adjective? What was the basis for people's choices?

What is a family?
Courtesy: John Birdsall Photography

Above **What is a family? This is a traditional family image. As you will see from photographs dotted throughout the rest of the book, there are many other family units.**
Courtesy: John Birdsall Photography

Below **What is a family?**
Courtesy: John Birdsall Photography

TASK 2:
What is a
family?

1   In groups of four, or with a partner, agree an order for the pictures. Place first the picture that raises most questions about 'What is a family?' Place last the one that raised least, and the others in between.

When you have done this, join with another group and compare your ordering. Reach a new agreement.

2   Write a short piece in which you give your own answer to the question 'What is a family?'

3   Choose one picture to study closely with a partner. Decide on ten questions to ask about the picture and write them down: who the people are, what they are thinking or saying, what is going on, what has just happened, is going to happen.

When you have asked your questions, start working out some answers. Use this as a basis for telling the group what you think is going on in your picture. Listen to the other presentations.

(The activities in Tasks 1 and 2 are closely based on activities in the excellent pack of photos and activities *What is a family?* produced by the Development Education Centre, Birmingham, and reproduced with thanks.)

TASK 3:
Family change
– an overview

In this task you are asked to read and think about the passage opposite and answer the questions which follow.

Families are changing
1   What is the difference between changing family *structures* and *patterns*?
2   What does 'role' mean? Why is this important in changing families?
3   Draw a simple diagram (like the one on p 15 of Part 1) to illustrate the different relationships between the children described in paragraph 4.

Prospects for the future
4   Is the fall in the birthrate in 1989 a result of people not getting married?
5   What is the pattern for marriage in the future suggested in the 'recent report'?

Divorce and remarriage
6   Sketch a simple pie chart to show the family size of divorcing couples in 1989. (*See* paragraph 1 only.)
7   How likely are divorced people to remarry?

Separation and cohabitation
8   Why are there no figures on the separation of cohabiting couples? What is likely to be happening?

Lone parent families
9   Sketch a simple pie chart to show the different categories of women who are lone parents. How do these proportions translate into numbers?

FAMILIES ARE CHANGING

Family *structures* are changing as divorce, cohabitation and remarriage are experienced by increasing numbers of adults and children, particularly those under five years old. Family *patterns* are changing as parents have fewer children, but four or even five generations may be alive at the same time.

Roles within families are changing in response to employment and unemployment patterns, greater equality for women, and parents sharing their child with a new partner or taking responsibility for their partner's child from a previous relationship. Such external changes in the way in which families are formed and parents and children live their lives are reflected in internal changes in the relationships between them and other important people in their lives.

We have already seen tremendous changes in family life and childcare over the last twenty years. Children may grow up with a male or female lone parent, natural or step-parents cohabiting or married, or with a parent who is in a male or female homosexual relationship.

Children may be growing up in one or two households, moving between them every week or month or only at holiday times. Children may be growing up with siblings who are full brothers and sisters, step-brothers and sisters, or half-brothers and sisters. Sometimes all three will be living within the same household. They may be relating to step-parents, step-grandparents and new aunts, uncles and cousins. There has been increasing use of foster parents for both short term and long term care and a decline in adoptive parents.

Family life is not static. Some children may go through several family transitions over a relatively short space of time. A child may be born into a two parent family, the parents may separate during the early years, one or both parents may have a cohabiting relationship before deciding to remarry and form a stepfamily.

Almost certainly there will be many early years workers whose own families are reflected within these changes in society and whose own circumstances, relationships and family may change while their own children are growing up.

PROSPECTS FOR THE FUTURE

Having a baby and bringing up children is still an ambition for most people. There has been much publicity about the fall in the birth rate in 1989 after several years of a slight increase, but the most significant trends are that more women are having babies outside marriage or at a later age, around 28 years, within marriage. Marriage remains very popular, although it may no longer last a lifetime.

A recent report looking at life in Britain in the year 2010 predicts that the majority of couples will cohabit before getting married, the majority of marriages will end in divorce, followed by remarriage. The emerging pattern for the future will be a dispersed extended family with parents, children and other family relations keeping in touch but where friends and neighbours may play an increasingly important role in providing support, advice and companionship. Marriage, or partnership outside marriage, will be regarded less as a lifetime commitment and more as a flexible arrangement which may be succeeded by another partnership.

Families are seen to be private places so children are recorded in official annual statistics only when they are born, when their parents divorce or when they take on a new legal family status, such as adoption. Children going into residential care are not officially recorded by their family background although this information would be contained within their personal files.

DIVORCE AND REMARRIAGE

In 1989, 103,962 couples with children were divorced. This affected 216,567 dependent children – on average 595 children every day, or one in every 70 children. A quarter were only children and, therefore, had no brother or sister with whom to share this family disruption or to turn to for comfort. Almost half (47%) of the divorcing couples had two children, and the remaining families therefore had three or more children. This is important when looking at the formation of stepfamilies as many of them may involve at least four children, possibly two from each partner's previous relationship.

A significant trend in terms of family change is that over half the children of divorcing couples are between three and nine years of age. They are old enough to remember the first family and young enough for both their parents to form new relationships, to remarry and create a second family, while they are still growing up and living at home.

In 1989 one third of all marriages was a remarriage for one or both partners. Research shows that almost three quarters of divorced women aged 25–34 remarry eventually, half within six years of the breakdown of the first marriage. Other research shows that about half the absent parents are likely to remain alone for only two years before remarrying.

At the moment the records on adults who remarry do not state whether or not one or both of them have any children from previous relationships. However, if the current trends continue, one in four children will experience their parents' divorce before they reach 16 and within five years at least half their parents will be remarried.

Current figures seem to indicate that second marriages are even more likely to fail than first ones. Divorcing couples where both partners had previously been divorced are a growing proportion of all divorcing couples. In over a quarter of the 150,872 couples divorcing in 1989, one or both parties had previously been divorced. For the children of those parents this was therefore their second or third experience of family disruption after the divorce of a parent.

SEPARATION AND COHABITATION

There will almost certainly be other children experiencing the separation of their parents, spending part of their childhood in a lone parent family and then in a step family. Even if parents do not choose to divorce after a separation they may still go on to have a new relationship. We do not know how many of the cohabiting couples with children may also have separated.

Unlike a marrriage, there is no official record of the partnerships of cohabiting couples, so they would not appear in any formal statistics on separation or divorce. However, they are likely to be subject to the same patterns of family stress and disruption and many of their children may also now be separated from one of their parents. Indeed, recent research from Sweden and the United States suggests cohabiting parents may be at increased risk of separation compared to married parents.

It is therefore likely that there are many more children in changing families than are accounted for in the published statistics.

STEPFAMILIES

Approximately 30,000 new stepfamilies with children and young people are created each year through the remarriage of one or both of their parents.

There will be an additional 75,000 stepmothers and 75,000 stepfathers by 1994. Since many parents cohabit after divorce there is possibly the same number again of stepfamilies created by parents living with a new partner but choosing not to remarry.

LONE PARENT FAMILIES

A recent major research survey has confirmed that at any one time there are over one million lone parents living in Britain, over one in seven families with a dependent child in 1989. That one million lone parents is a changing group of families, the one million today is a different set of families from those five years ago and will be another set of one million in five years time.

There are several patterns of lone parenthood, but the majority are lone mothers and the most common route is marital breakdown, separation and divorce. Divorced lone mothers account for 43% of all lone mothers, single lone mothers for 28%, separated lone mothers for 21% and widowed lone mothers for 8%. Since 1971 lone father families have accounted for just over 1% of all families.

Source: *Changing Families: A guide for early years workers,* published by VOLCUF, October 1991

TASK 4: Family figures

Study the chart opposite carefully, then answer the questions which follow.

1. (a) What proportion of families with dependent children were headed by a married couple in (i) 1971, (ii) 1988? How has the proportion of lone parent families changed in this time?

   (b) What proportion of families were headed by lone fathers in (i) 1971, (ii) 1988?

   (c) Which groups of lone parents have increased most in size between 1971 and 1988?

   (d) To what extent do these figures bear out the comments on changing families in the extract in Task 3? Be precise about any similarities and differences you spot.

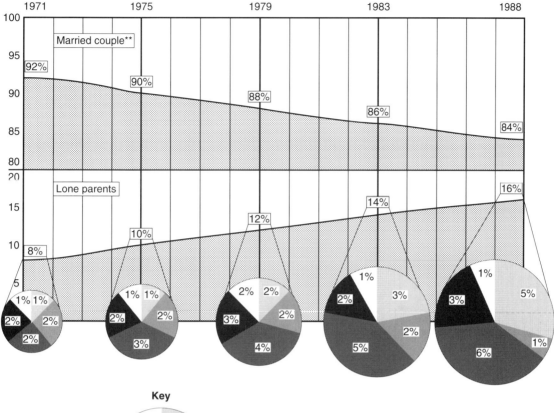

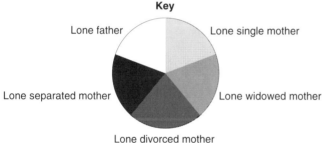

Key

Lone father   Lone single mother

Lone separated mother   Lone widowed mother

Lone divorced mother

* Persons aged under 16, or aged 16 to 18 and in full time education, in the family unit and living in the household
** Including married women whose husbands were not defined as resident in the household

Families with dependent children, by type and, for lone mothers, by marital status (1971–88)
Source: Figure 5 in Kathleen Kiernan and Malcolm Wicks, *Family Change and Future Policy*, published by the Family Policy Studies Centre, 1990

2 As you studied the chart, you may have noticed some unusual features in the way the information is presented.

- In each year, the percentage for families headed by married couple and lone parents adds up to 100%, but it does not look like it on the page. Did you notice that the space allocated for 80% is the same as the space allocated for 20%?

- It is generally accepted that pie charts should be used to show the proportions of the whole – how a pie is divided up. Pie charts are used here to show the detailed breakdown of a part of the whole.
- Is the pie chart for 1988 twice the size as the one for 1971?

Your task is to present the information in this chart in differently designed charts of your own. Work with a partner. Before you start, make sure you are clear about the number and type of charts you plan to use.

3 Figures for marriage and divorce in the EC are given on p 123.

Your task is to translate these figures, comparing 1981 and 1989, into a bar chart. You may like to use the chart on p 14 as a model.

Write a paragraph on the pattern of marriage and divorce in the EC to accompany your chart.

What is a family?
Courtesy: John Birdsall
Photography

Marriage and divorce: EC comparison, 1981 and 1989

Rates

	Marriages per 1,000 eligible population		Divorces per 1,000 existing marriages	
	1981	1989	1981	1989
United Kingdom	7.1	6.8	11.9	12.6[1]
Belgium	6.5	6.4	6.1	8.6
Denmark	5.0	6.0	12.1	13.6
France	5.8	5.0	6.8	8.4
Germany (Fed. Rep)	5.8	6.4	7.2	8.7[2]
Greece	7.3	6.1	2.5	
Irish Republic	6.0	5.0	0.0	0.0
Italy	5.6	5.4	0.9	2.1
Luxembourg	5.5	5.8	5.9	10.0
Netherlands	6.0	6.1	8.3	8.1
Portugal	7.7	7.1	2.8	
Spain	5.4	5.6	1.1	

1 1987
2 1988

(Source: Statistical Office of the European Communities. From *Social Trends* 22 1992)

**TASK 5:
Divorce and
children**

Below is an extract from a factsheet on the effects of divorce on children. Read and make notes on it. Use the three headings 'Practical', 'Emotional' and 'Social' effects of separation as the basis for your notes. You may wish to use these as the three main branches for 'spider' notes or as headings for linear notes. You may, as a separate exercise, wish to comment on the points made.

DIVORCE AND CHILDREN

In Britain in 1986, nearly 167,000 couples ended their marriages by divorce. Over half of them had dependent children, totalling more than 163,000 children (under 16 and, in England and Wales, up to 18 if in full-time education). A judge has to consider that the arrangements proposed for the children by divorcing parents are satisfactory or the best that can be devised in the circumstances. But the courts have little knowledge about children's actual access to the absent parent nor about their wishes.

Looking to the future, the Children Act 1989 is based on principles of parental responsibility and non-intervention by the courts. When it is implemented in England and Wales in 1991, there will be no residence (custody) or contact (access) orders unless specifically requested by parents.

It has been predicted that 37 per cent of marriages in England and Wales and 27 per cent in Scotland will end in divorce. Furthermore, it is also predicted that one child in eight is likely to experience parental divorce before reaching the age

▶

of 10 and one in five by the age of 16. At least 10 per cent will live with their fathers. An increasing proportion of these children of divorce are under five (33 per cent in England and Wales, 23 per cent in Scotland).

Divorce is a long process, and can affect children's lives in many ways: practically, emotionally and socially. The point of separation is more important than the actual divorce.

PRACTICAL EFFECTS OF SEPARATION

When one parent leaves the family home, with or without the children, those children face the first of many changes. Most of them have a lower standard of living and therefore poorer housing because there is only one adult potential wage-earner in the household; a mother has a lower earning capacity than a father; the absent parent often fails to pay maintenance and there is a higher incidence of divorce among manual workers. Some children have to change school and leave behind their former friends. Some children have more changes in custodial parent and in housing than is shown in official records.

In the face of so many actual or potential changes, children need as much continuation of routine as possible. They benefit from remaining in the matrimonial home, sometimes irrespective of which parent lives there. They are happier when their parents are seen to share responsibilities, but to move between two parental homes where parents share joint (residential) custody can be stressful and confusing for some children.

EMOTIONAL EFFECTS OF SEPARATION

The majority of children feel distressed and bewildered by the removal of one parent from their daily lives, and receive inadequate, or even no, information from their parents. While children might be relieved at the cessation of daily conflict between their parents, many of them are simply unaware that such conflict is serious enough to lead to a separation. Parents try to hide conflict and, for some children, it is part of their normal family life. Many do not believe that any separation is final, especially as many couples split up more than once before a final separation. Furthermore, parental conflict often continues after separation.

Pre-school age children tend to regress when their parents split up. Some children, and especially those under eight, blame themselves for the break up and

have fantasies about reconciliation; aged six to eight they feel a great sadness; nine to 12 an intense anger, and in their teens they have a profound sense of loss.

A study of six to nine year olds in school found their divorced families to be in three groupings: 'harmonious co-parents', 'conflicted co-parents' and 'absent parents'. Children in the third group were the least well adjusted, indicating that the loss of a parent was more disturbing than continued conflict.

Wallerstein and Kelly found that 'the overwhelming majority preferred the unhappy marriage to the divorce.' This is not to say that parents should stay together for the sake of the children but that, if they do split up, they should keep the children fully informed and make every effort to enable them to continue a loving relationship with each parent. They should also remember that 'divorce' is an adult word, often not understood by children.

Inevitably parents are in personal turmoil when a marriage breaks up and not in the best position to understand their children's feelings. Indeed, one study showed that custodial mothers were as likely to misinterpret their children's feelings as to understand them. Furthermore, children can deliberately hide their feelings out of concern for their parents. Children's loyalties are divided as they try to be fair to each parent. They can worry about how the absent parent is managing, and they are well aware of the distress of the parent with whom they live.

SOCIAL EFFECTS OF SEPARATION

The loss of one parent from a child's home life can be a severe shock, especially if it happens without the child's prior knowledge and/or the child is not told where the absent parent has gone. Among children from a cross-section of divorced families, one third lost touch with one parent as an immediate result of the separation and another third had lost touch five years after divorce. Children who lose touch with one parent might then also lose touch with grandparents, uncles, aunts and cousins.

For the child's peace of mind, there should be no delay in making access arrangements. The longer the delay, the more unsatisfactory is the subsequent relationship in terms of frequency and quality. Seeing a parent by appointment is an artificial situation and access needs careful planning by both parents: the absent one often has to take on an unaccustomed role, while the resident parent needs to co-operate in making arrangements. While most children long to continue a loving relationship with both parents, a few who have, for instance, experienced severe abuse from a parent can benefit from a clean break. If children are upset before or after seeing their absent parent, they are not necessarily resisting access. It could be that they are distressed by witnessing their parents' anger or by the need to part once again from a loved parent.

Reasons for absent parents, usually fathers, not seeing their children include the belief that it is in the child's best interests for the non-custodial parent to disappear, and that fathers will not have to pay maintenance if they have no access. Some are subtly prevented by their former spouses from seeing their children and some find access very upsetting.

Source: *Highlight No 93*, published by the Library and Information Service of the NCB/Barnardo's

---

**TASK 6:
Families on
the move**

What is available to a family moving into your area? Research the following.

1   A refugee family arrives in your area. What language tuition is available to the parents?

2   If a family moved into your street/block, how would they register with a GP? If there is a choice, which would you suggest?

3   How would a family with pre-school children get a playgroup or nursery place? How long would it take? What would it cost?

4   What facilities are available to a family with young children from Day 1 in your area? Check: One o'clock clubs, mother and toddler groups, playgrounds, libraries, swimming pool sessions. Any others?

5   Recommend one primary school and one secondary school in your area to a newly arrived family. Would the children be accepted automatically?

6   What other suggestions can you make on how to make links and feel at home in your area? Think about the needs of the parent or parents as well as the children: children 12–16, children 8–11, children 5–8 and pre-school children and babies.

**TASK 7:
Quick
reference**

Use your research on Task 6 as the basis for a leaflet suitable for newcomers to your area. Include useful names, addresses, hints and tips, and suggestions for feeling at home. Give it an appropriate title and layout.

Assignment 3

Life histories

TASK 1:
Different
families

Assignment 2 showed the many different kinds of family children grow up in. Some of the family types are reflected directly in statistics.

People in households: by type of household and family in which they live

Great Britain   Percentages

	1961	1971	1981	1990–91
Type of household				
Living alone	3.9	6.3	8.0	10.6
Married couple, no children	17.8	19.3	19.5	23.6
Married couple with dependent children[2]	52.2	51.7	47.4	40.8
Married couple with non-dependent children only	11.6	10.0	10.3	10.3
Lone parent with dependent children[2]	2.5	3.5	5.8	6.5
Other households	12.0	9.2	9.0	8.1
All people in private households[3]	100	100	100	100

2 These family types may also include non-dependent children.
3 The number of people in each census was 49,545 thousand in 1961, 52,347 thousand in 1971 and 52,760 thousand in 1981. The sample size of the General Household Survey in 1990–91 was 23,587.

(Source: Office of Population Censuses and Surveys)

In the questions below you are asked to offer interpretations of the figures you observe.

1   What percentage of people lived alone in (a) 1961, (b) 1991? What might be the age and circumstances of these people?

2   In which decade did the greatest increase in married couples with no children occur? Can you offer any explanation?

3   What percentage of households consisted of married couples with dependent children in (a) 1961, (b) 1991?

4   Which type of household has changed least between 1961 and 1991? Why do you think this is?

5   Comment on the changing percentage of lone parent families between 1961 and 1991. Work out what percentage this is of all families with

What is a family?
Courtesy: John Birdsall
Photography

dependent children in (a) 1961, (b) 1991. See if your answers are in line with the figures in Task 4, Assignment 2.

In the data and pictures in Assignment 2 and throughout the book, many of these types of family are shown:

- families with father, mother and two or three children;
- two person families – child and mother, or, more rarely, child and father;
- children and mother;
- chidlren and father;
- child and grandparents.

In addition, you may, in your discussion 'What is the family?', have included other forms of family: several unrelated children and a foster parent or parents; a child or children living with two adults of the same sex, children living with relatives, and other forms of family life.

**TASK 2:
A typical
family?**

The image of the 'typical family' of a married couple with two children is breaking down, but much more slowly than in reality. From the figures in Task 1 you saw that this group accounts for only 40% of all households, and the 1988 figure of 84% of families (in Task 4, Assignment 2) includes new families, with step-parents and children, an increasing group. In this task you are asked to compare the image of the typical family with the reality of your group's experiences of family life.

1 Study the *TV Times* or *Radio Times* to identify all the series, soaps and films featuring family life in the coming week and agree within the group who watches what. Make a note of the family relationships of the

127

characters in the programme(s) you have chosen to view. Identify a session next week in which you will pool your findings. Draw a large-scale diagram of relationships on a flip chart or large piece of paper as the basis for your brief talk summarising family relationships in the programme.

2   Discuss these points:
    (a)   Does British TV give a true picture of family life in the UK?
    (b)   Should it?
    Before you have the discussion, decide if you want to record it, and if so, how.

TASK 3:
Darren's family

Study Darren's family tree, below.
    Work with a partner. One person should take Darren's part and the other the part of the keyworker who drew up this chart with Darren.

I   The 'keyworker' asks 'Darren' ten or so questions to find out the basic factual information about Darren's family tree. Darren replies. You may want to record your questions.

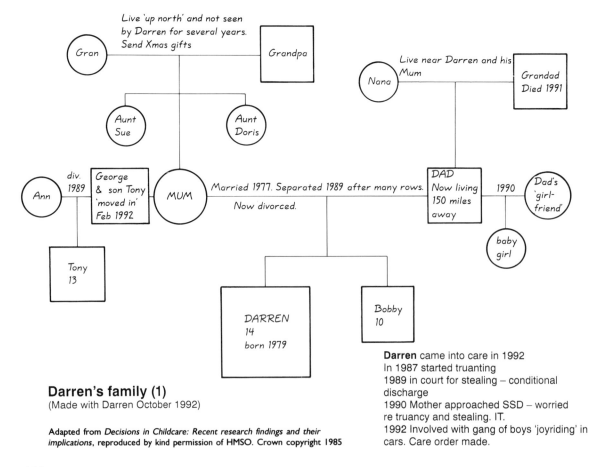

Darren's family (1)
(Made with Darren October 1992)

Adapted from *Decisions in Childcare: Recent research findings and their implications*, reproduced by kind permission of HMSO. Crown copyright 1985

Darren came into care in 1992
In 1987 started truanting
1989 in court for stealing – conditional discharge
1990 Mother approached SSD – worried re truancy and stealing. IT.
1992 Involved with gang of boys 'joyriding' in cars. Care order made.

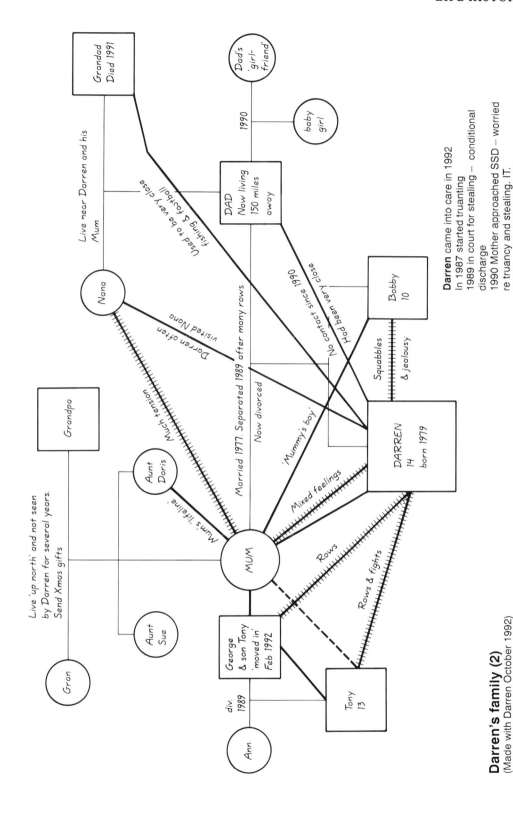

Darren's family (2)
(Made with Darren October 1992)

Adapted from *Decisions in Childcare: Recent research findings and their implications*, reproduced by kind permission of HMSO. Crown copyright 1985

The following text appears within the diagram:

Grandad Died 1991

Dad's 'girl-friend'

1990

baby girl

DAD Now living 150 miles away

Live near Darren and his Mum

Used to be very close fishing & football

Nana

No contact since 1990

Had been very close

Bobby 10

Darren came into care in 1992
In 1987 started truanting
1989 in court for stealing – conditional discharge
1990 Mother approached SSD – worried re truancy and stealing. IT.
1992 Involved with gang of boys 'joy riding' in cars. Care order made.

Darren often visited Nana

Married 1977. Separated 1989 after many rows. Now divorced

'Mummy's boy'

Squabbles & jealousy

DARREN 14 born 1979

Much tension

Grandpa

Aunt Doris

Mum's 'lifeline'

Mixed feelings

Live 'up north' and not seen by Darren for several years. Send Xmas gifts

Aunt Sue

MUM

Rows

Rows & fights

Gran

George & son Tony 'moved in' Feb 1992

div. 1989

Tony 13

Ann

129

2   Study the second chart of Darren's family. In this one positive and difficult relationships have been added.

Continue your role play of Darren and his keyworker. This time, the keyworker's task is to encourage Darren to talk about the relationships in his family. All the information you need to ask and answer the questions is on the chart, but you can add realistic detail.

3   Discuss with your partner what the next steps should be for Darren. What are his problems? What should be done about these? Where should he live? Which relationships should be encouraged? How?
   When you have talked through his situation, record your suggestions in one or two paragraphs.
   Present your suggestions to the whole group, and discuss any differences of views.

**TASK 4:
Your family**

Note to tutor: Before embarking on this task, establish to what extent it is appropriate to ask the group to share these experiences and which tasks you will undertake.

I   Draw a diagram to show the relationships in your family. Include all the members of your immediate family through the generations, and as many of your extended family as you can fit on a large sheet.

2   Work with a partner. Take it in turns to be the interviewer and the interviewee. The interviewer's task is to take the initiative in asking the

What is a family?
Courtesy: John Birdsall
Photography

interviewee about his or her family and relationships within it, and to sketch out a family tree as you go. The interviewee should explain and be as helpful as possible. But do respect each other's boundaries – find tactful ways of backing off from sensitive areas.

Decide which of the follow-up activities you wish to do:

(a) Working on your own family tree, indicate with coloured pens the positive and the difficult relationships.

(b) Give a short talk to the group introducing your family. Photos would be helpful.

(c) To what extent does your group reflect the range of family life in the UK? Compare your group with the family types in the statistical profiles you studied in Task 1, and present this in graphic form.

(d) Make a booklet entitled 'My family', with text and photos. A small photo album is a useful format – photos on one side complement the text, handwritten or word processed, or drawings, cut to fit, on the other. It also preserves the photos.

**TASK 5:
Lifelines**

A lifeline can be drawn in many ways and for many reasons. It can be a simple way of recording a complicated life history, so you can begin to understand someone else's life. It can be a way of reviewing your own life, to record and reflect on the things that stand out.

1   Below are some of the key events in Darren's lifeline. Copy it and add the missing ones (shown by date and lines only) using the charts in Task 3 above.

Darren's lifeline

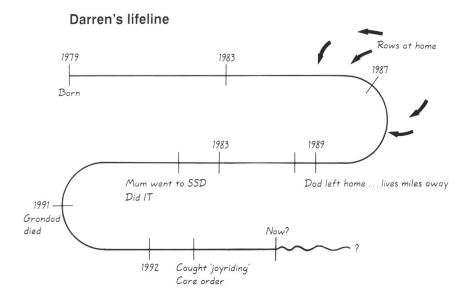

2   Draw your own lifeline, showing the events that are most important to you.

IN MY EXPERIENCE
by Alex Saddington

I was 14½ when I first came into care. I had been on the run for about three months. In my earlier school years I had many difficulties. I had to have special help because of a speech and hearing problem. I was in and out of hospital a lot at this time and so missed quite a few days at infant and primary school. In the 3rd year they moved me out of school because of my behaviour. I started to muck around in class. This was because home life was unbearable: there were always rows between my mother and stepfather. He would keep hitting me and my Mum till I couldn't take it any more.

When I was about 10, I was sent to my first special school, the first of six I was to attend in addition to two secondary schools. No-one really explained things to me and I was very bored there. I suffered a severe overdose of painting and drawing. That seemed about all we were given to do for the next 2 years. Because we had no interests to occupy our time, we ran wild. But instead of seeing that the school routine itself was actually making things worse, they put the blame on us. I got labelled 'maladjusted'. I was sent off to my first residential school (they are called EBD schools now – for 'emotionally or behaviourally disturbed' children).

I ended up at a school 200 miles away from my home. I was relieved to be away from my stepfather. But I hated it because it was so far away. I could go home only for main holidays and it was too far for any of the family to visit me. I could never go out alone, my incoming and outgoing letters were opened and read, phone calls were listened to and there was no freedom or privacy at all – it was like an open prison. No-one from outside ever came to visit me or ask how I was getting on.

Shunted Around

I went on to a further 2 schools like this one. The worst thing of all was being shunted around. No sooner had I begun to settle than I was uprooted and moved, I don't know why. Each time I had to leave my friends and in the end I never made any friends because I knew I'd be moving in the near future. The loneliness made me feel that nobody cared: I was out of sight, out of mind.

When I was 14 they decided residential school was not the answer. My problems really stemmed from home: so the Education Department was no longer willing to see it purely as an education problem and after 4 years sent me back home for Social Services Department to have a go. I knew it wouldn't work out at home and it didn't. The problems were just as bad as if not worse than when I left because my family had grown apart from me and I from them in the years I'd been away. I went on the run. My Mum put me in voluntary care. I agreed because I saw it as the only means of getting away from my stepfather.

First I went to stay with foster parents, then I moved to a children's home. There was a rule that you were taken to school in a yellow mini-bus with 'Social Services' written in large letters on the side. Any young person in care knows how that makes you feel and how degrading it is. Then I was moved back to the foster parents and they decided the school was too far away for me to travel there every day. They put me in a special school for physically disabled even though there was nothing wrong with me. Obviously it wasn't right so they moved me to a special school for 'maladjusted' kids: it was a joke. All we did was muck around for a couple of hours and go home. There were no proper lessons. Finally they found another secondary school where I settled for the last year of my education. Very little was expected of me because I had missed out so much and because I was in care. Two weeks before I was due to take exams, the Social Services Department moved me 20 miles away from my school. Because of the upheaval and stress, I didn't take them. I left the school aged 16 without any qualifications at all.

Not Giving Up

But I was still determined to get a decent education. After leaving school, I was lucky enough to get a place in college to study 'O' levels. Halfway through the course, I decided with Social Services that I no longer wanted to be in care. So it was agreed that I left care and went to live with my grandparents. I was forced to give up college though, as I couldn't get a grant or DHSS money. No-one told me I could have applied for a grant from the Social Services. (Under Section 27 of the 1980 Child Care Act.)

I went back to college: this time it was an 'A' level course, which I am now halfway through. I hope to go to University and one day work in social work management or in politics. At the moment I am Chairman of NAYPIC (London and South). I am still coming to terms with all that has happened to me, but feeling more hopeful at last.

I believe that:

- **No-one should be moved around in care or at school more than once or twice at the most.**
- **Children should not suffer because of professional blunders either by Education or Social Services Departments.**
- **No-one should be sent 200 miles away from home: they should be sent somewhere within reasonable travelling distance.**
- **Children should have somewhere in a children's home for studying in peace and someone to take an interest in their work.**
- **What social workers demand and expect for their own children should be what they demand and expect for children in their care – they shouldn't say or think that it is no part of their job to provide for a child any better than its own parents could have done.**
- **The Education Department have got to allow for our problems: after all we didn't physically, sexually or emotionally abuse ourselves.**
- **All children should be given the opportunity of learning even if they are 'different' and not be made to paint or draw all day.**
- **Social Services should be a good parent and all good parents want their children to have success in education.**

Source: Alex Saddington, 'In my experience', in *Who Cares?*, published by the NCB

TASK 6:
Lifelines and
life stories

Opposite is another life story. Draw a lifeline and mark on it the significant dates and events in Alex's life.

Discussion points Did you all pick out the same events as significant? Can you see linked events?

Assignment 4

L'Europe sans frontières

TASK 1:
Eurodata

Opposite is a map showing the countries of the European Community (EC), and some basic statistics. Use them to answer the following questions.

1   You will notice that in the data, the countries are represented by initials. What is the name of the country in (a) the language of the country, (b) in English?

2   List the countries of the EC in descending order of (a) geographical size, (b) population.

3   Consider your two lists. Which four countries are (a) most densely populated, (b) most sparsely populated? Compare your findings with the 'Population density' pie charts shown.

4   Compare the figures for the population of the countries of the EC as a whole with those of the USA and the countries of the former Soviet Union. Consider (a) geographical size, (b) population, (c) population density. Comment on your findings.

5   The projected rate of change in the population of each EC country by year 2000 is given as a percentage of current population.
    (a)   Work out what this represents in numbers. You may wish to use a calculator.
    (b)   Devise an effective way of showing the changes, country by country.
    (c)   Comment on the differing rates of change in EC countries, and suggest reasons for this.
    (d)   Compare the rate of population growth in Europe with that of the USA and the former USSR.

TASK 2:
The four
freedoms

On 1 January 1993 the Single European Market came into being.
    When you have read the extract below, answer the questions which follow.

FREE MOVEMENT OF PERSONS

European Community nationals and foreign tourists will no longer be subject to checks at the frontiers between the Member States but will be able to move freely within the Community. Increased cooperation between the

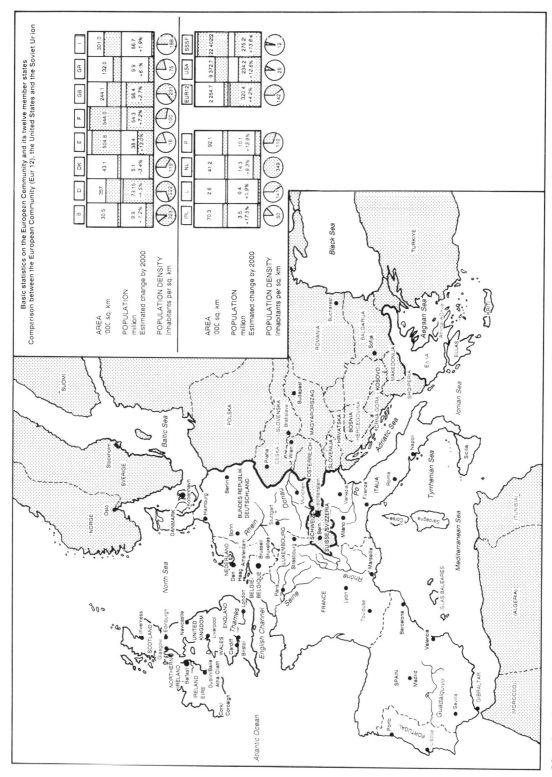

Member States of the European Community

Adapted from publications of the Commission of the European Communities 1987 and 1991

government departments responsible for dealing with drug trafficking and terrorism could make this possible.

Students will be free to choose their university and will be able to study in more than one Member State. Their degrees and diplomas will be recognized throughout the Community.

Workers, employees and the self-employed; mechanics and accountants; teachers and researchers; doctors and architects – all of them will be able to work in the Member State of their choice, on the same terms and same chances of success as nationals of the country in question.

FREE MOVEMENT OF GOODS

Goods will move freely throughout the Community, without being delayed at the one-time internal frontiers, thanks to the disappearance of fiscal and administrative constraints, along with paperwork.

Producers will have access to a genuine market of 324 million consumers. The harmonization, or mutual acceptance, of technical standards, production techniques and make-up of products will result in the disappearance of technical barriers to trade.

Economies of scale will enable manufacturers to be more effective as regards research and development and to offer consumers a wider range of better and cheaper products.

The health and safety of consumers will be safeguarded even more than at present, thanks to the approximation of national laws and regulations.

Firms as well as individual traders will enjoy considerably greater facilities to prospect the Community and set up shop.

FREE MOVEMENT OF SERVICES

Companies will be able to offer their services throughout the Community, while consumers will be free to choose the best offer at the best price.

The airlines will operate numerous flights to a wide variety of destinations. Fares will be the lowest possible, service will have improved and safety standards will be of the highest.

Road transport will be organized so as to allow a more rational use of the Community's fleet of trucks. There will be less paperwork, lower costs, more competition and increased safety.

The range of telecommunication products and services on offer will be highly diversified. They will be based on the latest technologies, thanks to a better utilisation of the results of scientific research.

European television without frontiers will offer a larger number of channels, programmes and services, thanks to more satellites and the introduction of new technologies. European creativity will be encouraged.

FREE MOVEMENT OF CAPITAL

Pending the development of a common currency, the ecu, the Community's citizens will be able to travel throughout the Community with the currency of their choice, without restrictions.

Individuals as well as companies will be able to transfer funds freely in all the Member States. Everyone will be free to save or invest wherever he likes within the Community.

The liberalization of capital movements and of financial services will make possible the freedom to choose in a large number of fields, including banking, savings and investments, mortgages, leasing and insurance, even while enjoying the best guarantees throughout the entire Community.

(Source: 1992: *The Frontiers Open*, published by the Commission of the European Communities/European Parliament)

1   What difference do you think the Single Market will make (a) to you and your family going on a camping holiday, driving through France and Italy; (b) to a school leaver with A levels planning to go to university; (c) to you, in thinking ahead about your working life?

2   (a)   Explain the meaning of the following: one-time internal frontiers; fiscal constraints; harmonisation of technical standards; technical barriers to trade; economies of scale.
    (b)   In a sentence, briefly summarise the effect of the Single Market on firms and individual traders in the EC.

3   What are the four examples of 'services' from which 'consumers are free to choose' in the Single Market?

4   (a)   What is the ecu?
    (b)   Find out the name of the currency in each country in the EC.
    (c)   What would you get in each of these currencies for £10?
    (d)   You are now free to open a bank account in any country in the EC. Find out the name of a bank in four countries of the EC.

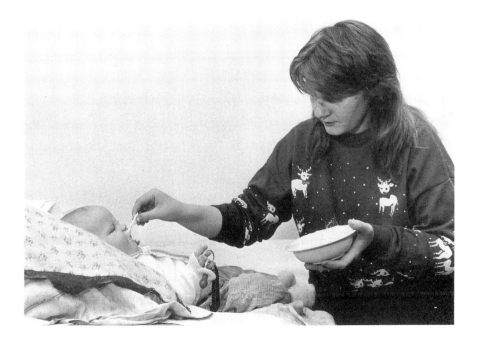

What is a family?
Courtesy: John Birdsall

**TASK 3:
Childcare in
the UK**

Study the table below.

Education and day care of children under five

United Kingdom   Thousands and percentages

		1966	1971	1976	1981	1986	1988	1989	1990
Children under 5 in schools[1]									
(thousands)									
Public sector schools									
Nursery schools	– full-time	26	20	20	22	19	18	17	17
	– part-time	9	29	54	67	77	80	65	67
Primary schools	– full-time	220	263	350	281	306	314	317	346
	– part-time	–	38	117	167	228	243	273	286
Non-maintained schools									
	– full-time	21	19	19	19	20	23	26	27
	– part-time	2	14	12	12	15	17	18	19
Special schools	– full-time	2	2	4	4	4	4	4	4
	– part-time	–	–	1	1	2	2	2	2
Total		280	384	576	573	671	700	722	769
As a percentage of all children aged 3 or 4		*15.0*	*20.5*	*34.5*	*44.3*	*46.7*	*48.4*	*49.1*	*51.2*
Day care places (thousands)									
Local authority day nurseries		} 21	23	35	{ 32	33	34	34	33
Local authority playgroups					5	5	6	4	3
Registered day nurseries		} 75	296	401	{ 23	29	40	49	64
Registered playgroups					433	473	479	480	491
Registered child minders		32	90	86	110	157	189	216	238
Total		128	409	522	603	698	747	783	830

1 Pupils aged under 5 at December/January of academic year.

Source: Department of Health; *Education Statistics for the United Kingdom*, Department of Education and Science; The Scottish Office Social Work Services Group; Welsh Office; Department of Health and Social Services, Northern Ireland.

1 What is the trend in nursery schools for (a) full-time, (b) part-time provision?

2 How many children had part-time places in nursery classes in primary schools in (a) 1971, (b) 1990? Comment on the change.

3 Have the numbers of children in full-time places in nursery classes of primary schools changed in the same way? Why do you think this is?

4 What is a 'non-maintained school'? Describe the trend in nursery provision in these schools. What percentage of children aged 3–5 attended these schools in 1990?

5 Comment briefly on the provision of places for children with special needs.

6 Draw a graph to show the changing percentage of children aged 3 or 4 attending schools.

7 Explain the difference between a 'local authority' and a 'registered' day nursery and playgroup. Which groups of children have priority for local authority places? Identify a number of providers of 'registered' provision.

8 How have the numbers of children catered for in (a) local authority, and (b) registered day nurseries and playgroups changed between 1981 and 1990? Can you suggest reasons for this?

9 How many children were looked after by registered childminders in (a) 1966, (b) 1990? Comment on the changes in the years between.

10 (a) Draw a pie chart showing the proportions of children in 1990 in *either* the various types of school provision *or* in different forms of day care.

 (b) Choose a year which you think contrasts with 1990 in at least one important respect. Draw a pie chart showing the proportions of children in that year in schools or day care, depending on what you chose above. Comment on the differences.

TASK 4: Children in Europe

1 Study the chart on p 140, and answer the questions that follow.

 (a) What is the average number of children per woman for the EC as a whole in (i) 1971, and (ii) 1990?
 (b) In which countries did people have more children than average and in which did they have fewer in (i) 1971, (ii) 1990?
 (c) In which countries has the greatest change in the birth-rate taken place? Can you suggest any reasons for this?
 (d) What is the trend in the birth-rate in the EC?

2 Your task is to find out about patterns of child care in one other EC country in the form of statistical data. Ideally, at least one member of your group should study each EC country. Where more than one person chooses the same country, work together.

The tasks set so far in this assignment will have given you an idea of how to extract information from data by asking yourself questions. Point out important features, changes and trends, and comment on what you find.

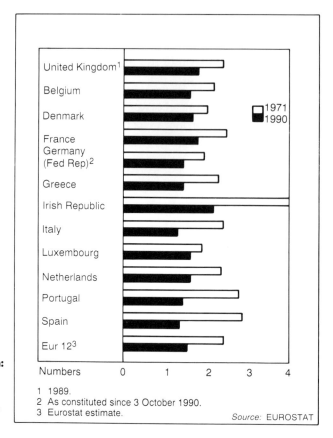

Average number of children per woman: EC comparison
Source: *Social Trends 22.*
Reproduced by kind permission of HMSO. Crown copyright 1992

TASK 5:
Europe and
the UK

1 Find out more about at least **one** of the forms of child care shown in the data for the EC country you studied. You may be able to find out about funding (who pays); location (near the child's home or parent's work); hours; facilities; numbers of children in one setting; provision for children with special needs, language, social or behavioural difficulties.

2 Compare your findings in Task 4 and question 1 above with UK provision profiled in Task 3.

3 Find out about jobs in child care in the country you studied. Aim to include training and qualifications, rates of pay, the scope of the job, employment conditions.

TASK 6:
Presentation

As a whole group, consider the following methods of presentation and choose the form in which you want to record your findings.

1 Display, in either a wall display or booklet form, your findings from Tasks 4 and 5 on different patterns of child care in Europe, country by country.

2   Give a talk to your group, with appropriate visual material, on child care in your chosen country. You may wish to compare it with the UK.

3   Write an article of about 500 words on 'Childcare in (EC country) and the UK' for publication in a magazine. Your style will depend on your choice of magazine. Type it, using a word processor. You may be able to design the page to include a picture (from a magazine) and some of your graphical data. Give it a headline and a bold introduction to encourage the reader to read on.

Assignment 5

Children's rights

TASK 1:
The UN
Convention on
the Rights of
the Child

The UN Convention on the Rights of the Child is an international human rights treaty, which was adopted by the UN General Assembly on 20 November 1989 and came into force on 2 September 1990. The UK government ratified the Convention with some reservations on 16 December 1991. The convention is now binding on those countries which have signed.

However, unlike the European Convention on Human Rights there will be no judicial machinery to enforce the law and no right of individual complaint. Each country will be placed under a duty to publicise the Convention's provisions and report progress to a specially constituted UN committee.

Source: *Childright*, No. 63, January/February 1990, published by the Children's Legal Centre

1 (a) What is 'judicial machinery'? What happens if there is no judicial machinery?

   (b) Can an individual child (through a lawyer) complain about a breach of rights?

   (c) Why do you think the UK government had 'some reservations' about ratifying the treaty? (These points are explored further on p 144.)

2 Below is an extract from the 'Unofficial summaries' of some of the articles of the Convention.

The United
Nations
Convention on
the Rights of
the Child

UNOFFICIAL SUMMARY OF MAIN PROVISIONS

Article 5
Parental guidance and the child's evolving capacities
The State's duty to respect the rights and responsibilities of parents and the wider family to provide guidance appropriate to the child's evolving capacities.

Article 6
Survival and development
The inherent right to life, and the State's obligation to ensure the child's survival and development.

Article 7
Name and nationality
The right to have a name from birth and to be granted a nationality.

Article 8
Preservation of identity
The State's obligation to protect and, if necessary, re-establish the basic aspects of a child's identity (name, nationality and family ties).

Article 9
Separation from parents
The child's right to live with his/her parents unless this is deemed incompatible with his/her best interests; the right to maintain contact with both parents if separated from one or both; the duties of States in cases where such separation results from State action.

Article 12
The child's opinion
The child's right to express an opinion, and to have that opinion taken into account, in any matter or procedure affecting the child.

Article 13
Freedom of expression
The child's right to obtain and make known information, and to express his or her views, unless this would violate the rights of others.

Article 14
Freedom of thought, conscience and religion
The child's right to freedom of thought, conscience and religion, subject to appropriate parental guidance and national law.

Article 18
Parental responsibilities
The principle that both parents have joint primary responsibility for bringing up their children, and that the State should support them in this task.

Article 19
Protection from abuse and neglect
The State's obligation to protect children from all forms of maltreatment perpetrated by parents or others responsible for their care, and to undertake preventive and treatment programmes in this regard.

Article 20
Protection of children without families
The State's obligation to provide special protection for children deprived of their family environment and to ensure that appropriate alternative family care or institutional placement is made available to them, taking into account the child's cultural background.

Article 25
Periodic review of placement
The right of children placed by the State for reasons of care, protection or treatment to have all aspects of that placement evaluated regularly.

Activity 26
Social security
The right of children to benefit from social security.

Article 27
Standard of living
The right of children to benefit from an adequate standard of living, the primary responsibility of parents to provide this, and the State's duty to ensure that this responsibility is first fulfillable and then fulfilled, where necessary through the recovery of maintenance.

Article 37
Torture and deprivation of liberty
The prohibition of torture, cruel treatment or punishment, capital punishment, life imprisonment, and unlawful arrest or deprivation of liberty. The principles of appropriate treatment, separation from detained adults, contact with family and access to legal and other assistance.

Go through the summaries of the articles here. For each, decide in what circumstances, in the UK or elsewhere in the world, the child's rights might be or are being infringed. To summarise your discussion, you may wish to set out your examples in columns.

3   Below is an extract from *Childright*, a publication concerned with promoting the rights of children. It suggests that the UK might be in breach of some of the articles of the Convention. Which are these? In what circumstances might this be the case?

Although the Convention is framed to accommodate minimal standards of the developing world, the UK cannot be complacent about all its provisions. Our immigration policies were at odds with the original drafts and even now immigrant children may be separated from their parents in breach of Article 9; the child's voice is not heard in some administrative or judicial procedures (such as education decisions or non-contested family proceedings) despite Article 12; our law condones the hitting of children despite Article 19; boys of 15 and 16 are being remanded in prisoin with adults despite Article 37, and can children who live for years in bed and breakfast accommodation or whose family income is below basic social security be said to receive an adequate standard of living in line with Article 27? It remains to be seen if the UK will ratify the Convention as a whole or enter reservations about some Articles.

Source: *Childright*, No. 63, January/February 1990, published by the Children's Legal Centre

4   Over the next two weeks collect newspaper articles or pictures which you think illustrate some abuse or neglect of children's rights. They do not have to relate precisely to the extracts above.

Shackles and handcuffs bind boy in US court

Nine year-old Jeffrey Bailey appeared in Florida's Osceola County Court in the United States wearing leg shackles and handcuffs when he was charged with killing a boy aged three.

At the request of his lawyer, he is to be tried as an adult for the murder, and, if found guilty, could face life imprisonment – or even, in principle, capital punishment. Florida has no minimum age for imposing the death sentence.

Jeffrey is accused of killing the child by pushing him into a motel swimming pool and watching him drown. There are no eyewitnesses to the incident, but Jeffrey told police he pushed the boy into the pool.

Asked about why it was necessary to handcuff and leg-iron the boy, Jeffrey Bailey's lawyer replied that it was the policy of the detention centre where he is being held.

Defence for Children International (DCI) reporting the case, point out that Standard Minimum Rules for the Treatment of Prisoners state 'chains or irons shall not be used as restraints. Other instruments of restraint shall not be used except . . . as a precaution against escape during a transfer, provided that they shall be removed when the prisoner appears before a judicial or administrative authority'. The Standard Minimum Rules have no binding force. DCI also point out that the Draft Convention on the Rights of the Child contains a provision outlawing the imposition of life imprisonment and capital punishment for crimes committed by young people under 18. More than 30 young people are awaiting execution in US jails because of crimes committed when they were under 18■

Source: *International Children's Rights Monitor*, Vol 3 No 4, Defence for Children International, PO Box 88, CH-1211 Geneve 20, Switzerland

London's illegal young workers

Only one child in seven with a part-time job in London is properly registered for employment with the local authority, according to a survey by Defence for Children (DCI)-UK.

The survey discovered many children working illegally in factories as machinists or in commercial kitchens and restaurants. Some ten year-olds working on milk floats or delivering newspapers start work as early as six in the morning. Children who work illegally earn on average 50 per cent less than those in legal employment.

Less than half the 22 boroughs surveyed make enquiries about children working illegally and only two employ specialist officers to tackle the problem■

DCI-UK, Richard Murphy, c/o Spectrum Children's Trust, Memorial School, Mount Street, Taunton, Devon. *A study of child labour in London*, further information from Leah Levin, 01 405 6018 or 267 6785.

Double standard for black and white children

Organisations such as the British Agencies for Adoption and Fostering (BAAF) are worried about the issue of inter-country adoption – the practice of bringing babies into Britain from countries such as Latin America and Asia for the purposes of adoption. Back in 1985 a working party was set up which helped formulate a policy statement, detailing specific areas of concern and criteria and recommendations relating to children; the biological parents or guardians; the adoptive parents, and the current practice and procedures relating to inter-country adoption.

Source: *Childright*, May/July/August 1987, published by the Children's Legal Centre

TASK 2:
The full text

Note to tutor: It is advisable to contact these organisations yourself to check whether it is appropriate for students to send these letters. Advice on letter layout is given on pp 276–8, *A Practical Approach to Caring* (Pitman Publishing, 1991) by Kate Williams in this series.

Obtain a copy of the full text of the United Nations Convention on the Rights of the Child. Write to one of the following organisations:

- The Children's Legal Centre, 20 Compton Terrace, London N1 2UN, Tel. 071-359 9392;
- CRDU, 235 Shaftesbury Avenue, London WC2H 8EL, Tel. 071-240 4449.

Be sure to enclose a large self-addressed envelope with your request.

TASK 3:
Not in the West!

For this task you need the full text of the Convention.

1 Read the extracts from newspapers on p 145, and identify the articles of the Convention you consider the incidents described to be in breach of. Write a short paragraph explaining why.

2 Look carefully at the collection of articles and pictures you started in Task 1. Can you be more precise about which articles these are in breach of?

3 Devise a way of displaying your work. Your purpose is to try to put a new perspective on many of the stories of children's ill fortune we regularly see and hear about. Your purpose is to convey that children have rights.

TASK 4:
Rights and responsibilities

In the contexts you have been looking at, the child is the vulnerable party whose rights need protection. On a personal level, it is important in work with children to convey that rights bring responsibilities. An example of this work to encourage the idea of fair play is shown opposite.

1 Complete these statements in terms that children you work with or know will be able to relate to.

2 With a partner, identify four more everyday rights of children, and develop these into statements like these. Ask another pair to complete the statements.

3 Compile the lists from the whole group, and consider how you might use them in work with children.

RIGHTS AND RESPONSIBILITIES

1   I have the **right** to be treated politely. Therefore, I have the responsibility to

_____

2   I have the **right** to my own space and to my own belongings. Therefore, I have the responsibility to

_____

3   I have the **right** to be safe and not to be hurt by others. Therefore, I have the responsibility to

_____

4   I have the **right** to be treated kindly and fairly by all. Therefore, I have the responsibility to

_____

TASK 5:
Rights in care

Read carefully the Charter of Rights for young people in care.

Charter of rights for young people in care

We have drawn up this charter for 'young people' because we feel it is the responsibility of the residential worker and social worker to make sure that younger kids get a good deal.

1   The right to be accepted and treated as an individual member of society. Also the right to be treated with the same respect given to any other valid member of the human race.

2   The right to know who we are. To know our parents and brothers and sisters. To have factual information about our family origins and background.

3   The right to be able to make our own decisions and to have real influence over those decisions we are sometimes considered too thick to participate in.

4   The right to privacy. We understand that in care it is not always possible to choose who we are going to live and share our lives with. But we are still human beings and are still entitled to the essential amount of privacy needed before cracking up.

5   The right to be given an insight into the use of money by handling it, using it and paying the consequences if we misuse it, e.g. being

given the money in our hand to buy the clothes our clothing allowance will allow.

6 The right to choose those who will represent us whether it be legally or otherwise, e.g. social workers. Also the right to choose those whom we wish to confide in.

7 Finally, the right to be as much a part of society as the next person and not to be labelled in any way. In short, to live.

These rights can be interpreted how you like. But don't misuse them or distort them for your own devices.

Source: G Clark and R Page *Who Cares? Children in Care Speak Out*, NCB 1977

1 Which of these rights are also written into the UN Convention on Children's rights?

2 Which of these rights do you think apply to children not in care, living in their own families?

3 Are there any other rights you think should be included in this Charter? Look at Alex Saddington's comments in Assignment 3 (p 132). Do you think the Charter covers the points he makes? Make any amendments you think are merited, arising from his comments and your group's views. Redraft and retype the Charter if you have made changes.

TASK 6: **Research or report**	Choose one aspect of children's rights to research or survey. Work with a partner. Below are some suggestions – you could, for example, consider the rights of children:

- at home;
- at school;
- with the police;
- over forms of punishment;
- with disabilities;
- black and ethnic minority children;
- in hospital;
- victims of war;
- refugees.

Some of these subjects would best be explored through a **survey**, others through a **project**. Agree with your tutor which you will do, and present a **plan of action**. This may include:

- reading about the subject – for example, elsewhere in this book, in libraries, in specialist publications, in newspapers;
- drafting a questionnaire;
- writing letters for information or permission to carry out a survey;

- getting your letters or questionnaire translated into other language(s), put on tape or in braille if you want to contact people who would not otherwise be able to respond;
- carrying out a *pilot* survey and making changes;
- deciding on who to contact and the size of your sample for a survey;
- collating your results, and presenting your data in as clear a form as possible, using charts where possible.

Check the index under *survey*, *questionnaire* and *report writing* for advice on these stages of your research.

Assignment 6

Milestones in child development

At what age did you learn to pile up three bricks, walk and talk? The chances are, you don't know. And it really doesn't matter when you learnt it – the fact is, you did. We all know people who are better at doing certain things than we are. Equally, we can all think of particular things we do well. As adults, we know we got there.

To parents of young children, it does not always feel like this. Any parent will be anxious about some aspect of their child's development. 'Is it normal?' will be a spoken or unspoken concern to many parents. If you work with children, you will have a different perspective; you will see the great range of what is 'normal'. One child will be walking well at one; another crawling fast and confidently; another hardly moving at all. Yet they are all quite 'normal' stages of development for a one-year-old.

So development can be seen in terms of 'milestones' – a point that is

Courtesy: John Birdsall
Photography

150

passed sooner or later. There *is* a range of 'normal' development; sometimes everything is not all right. So people who work with children have to be sensitive to parents' worries and know when to encourage them to seek advice.

Where children do have a disability or special need, development in a particular area may be delayed. There are all sorts of causes for this: impaired hearing may affect speech; a physical difficulty with movement will make many standard measurements of intellectual development meaningless. Children with special needs still develop, but milestones may be passed later – sometimes much later, when these successes are also a measurement of the achievement made by the child, the parents and the caring services.

TASK 1: Charting the milestones	On pp 152–3 you will find

- a guide to development from birth to five, and
- a development summary chart.

Your task is to redraw and complete the chart using the information from the guide. Draw a bar showing the span of ages at which each development takes place, and write neatly in each bar. It will help the overall appearance if you plan roughly what goes where before you start detailed drawing.

TASK 2: A closer focus

1 Draw up a similar chart for ages 4 and 5 only, and complete it, drawing selectively on the material in the developmental progress chart given for Task 1.

2 Identify an age or span of ages that particularly interests you. Draw an enlarged chart allowing you to show more detail. Complete it by using selective information from the chart in Task 1.

TASK 3: Special needs

1 Find out about illnesses and conditions that result in children having a developmental delay and special needs in education.

2 Research one of these conditions in greater depth. You may be able to visit a ward, school, unit or centre that specialises in help for these children.

3 Write up your research. Below are some suggestions for headings. You may think of others:

- causes/symptoms;
- treatment/therapy;
- services to help;
- experiences of individuals and families, effects on families.

A Guide to Development

This guide gives an idea of the age range within which *most* children gain certain skills. The ages given are averages. Lots of perfectly normal children gain one skill earlier, another later than average.

Movement

Most children:

☐ lift their heads by about 3 months.

☐ sit without support between 6 and 8 months. If your baby is not sitting unsupported by 9 months, talk to your health visitor or doctor.

☐ start *trying* to crawl around 6 months. Some crawl backwards before they crawl forwards. Crawling may really get going around 9 months. But some children learn to walk without ever crawling at all. Others are bottom-shufflers.

☐ pull themselves upright and stand, holding onto the furniture, between 6 and 10 months.

☐ walk alone between 10 and 16 months. If your child is not walking by 18 months, talk to your health visitor or doctor.

☐ learn to kick or throw a ball between 18 months and 2 years. Throwing sometimes takes longer than kicking.

☐ learn to pedal a trike between about 2 and 3 years.

Handling things

Most children:

☐ will reach out for objects between 3 and 5 months.

☐ can hold an object and will lift it up to suck it between 5 and 8 months. At first, babies can hold objects but not let go. At about 6 to 7 months, they learn to pass things from hand to hand, maybe via their mouths. They learn to let go of things (for example, to drop something, or give it to you) at about 9 to 10 months.

☐ use both their right and left hands, without preference, until about 3 years old.

☐ can feed themselves the sort of foods they can pick up and hold at about 10 months.

☐ begin to feed themselves, very messily, with a spoon sometime after 14 months.

☐ begin to take off easy clothes (like loose, short socks) from about 14 months.

☐ begin to be able to build bricks between 15 and 18 months. Large bricks are easiest to start with.

☐ enjoy scribbling with a crayon from about 18 months onwards.

☐ can draw what you can see is a person (with a face and maybe arms and legs) between 3 and 4 years old. Like much else, this depends a lot on how much practice and encouragement they get.

Hearing and talking

Most children:

☐ are startled by sudden, loud noises from birth.

☐ make cooing noises from about 3 months.

☐ by 3 months will quieten to the sound of a parent's voice, and may turn towards the sound.

☐ by 6 months are making repetitive noises, like 'gagaga . . .' and enjoy making more and more different sounds.

☐ start to use particular sounds for particular things between 10 and 14 months.

☐ say something like 'mama' and 'dada' to anyone from about 6 to 9 months and to their parents from 10 to 12 months.

☐ by 18 months, can say between 6 and 20 recognisable single words, but understand much more than they can say. They also start to use language in play – for example, when feeding a teddy or doll, or talking on a toy telephone.

☐ can put at least two words together by 2 years old, and can point to parts of their body.

☐ can talk well in sentences and chant rhymes and songs by 3 years old.

☐ by 3 years old are talking clearly enough to be understood by strangers. A few 3 year olds may still be difficult to understand. It is normal for a 2 year old to pronounce words wrongly.

Seeing

Babies can see from birth, but for a few months they can only focus on what is close to them. So to begin with, the other side of a room, for example, is a blur, but a face close in front of them is clear – and interesting. The distance they can see gradually increases.

Many babies squint at birth. If you still notice the squint after three to four months, you should ask your doctor about it.

Most children:

☐ begin to recognise their parents by 2 weeks, and start to smile at around 4 to 6 weeks.

☐ in the first few weeks, especially like looking at faces. They will focus on a face close in front of them, and follow it. They prefer the face of a parent, or a known face, to a strange one.

☐ can follow a brightly coloured moving toy, held about 20cm/8ins away, by about 6 weeks.

☐ can see across a room by about 6 months.

Source: *Birth to Five: A guide to the first five years of being a parent*, published by the Health Education Authority

Development Summary Chart

		Months	Years
Movement			
Handling things			
Seeing hearing and talking			
Months	1 2 3 4 5 6 7 8 9 10 11 12 13 14 15 16 17 18 19 20 21 22 23 24 27 30 33 36		
Years	1	2	3	4

TASK 4:
A special child

To complete this task you need to spend some time with a child with special needs.

1 If the child is under 5, use your completed development summary chart as a basis for observing the child's development. Consider the child's development under the headings Movement, Handling things, Seeing, hearing and talking. You may find it helpful to use a blank chart to mark in your child's development.

If the child is over 5, you need to prepare for the visit by making sure you know what development you would expect to see in a child of that age.

2 Talk to the child's parent or carer to find out what they are doing to help the child's development, and what developments are taking place.

3 Write up and present your study in whatever way you think best conveys the difficulties and achievements of your special child.

NOTE *Tasks 1, 3 and 4 of this Assignment are taken from* A Practical Approach to Caring *(Pitman Publishing, 1991) by Kate Williams.*

Assignment 7

Children's needs and expectations

TASK 1:
Quality care

Below is an extract from The Children Act 1989 Guidance and Regulations. Read it carefully, and answer the questions that follow.

CHILD DEVELOPMENT

6.27 This involves focusing on the child's experience in terms of the potential advantages and disadvantages that the experience offers the child and the possible effects of the care upon child development. One aspect of good quality care is that it is developmentally beneficial to the child, and poor quality care is that which inhibits, or at least does not facilitate, child development. Most research on quality has been explicitly or implicitly guided by this approach.

RIGHTS OR EXPECTATIONS OF CHILDREN

6.28 Children have a right to an environment which facilitates their development. An approach based on children's rights would encompass all the factors necessary for their development. However, depending upon the values held by society at large, the child may be regarded as having rights which go beyond the provision of an environment which can be empirically demonstrated to facilitate development. For example: children should have the right to be cared for as part of a community which values the religious, racial, cultural and linguistic identity of the child. The justification for the awarding of such a right would be in terms of fostering the child's sense of identity. Children's sense of identity is a fundamental aspect of their development and so such a right could be included within a definition based upon the facilitation of child development. Other examples of rights which might be assigned to children include the right to health, individuality, respect, dignity, opportunities for learning and socializing with adults and children, freedom from discrimination such as racism or sexism and cultural diversity. The extent to which a day care setting fulfils these rights may be used in defining the quality of care for that setting. All these rights can be regarded as potentially contributing to children's physical, intellectual, social and emotional development.

Source: *The Children Act 1989 Guidance and Regulations Vol. 2*
Family support, day care and educational provision for young children, HMSO, 1991

1   What are the definitions of good quality care and poor quality care given in s. 6.27?

2   List all the rights of children identified in this extract.

3 Why should a child's religious, racial, cultural and linguistic identity be valued?

4 Is it proven that respecting these rights helps a child's development?

5 By what criteria will the quality of day care be judged under the Children Act?

6 What areas of a child's development are helped by a day care setting that respects the child's rights?

7 Explain in your own words what you feel the Children Act is trying to achieve in laying down standards for the day care of children.

TASK 2: Children's needs

In a booklet for parents, the NSPCC identifies emotional, physical and intellectual needs as the three essential types of needs. The elements of these needs they list are: love, praise, physical care, routines, stimulation, talking, independence, respect.

Courtesy: John Birdsall Photography

With a partner or in small groups, refer back to your work on children's needs on p 154 and compile your own list of what you consider children's needs to be. Offer an explanation for each one you suggest. When you have agreed your list, design a simple leaflet for *either* parents *or* child care workers to increase their awareness of the needs of their children and to encourage a positive response. Make sure your advice is positive and does not expect your readers to be superhuman!

156

TASK 3: Have you hugged your child today?

From your booklet on children's needs (Task 2), pick one message about caring for children that you want to communicate to parents and/or carers. Design a poster with a clear slogan and good visual impact.

Courtesy: G A Clark ARPS

TASK 4: Child abuse

Note to the tutor: This task raises issues about child abuse that should be talked and thought through by everyone working with children. Child abuse is touched on elsewhere in this book (*see* particularly Part 1, Chapter 7), and you may find Assignment 13 'At Risk?' in *A Practical Approach to Caring* (Pitman Publishing, 1991) by Kate Williams a useful introduction to the topic.

People who work with children will at any given moment have children in their care whose parents have widely differing views about upbringing and discipline, and widely differing circumstances. You have to be aware of imposing your own views and values on children and families, and of the possibility of misinterpreting the workings of another family. It is important to develop and maintain close working relationships with parents, to talk to them about what their children did in the day, to mention any concerns you have or problems the child seems to have. This day-to-day communication is the basis of a partnership in caring for their child.

Abuse, however, does happen, and no culture tolertes the abuse, neglect or sexual exploitation of children. As a child-care worker your first duty is to the child, so you must rehearse your feelings if you were to find yourself suspecting abuse or neglect and know what you would do.

Your work on child development and experience of a range of children is the bedrock on which you build. Your knowledge of the range of normal behaviour in children will help you to see when a child has a particular problem, but there are always many possible reasons for a problem. Experienced workers readily take advice on their observations, and share their concerns.

Opposite is a flowchart which shows what a child care worker should do if abuse is suspected.

Work through each of the three sections in this flowchart, referring to the material on child abuse in Part 1, Chapter 7, and below.

1 Section A:
   (a) What in the child's behaviour/appearance might give cause for concern?
   (b) What should the worker do then?
   (c) Who is the equivalent to the 'senior playworker' in your work setting?
   (d) Who would the senior worker inform in your work setting?
   (e) At what point would the senior worker talk to the other workers?
   (f) Who talks to the parents about staff concerns?
   (g) Who contacts social services? When?

2 Section B:
   (a) What sorts of physical injuries would cause you concern?
   (b) Describe the procedure to follow if you were a playworker who suspected abuse. Model your account on the step-by-step account above.

3 Section C:
   (a) What, in a child's accounts of experiences, would you feel constitutes 'abuse'?
   (b) Describe the advice on processes to follow here.
   (c) What is different about the possible outcomes of C to the outcomes of A and B?

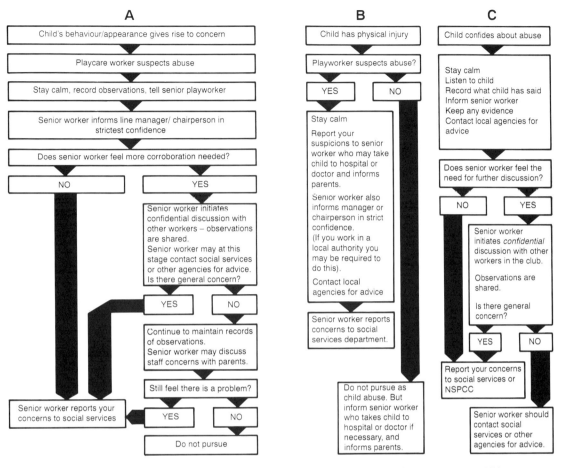

Source: *The role of playcare workers in the protection of children from abuse*, published by the Kids Clubs Networks, June 1992

The flowchart makes the following points clear:

- The individual child care worker is not an expert in child abuse, they are not expected to be, nor should they aim to become one. They must make contact with people who are.
- Each worker is part of a caring network looking after children. Even if you are on your own as a childminder, or feel isoalted in your work setting, there is someone outside to talk to – health visitor, day care organiser, social worker, social services duty officer, NSPCC, PPA organiser. Find out the name, address and phone number of all these people in your area.
- A worker who has concerns must share them with the senior worker or an independent agency.

Child abuse

When might you suspect abuse?

Every child will react differently to abuse. The following signs might arouse your suspicions that a child is being neglected or physically or sexually abused, but don't jump to conclusions too quickly. There could be perfectly legitimate and reasonable explanations for all of them.

GROWTH AND DEVELOPMENT

Children who are being emotionally deprived often fail to thrive for no specific medical reason. They may seem undernourished, and small in height and weight. If you think a child looks smaller than his or her friends, talk to a health visitor: there may be an obvious explanation.

GENERAL APPEARANCE

Children who are being neglected often seem ill-kept. Their clothing may be inappropriate and ill-fitting; they may be grubby or smelly. But don't forget that well turned-out children can also be victims of abuse.

EATING PROBLEMS

If a child always appears ravenously hungry, they may be receiving insufficient food at home.

PHYSICAL CHANGES

There may be sudden physical changes. The child might start wetting, get tummy pains with no medical reason, or get constipated. Such changes may not be due to abuse but in any case you should get medical attention.

BEHAVIOURAL CHANGES

The child may become very quiet, very aggressive, or very detached. When sexual abuse is occurring they may behave in a sexually explicit way (playing sexual 'games', masturbating, and showing the sexual awareness of a much older child). However, don't automatically assume that sexual behaviour is unnatural.

BRUSING, CUTS OR BURNS

All children get injuries and bruises in the normal rough and tumble of play. However these usually occur in specific places, such as the elbows, knees and shins. If you notice bruising on the cheeks, ear lobes, upper arms, chest, stomach or buttocks, this may suggest that

▶

the child has been gripped or slapped.

Burns that cannot be explained are also suspicious – in particular, cigarette burns, which have a typical circular appearance, and iron burns, which appear triangular.

Children who are being abused are frequently reluctant to discuss how they got their injuries, whereas most children who have fallen over or fallen off their bike are only too ready to explain what has happened and to tell everybody about it.

You may need to take expert advice on the appearance of injuries on a black or brown skin. There have been cases where black families have been wrongly suspected of child abuse because the professionals mistook uneven skin pigmentation for bruising.

RELATIONSHIPS WITH PARENTS

A child who is being abused may seem to be frightened of the parents, or only seem happy with you and the other workers. If one of the parents is also being abused, the child may cling to them and be reluctant to leave them.

CHILD'S OWN STATEMENT

Very occasionally, a child will trust you enough to tell you that they are being abused in some way. However unlikely you may think it is, it is very important to believe what the child says, at least until proven otherwise. Make a written note of what the child actually said as soon as possible. Children may fantasize and enjoy telling stories but will rarely, if ever, tell lies about abuse.

(Source: *Keeping Children Healthy: A guide for under 5s workers* in the Starting Points series published by VOLCUF)

This is hard for any worker. Professional advice tells us:

- to acknowledge our own feelings. We will worry about what will happen to the family. Will the child be taken away? Suppose I'm wrong? Are people going to think I am a busybody or a nutter?
- to get help from an outside agency if our own feelings become too strong, or if our thoughts about the child's condition arouse memories of harm we experienced ourselves, even if it was a long time ago. The NSPCC is a good place to start for advice and help.
- that parents do not want to harm their children, and may need help and support to achieve this.

4 Draw three flowcharts modelled on the ones above, showing what to do if a junior worker in your workplace/placement suspected abuse. You may add any details you think would be helpful arising from your work on this section.

Assignment 8

Don't put mustard in the custard

Recommended reading: 'Don't', a short poem by Michael Rosen in the collection *Don't put mustard in the custard*. It ends:

Who do they think I am?
Some kind of fool?

Much of what we do and don't let children do depends on the attitudes and values – and personal foibles – that we have formed over the years. This assignment explores some of them.

Note to the tutor: This assignment should be undertaken when members of the group feel safe with one another.

TASK 1:
Your views

1   Working on your own, complete the questionnaire opposite, giving a mark in the column on the right next to each statement to show how strongly you agree or disagree with it.
10 = strongly agree
 1 = strongly disagree

Courtesy: John Birdsall
Photography

1	When we become parents, we often treat our children the way our parents treated us.	
2	Adults should make clear rules; young children should obey them.	
3	Boys and girls are born different; therefore they will behave differently.	
4	Black British people do not get a fair chance.	
5	Children should be looked after at home for the first three years of life.	
6	Children should not be allowed to play with guns and war toys.	
7	Women and girls are treated unfairly in our society.	
8	Television is the most damaging influence on young children's development.	
9	Children in single parent families are deprived.	
10	If someone really wants a job, they will be able to find one.	

Based on p 45, *Working with children: a curriculum for the early years*, NCB

2   Working as a whole group, take each statement one at a time, and line up across the room, with people who gave a statement a high mark on one side, those with a low number on the other, and people with numbers in between lining up in order. When a line is formed for each statement, ask each person to explain why they have placed themselves where they have.

Discussion will help you to discover the reasons for your beliefs and values.

3   **An accurate record.** One person (a different one for each statement) does not line up, and instead records the views of the people in the line.

When the line-up for each statement has been completed and recorded, each recorder has the task of checking that they have faithfully recorded the views explained earlier. Pass your records around for the group to read. When anyone feels their views have not been recorded accurately, discuss these with the recorder and the wider group if necessary. Your purpose is to reach agreement about the accuracy of the record.

**TASK 2:
... and don't
chuck jelly at
the telly**

1   Write down three rules you were brought up with as a child – words said to you by your mother, father, teacher, grandmother ... Record how you reacted to them. Did you obey? resist? rebel? What happened if you did/not comply?

2   Share your experiences with a partner. Are there similarities in the rules you grew up with? Differences? What are your views of the three rules now?

3   Working in pairs, make a list on a large sheet or flipchart of the rules enforced:
    (a)   at home
    (b)   at your workplace.
    In your pairs, present these rules to the group, and explain whether they are fixed or flexible. Do they get bent sometimes? If so by whom, and when?

4   As a whole group, consider which rules are most commonly held, and which are particular to individual settings.

**TASK 3:
... and don't
throw fruit at
the computer**

How do we convey rules to children?
    The PPA suggests a number of strategies to try to achieve acceptable behaviour in day care groups.

Strategy 1: Make sure they know the rules

For many children, playgroup is the first public situation they have been in and the first time they have had to accept the authority of people other than their parents. The playgroup may need to have rules quite different from those of home. This can be confusing at first for a young child.

CONSISTENCY WITHIN THE GROUP

Do all adults in your group handle children in the same way? There is little wonder children become confused or 'try to score' if everyone has a different approach. Everyone needs to know how the adults will react if a child persistently throws sand on the floor – will s/he be expected to sweep up the mess, have a ticking off, be removed to another part of the playroom, be told s/he cannot play in the sand any more for the rest of the morning? Will that policy then be adhered to by all the adults?

    To create a stable, disciplined framework for the group's activities, all the adults need to be agreed about the 'rules', and about the thinking behind them. These are some of the things you might need to discuss:

▶

- Are the children allowed to run about indoors?
- Is it permitted to 'mix up' the equipment?
  For example, may children
  - use Lego bricks/playdough/jigsaw pieces for 'cooking' in the home corner?
  - add water to the sand?
  - add sand to the water?
- May the children:
  - play with guns brought from home?
  - play with guns made on the spot with Lego etc?
  - play at guns by pointing and saying 'Bang', for example?
- When children are wearing dressing-up clothes, may they:
  - play with the water?
  - go on the climbing frame?
  - use the clay?
- What is expected of children who have finished with a piece of equipment?
  Should they:
  - leave all jigsaws complete?
  - put Lego back in the box?
  - replace books on the shelf/table?
- What about small accidents?
  Are children expected to:
  - pick up the beads which have rolled on the floor?
  - mop up spilled water?
  - sweep up spilled sand?

Once you have agreed about all these issues, there are more questions to answer:
Do all the adults know?
Do all the children know?
Do all the adults enforce all the decisions in the same way all the time?

Source: *Behaviour in Playgroups*, Information Sheet 10, published by the PPA

1 In small groups discuss each point here, and decide what rules you would decide on if you were a day care staff group.

2 When you have decided on your policy in each case, discuss the strategies you would use to achieve it. Suggestions from a number of sources are noted overleaf.

3 Divide the situations up between the members of your group. Summarise your discussions by writing a prompt list of questions, comments and strategies the child care worker might use in each situation.

4 Write your key points on a flip chart and present your strategies to the whole group.

Think before you say 'no' but then mean it – it's fine to avoid clashes when you can and keep your limits wide, but once you've said 'no', stick to it. Children need to discover that there's no point in going on fussing/making a scene.

STRATEGY 2: Make sure you are communicating.
Does the child understand the language you are using? Just because one four year old understands you, it does not mean another one will!

Rewards work much better – praise, approval and hugs as well as tangible things like ice-lollies or presents – because rewards motivate people and make them want to please.
   Think of yourself: would you work harder for a boss who offered overtime when you stayed five minutes late or one who docked your wages when you arrived five minutes late?

STRATEGY 7: Never 'label' children
If you refer to the "bully" or the "bad lads gang" you will begin to think of the children in a very negative and unproductive way. They will also live up to the label you have given them, so that all that is achieved is a reinforcing of undesirable behaviour.

Try to be positive:

'Do' works better than 'don't': rewards work better than punishments

- Show and tell what they **should** do - not just what they shouldn't.
- **Explain** your real reasons - "because I say so" teaches nothing for next time.
- Try to say **"yes"** and "well done" at least as often as **"no"** and "stop that".
- Be as ready to **praise** behaviour you like as to **scold** for behaviour you don't.
- Rely on **rewards** like hugs and jokes, not **punishments** like smacks and yells.
- **Ignore** minor silliness and "cheek". The more you nag the less they'll listen.
- When they do something wrong explain what it is and **how to put things right**.
- Even when you **dislike your child's** behaviour, **never suggest that you dislike your child**.

Introduce important values like truth, honesty and unselfishness through everyday experience. That the playgroup would have no books if everyone took them home; everyone wants first go on the swing so it's fairest to take turns . . .

STRATEGY 3: Reward the behaviour you want to encourage.
A child who misbehaves in order to seek adult attention is clearly not getting enough attention on the occasions when s/he is being 'good.' Find something to praise, and praise it.

STRATEGY 8: Watch your own behaviour
If you find yourself getting angry,
   – Relax. Breathe slowly.
   – Lower your shoulders.
   – Lower your voice.
   – Remind yourself 'I can handle this' and count to ten.
   – Move yourself away from the situation to give yourself time and space to decide on the best thing to do next.
   – Breathe in
   – Hold
   – Breathe gently.

Do expect some showing off, and 'silliness': 'rude' rhymes and noisy, boisterious behaviour that tends to send things flying! This is an age for experimenting with words and physical actions, and copying other children.

(From material published by PPA and EPOCH)

166

TASK 4:
Behaviour and
sanctions

The Children Act sets out the legal position on behaviour and sanctions very clearly:

Behaviour and sanctions

6.21. People responsible for running a day care facility need to have an agreed policy on its day to day operation and to develop procedures for modifying unacceptable behaviour in the children which will include appropriate sanctions. It will encourage development of a sense of right and wrong behaviour if children are encouraged to co-operate in the social organisation of the facility. The sanctions applied in the case of unacceptable behaviour must take account of the age and stage of development of the child, be given at the time, be relevant to the action or actions and be fair. The child should always be told why his behaviour is not acceptable and the reasons for applying a particular sanction. Providers and childminders should ensure that parents are fully informed about and support the policy on modifying unacceptable behaviour and the range of sanctions.

6.22. Corporal punishment (smacking, slapping or shaking) is illegal in maintained schools and should not be used by any other parties within the scope of this guidance. It is permissible to take necessary physical action in an emergency to prevent personal injury either to the child, other children or an adult or serious damage to property.

Source: *The Children Act 1989 Guidance and Regulations, Vol. 2*, HMSO, 1991

Corporal punishment by any child care worker is illegal. Overleaf are some of the arguments and evidence which led to this statement in the Act, and which are now being put forward by organisations who want to see all forms of corporal punishment by parents made illegal.

Use these as the basis of a short radio talk, suitable for broadcasting on 'Woman's Hour', designed to persuade parents not to smack their children. Decide on the format of your talk:

- a short talk;
- an interview, one person being the interviewer, the other the interviewee;
- a discussion, one person chairing a discussion between two people with opposing views.

Prepare your talk, then tape record it.

TASK 5:
Feeling good

Much of this assignment has focused on how children modify their behaviour in response to the positive – or negative – feedback they get from others. The same is true of us all...

Praise is a powerful thing. We need to be clear about what it is we are praising.

1   Work in twos or threes. Compile a list of the expressions of praise you have used or heard used. Use the exact words as far as possible.

"Children are entitled to care, security and a good upbringing. Children are to be treated with respect for their person and individuality and may not be subjected to corporal punishment or any other humiliating treatment".

Swedish Parenthood and Guardianship Code

Look at the basic message the child receives from the smacking parent: that someone they love and respect believes that using a degree of violence is a useful way of sorting out conflicts or problems: the absurdity of the parent in the supermarket slapping her child and punctuating the slaps with "I - will - not - have - you - hitting - your - little - brother".

The model is well learned, and there is a mountain of research evidence that if a child is physically punished, he or she is more likely to develop violent attitudes, to get involved in bullying at school, and later domestic violence and violent crime.

John and Elizabeth Newson's long-term study of UK childrearing finds a "very clear association" between the frequency of physical punishment at 11, and the child's later delinquency. The Newsons also concluded: "The measures that stand out as being most predictive of criminal record before the age of 20 are having been smacked or beaten once a week or more at 11, and having had a mother with a high degree of commitment to formal corporal punishment at that age".

"A child shall be brought up in a spirit of understanding, security and love. He shall not be subdued, corporally punished or otherwise humiliated. His growth towards independence, responsibility and adulthood shall be encouraged, supported and assisted".

Finland: Child Custody and Rights of Access Act 1983.

A recent survey reported in *Woman's Own* found that a quarter of the thousands of respondents who smacked their children admitted that they had "lost control" at least once while administering physical punishment.

Research in the UK, the US, Finland and other countries shows that when serious physical child abuse is investigated, parents frequently explain that the incident began as "ordinary" punishment. For example, an intensive review of 66 cases of prosecuted child abuse in the United States, published in 1981, concluded that child abuse most often occurs as "extensions of disciplinary actions which at some point and often inadvertently crossed the ambiguous line between sanctioned corporal punishment and unsanctioned child abuse".

Most recently, an EPOCH survey of UK child protection co-ordinators in 1990 found 13 per cent of responding authorities reporting that physical punishment is the explanation in over half the cases they investigate; a further 63 per cent report it in up to half of all cases: "There are relatively few cases of deliberate cruelty and the vast majority of incidents dealt with represent over-chastisement or a loss of control in administering physical punishment" (Salford); "Normally explanation is over-chastisement . . ." (Warwickshire).

To be effective, a disciplinary technique must do two complementary things: it must set external limits on children's behaviour so as to keep them safe and acceptable to their parents and others, and it must help them to develop the self-discipline that will gradually replace those external controls with the internal controls we call "conscience". Physical punishments do neither. They cannot show children where the limits are because they are only smacked or beaten when those limits have already been overstepped. They cannot help in the development of self-discipline because they only tell children that they have done wrong; they neither describe the crime nor suggest the preferable alternative.

Learning how to behave is exactly like other kinds of learning in that it depends on children understanding what is wanted of them; being motivated to co-operate and make efforts, and being set a good example. Children who are hit often misunderstand the cause of the punishment. Many spankings are the result of cumulative parental stress in which one last small misdemeanour is one too many. The child sees the parental anger but relates it only to that last event and believes he was hit for "spilling my drink" or, more accurately "because you were cross". Premeditated punishment for carefully explained reasons fares no better: the hurt, anger and humiliation caused by the punishment deafens children to the reasons for it. And even if the reason is understood, those feelings leave no room for remorse or determination to do better.

Corporal punishment is "an evil which must at least be discouraged as a first step towards outright prohibition. It is the very assumption that corporal punishment is legitimate that opens the way to all kinds of excesses and makes the traces and symptoms of such punishment acceptable to third parties".

Committee of Ministers of Council of Europe, Recommendation R85/4, Explanatory Memorandum.

More than seven million children in Europe now live under legal protection from all forms of physical punishment and humiliating treatment. In 1979 Sweden became the first country to ban all physical punishment of children. Similar reforms quickly followed, in Finland (1983), Denmark (1985), Norway (1987), and Austria (1989). (In 1992 the German government committed itself to a similar reform.) The purpose in each case has been to change attitudes to children, not to increase prosecution of parents, or state intervention in family life. In Sweden in 12 years there has been just one prosecution of a parent for "ordinary" physical punishment: a father was fined the equivalent of £10 for spanking his 11 year-old son (in the other countries there have been no prosecutions). And the rate of state intervention in family life in Sweden is very much lower than in the UK and reducing.

Opinion polls have shown a dramatic change in the attitudes of Swedish parents: between 1965 and 1981 the proportion believing that children should be raised without physical punishment increased from 35 to 70 per cent.

Legal reform was accompanied by an intensive education programme. Pamphlets were circulated to all families with children. Milk cartons, commonly used as vehicles for public information campaigns in Sweden, carried a cartoon of a little girl saying "I shall never, ever hit my child", and an explanation of the law. In schools, the message was built into the national curriculum.

Source: *Hitting people is wrong – and children are people too*, published by EPOCH

2 Review your list. What **activities** is the child being praised for? (You do ride that bike well / What a lovely castle/painting/sticking.) What **qualities** are you praising the child for? (You did do that quickly/neatly/quietly.)

3 Compare your pattern of praise with another group's. What activities and qualities attract praise? Are these the ones you want reinforced? Are boys and girls praised for the same or for different qualities and activities? Are noisy children praised when they are not

grabbing attention? Are quiet children praised for their efforts to engage?

And finally – it can be hard to give praise and even harder to accept it. Before you go, find a nice thing to say to each person you have been working with today. And smile when they say a nice thing back . . .

Assignment 9

Minding children

This assignment is linked with Case Study 1, Lena's children.

**TASK 1:
Each child's
needs**

If you have worked through Case Study 1, use the schedule of Lena's week (Activity 3) as the basis for this task. If you have not, refer to the case study and extract from it the names and ages of all the children Lena has been asked to look after.

1 Lena will be expected to have appropriate toys and play equipment for the children she cares for. Refer to the Good Toy Guide in Assignment 10 and the guide to child development on p 152. Consider each child's likely stage of development and make suggestions for three toys or play opportunities you would like to see for each child in Lena's care. For each, draw a diagram like the one below, write the activity in the middle of the page and show under the six headings the ways in which the activity you suggest might help development in each area. Work with a partner. You may wish to compare this with the skills developed through play identified in the extract on p 83.

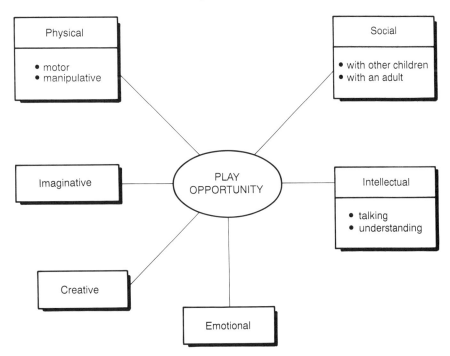

**Areas of
development
through play**

NOTE This approach to considering the potential of playthings is also explored in Assignment 10 of *A Practical Approach to Caring* (Pitman Publishing, 1991) by Kate Williams.

2 Check your assumptions! Work with a new partner. If you change the sex of each child, would you want to change your suggestions in any way? Compare your suggestions with your new partner's and review them — are Simone's and Simon's needs the same?

TASK 2: TV and video

How much TV/video should children watch?

1 In small groups agree on what you think is the overall maximum amount of TV/video each child in Lena's care (including her own!) should watch in a day.

2 Below is one day's TV. Within your agreed overall limit, choose programmes you consider appropriate for each of Lena's children.

TELEVISION AND RADIO

BBC 1

6.0am Pages from Ceefax. **6.30** Breakfast News. **9.05** Perfect Strangers. **9.30** Labour Party Conference 92. Covering the debate on electoral reform. **10.0** News; regional news. **10.05** Children's BBC: Playdays; **10.25** Jimbo and the Jet Set **10.35** Labour Party Conference 92. **12.55** Regional news. **1.0** News; weather. **1.30** Neighbours **1.50** Going for Gold.

2.15 FILM: Trottie True. Pleasantly entertaining costume comedy. Jean Kent stars in this 1949 charmer as a music hall artist who marries into the aristocracy.
3.50 Children's BBC: Puppydog Tales; **3.55** Noddy; **4.10** Star Pets; **4.20** Get Your Own Back; **4.35** Uncle Jack and the Dark Side of the Moon; **5.0** Newsround; **5.05** Blue Peter.
5.35 Neighbours.
6.0 News; weather.
6.30 Regional news magazines.
7.0 Top of the Pops.
7.30 EastEnders.
8.0 As Time Goes By. Judi Dench and Geoffrey Palmer as the couple trying to rekindle a very old flame.

BBC 2

6.45am Open University: The Search for the W and Z. **7.10** Interval. **8.0** Breakfast News. **8.15** Arthur Negus Enjoys. **8.30** Play Better Golf. **9.0** Daytime on Two: Play it Safe! **9.10** Global Environment; **9.30** Let's See: Go 4,5; **9.45** You and Me; **10.0** Mathscope; **10.15** Over the Moon; **10.30** Ghostwriter; **11.0** Thunderbirds; **11.05** Q and A; **11.10** Landmarks; **11.30** Lern-express; **11.45** History File; **12.05** The Geography Programme; **12.25** Lifeschool; **12.50** Business Matters; **1.20** Bertha; **1.35** Crystal Tipps and Alistair; **1.40** Music Time; **2.0** News; You and Me.

2.15 Labour Party Conference. From Blackpool: the debate on international affairs. Including **3.0** News;(T) **3.50** News; regional news.
5.30 News from Every Angle. (R) Nicholas Witchell explains how the BBC's newsroom works.
6.0 FILM: Carry On up the Khyber. For the true Carry On connoisseur this is vintage stuff. Sid James stands for Queen and Empire against the forces of rebellion led by Kenneth Williams.
7.30 Ps and Qs. Etiquette quiz.
8.0 A Cook's Tour of France:

ITV London

5.30am News. **6.0** TV-am. **9.25** Win, Lose or Draw. **9.55** Regional news. **10.0** The Time, The Place. **10.40** This Morning. **12.10** The Riddlers. **12.30** News; weather; regional news. **1.15** Home and Away. **1.45** A Country Practice.

2.15 TV Weekly.
2.45 Take the High Road.
3.10 News; regional news
3.20 GP. Another Aussie soap! Set in a doctor's practice, where the returning medic finds his partner has been ousted.
3.50 Children's ITV: The Ratties; **3.55** Captain Zed and the Zee Zone; **4.20** Rolf's Cartoon Club; **4.50** Art Attack; **5.10** Who's the Boss?
5.40 News; weather
5.55 Thames Help.
6.0 Home and Away.
6.30 Thames News.
7.0 Emmerdale.
7.30 Jimmy's. More real-life dramas from the wards of the Leeds hospital.
8.0 The Bill: Tip Off.
8.30 This Week: Are You Sitting on a Toxic Time Bomb? The Government wants to register land contaminated by past industrial use — and such land would have to be cleaned up at the cost of about £100,000 per acre before being redeveloped.

Channel 4

5.20am 4-Tel on View. **6.0** Cartoons. **7.0** The Big Breakfast. **9.0** You Bet Your Life. **9.30** Schools: Scientific Eye; **9.52** Time for Maths; **10.04** Our World; **10.21** Science and Technology; **10.40** Geography Today; **11.02** All Year Round; **11.19** Story World; **11.32** Stop, Look, Listen; **11.44** Project IT. **12.0** Flight Over Spain; **12.30** Sesame Street. **1.30** Take 5.

2.0 Check Out 92.(S) (R) Tuesday's programme looking at public houses and public loos.
2.25 Racing from Newmarket. Introduced by Brough Scott.
4.30 Fifteen-to-One.
5.0 The Oprah Winfrey Show. Patrick Swayze, teen heart-throb from Dirty Dancing, tells how his latest film City of Joy has changed his life — through working in Mother Theresa's Clinic for the Dying, and through dealing with Muslim resistance during filming.
5.55 The Bunbury Tails.
6.0 My Two Dads.
6.30 Gamesmaster. New series of the cult computer game show.

Source: *The Guardian*, 1 October 1992

3   Lena has one TV and one living room. If you were Lena, what would you do to ensure that the TV was not on all the time, while each child views his/her favourite programmes?

TASK 3:
Out and about

Lena lives in a maisonette on the third/fourth floor of a postwar block of flats. She takes her children out every day. Over the years, her outdoor/out-of-house activities have included the following:

- the park – playground, One o'clock Club, café, feed the ducks, bike/trike riding, collecting conkers, etc.;
- shopping – supermarket and shopping centres;
- visiting friends with children or minders;
- coffee mornings and outings with the local childminders' group;
- toy library;
- library – exchange books, story telling sessions;
- baby bounce, occasionally swimming, music classes;
- parent/carer and toddler group;
- art gallery/museum.

I   Find out what is available to childminders in your area:
   (a)   within walking distance;
   (b)   **one** bus ride away.

2   Find out hours, costs and access.

TASK 4:
Sharing
information

Design a leaflet to present the information you researched in Task 3 in a clear and attractive way, suitable for distribution to child carers in your area. Include a simple map showing locations and appropriate bus routes. You will have drawn up a valuable resource. Discuss with your tutor ways of making it available to child carers in your area.

TASK 5:
Planning a
week

Draw up a schedule for a week for a childminder in your area. If you have worked on Case Study 1, base this around Lena and the children she cares for, their days and times.

I   Decide on what you think is a balanced structure for a day, allowing time for taking and fetching, time in the home, time for structured activities, quiet/sleep times, time outdoors and out of the home. Note the times the TV is on.

2   Plan a week with a balance of activities, and a balance of needs, including Lena's. Be realistic – don't suggest a programme of activities that would leave Lena (and her children) exhausted at the end of one week!

TASK 6:
What would
you do if . . . ?
Problem page

Working in pairs or small groups, decide what you would do if you were the childminder in the situations below. When you have reached agreement in your small group on how you would deal with each situation, compare your approach with those of the other pairs/small groups. Discuss any differences of view.

1   A new child is tearful when he arrives at your home, clings to his mother, and sobs hysterically. Do you:
    (a)   suggest she stays until he calms, and you both talk to him;
    (b)   prise him off her and tell her to go quickly;
    (c)   let his mother sort him out and take over when she is ready;
    (d)   any other ideas?

2   A child you care for is used to a different sort of discipline at home. It is hard work to show her that you mean what you say, and that some behaviour is not acceptable. Her mum tells you to give her a little smack when she is really naughty. What do you do?

3   A child comes from a vegetarian family, and the parents have asked you to ensure that he eats no meat or fish. What are the pros and cons of each of the following approaches?
    (a)   Give him the same as you cook for your family, but leaving out the meat.
    (b)   Ask the parents to supply his food.
    (c)   Cook only vegetarian food for the whole family when he is with you.
    (d)   Any other ideas?

4   You come home with the children you care for to find your washing machine has flooded through the kitchen into the living room. The kitchen is awash, living room carpet soaked, books soggy. You know there is underfloor wiring. What are the pros and cons of each of the following solutions?
    (a)   Phone all the parents at work/college and ask them to come and collect their children immediately.
    (b)   Take them to a childminder friend (whom they know because you spend time together) and ask her to look after them while you mop up and wait for the plumber.
    (c)   Ask your 15 year-old son to take them to the park.
    (d)   Keep the children in the bedroom while you organise the clear-up.
    (e)   Any other ideas?

5   A parent phoned you to arrange to come and discuss the possibility of you looking after her child. When she arrives she says, 'Thank God you're not black. I wasn't sure on the phone . . .' What do you do?

6   When Mark's dad came to pick him up, Mark was setting out the cups and saucers and offered him a cup of tea. The next day his mum asks

you not to let him play with girls' toys. His dad thinks he is becoming a sissy. Do you:

(a) gently steer him into less 'girlish' activities;

(b) tell his mum that you do not agree with her view of how Mark should play;

(c) make no changes and assume that they won't know;

(d) offer to see his dad;

(e) any other ideas?

7 Review the questions above. Which situations and options have legal implications? What are they?

TASK 7: Forming a policy

In the course of this assignment and Case Study 1, you have touched on many of the key areas relating to childminding. As a whole group, draft a 'Code of Good Practice' for childminding in your area.

You may want to do this in two stages:

1 A brainstorming session in which you make suggestions as to which points should be included. Record all suggestions.

2 A drafting session, in which you agree areas to include in your Code, and thrash out the wording. Minute the outcomes of this meeting precisely.

Type up your Code of Good Practice and present it to a new audience. Be prepared to speak about your proposals, and to answer questions and criticism. It could be to another group following a similar course, or, if you make the contact sufficiently far in advance, you could invite or go and meet an outside group, a voluntary agency, community group or the local authority childminding adviser.

Assignment 10

Equipped for the job

TASK 1:
At what age?

Below is a chart which links child development with playthings and an explanation of how these encourage the child to develop new skills.

TOY GUIDES

When a child can:	Provide:	To encourage:
0–6 months		
Follow objects with eyes. Attention caught by sounds.	Mobiles to fix on cot – musical or silent. Baby mirror on side of cot.	Listening, eye movements and following. Attention to movement.
Kick legs.	Soft balls and foam bricks. Rattles with varying sounds.	Awareness of its own movements.
Begin to reach and grasp (but cannot yet sit without support).	Toys to string on cot and pram. Small light rattles easily grasped by baby.	Aiming and grasping. (Baby associates movement made with the sound.)
6–12 months		
Beginning to put its hands to mouth.	Toys that are light, safe, suitable for mouthing, e.g. teethers.	Discovery of mouth.
Sit supported at first and visually alert.	Toys with suction base that can be fixed on to play tray. Toys that can be hung where baby can reach and grasp. Toys that move easily when touched.	Movement of eyes and hands together. (Child's action produces a result.)
Lie on tummy.	Toys that move when touched.	Movement in lying position e.g. rolling over.
Sit with support.	Activity centres. Textured balls.	Exploring different effect caused by hand movement. Exploring different textures using two hands.
Manipulate with fingers and use two hands together.	Objects that can be explored with fingers.	Two-handed play and five finger movements.
Give and take objects.	Objects that can be grasped and transferred from one hand to another, e.g. rattles, plastic cotton reels.	Practice in grasping and releasing. Bringing hands together in the middle. Giving and taking objects with adults.

176

When a child can:	Provide:	To encourage:
12–18 months		
Spontaneously bang on table.	Drum. xylophone, hammer toys.	More precise use of the hands and eyes.
Crawl and push objects along.	Balls of various sizes. Various push-along toys especially those on short rigid handles.	Increase in range of mobility and hence exploration.
Walk with support. Without support.	Baby walkers and other pushtoys on wheels. Pull-along toys.	Confidence and independence. Better control of body movements. Refinement of balance and walking skill.
Imitate sounds. Understand simple phrases and words.	Rag books and picture books. Telephone. Baby mirrors.	Simple imitation in a social context. Understanding of first picture symbols.
Co-ordinate objects. Relate objects to a container.	Plastic pots and pans. Simple posting boxes (i.e. with round and square shapes). Bricks and coloured cotton reels to put in and tip out. Large cardboard boxes and laundry baskets.	Moving eyes and hands together. Shape discrimination and putting into containers.
Begin to imitate parents' domestic duties.	Simple domestic items, brooms, duster, plastic cup and spoon, hairbrush, flannel.	Simple domestic play.
19 months–2 years		
Drum with two sticks.	Drums, xylophone and other 'banging' toys such as hammer pegs.	Moving eyes and hands together and to channel 'banging' into constructive activity.
Hold pencil.	Paper and jumbo pencil and crayon.	Improve the use of hands and eyes. Scribbling and later copying.
Build several bricks into a tower.	Building beakers and other stacking toys.	Simple building activity.
Use thumb/finger grasp. Still preoccupied with container play.	All toys using peg people.	Controlled use of hand, fingers and eyes. Early representational play.
Enjoy simple picture books and other simple pictures.	First picture books. Lift out puzzles with pictures underneath. Inset puzzles.	Talking, listening and conversation.
Recreate domestic situation.	Simple domestic play, e.g. cookers and pans, tea sets, cleaning sets, prams, or push chairs.	Early make-believe. Relating several 'pretend' items together.
2–3 years		
Push and pull large items. Climb steps with some agility.	Large push-along vehicles, trundle toys, wheelbarrows.	Climbing on and off. Overcoming problems of balance and steering.
Throw or kick a ball.	Large plastic skittles and ball. Football.	To help develop aim and taking turns in games.

When a child can:	Provide:	To encourage:
By 3 years		
Begin to pedal.	Tricycle.	Balance, steering and control of parts of the body.
Begin to get dressed alone.	*Simple* dressing up items, cloaks, hats and accessories (without buttons).	Make-believe play. Dressing skills, body image games.
Assemble toys which screw together.	Toys wth screw fittings.	Practice, so that more advanced construction toys are possible.
Begin to copy simple figures and draw.	Chubby crayons and thick pencils.	Interest in drawing. Can then introduce templates and other tracing activities.
Begin to match 2 or 3 primary colours and name them.	Matching games using colour. Colour snap, colour matching dominoes.	To group together things which are the 'same' and 'different'.
Enjoy picture book, recognising fine details. Match four pictures.	Simple picture lotto.	To discriminate details.
Pour water from one cup into another.	Various containers for water play. Include funnel, and water/bath toys.	Improving the control of both hands and eyes together.
3–4 years		
Push and pull large toys while walking and running. Ride tricycles.	Scooters and barrows. Tricycle and pedal cars.	Agility and balance. Confidence in ability.
Throw, catch and kick ball. Show agility in climbing.	Football, games involving bat and ball. Access to climbing frame, ropes, etc.	Muscular strength.
Cut with scissors.	Materials for cutting, sticking, collage.	Fine hand movements. Creative play.
Copy and trace shapes.	Wooden templates. Tracing activities.	Refinement in use of pencil and crayon.
Sort and compare materials. String beads.	Threading beads and sorting materials.	Fine observation of details. Fine finger movements.
Complete more complex jigsaws.	Increasingly difficult puzzles.	Distinguishing simple shapes and colours. Problem solving and development of speech.
Show awareness of numbers.	Number dominoes and simple games involving dice and counting.	Understanding numbers. Simple games with rules.
Draw a simple person.	Paints, paper, brushes.	Being creative.
Make believe and show imaginative play especially with others.	Playgroup or other group experience. More varied 'dressing-up'. Small objects for 'pretend' – small dolls, people. Larger props for group domestic play. Shops.	Development of language and co-operation. Planning more elaborate games and acting out real-life situations.

When a child can:	Provide:	To encourage:
4–5 years		
Skip, hop.	Skipping rope and hop-scotch mat.	Better control of muscles and limbs, strengthening of muscles. Singing games, balance.
Copy shapes and letters.	Magnetic letters. Letter shapes. Chalk blackboard. Tracing, maze patterns.	Recognising letters and simple spelling. More precise control in writing.
Plan and build constructively.	Layout and creative kits. Playmats, farms, zoos, Noah's Ark, garages, train layouts.	Practice in planning construction. Use of language to plan and explain actions to self and others.
Understand the rules of games – become competitive.	Simple competitive games – snakes and ladders, draughts, noughts and crosses, racing games, hide and seek.	Practice in winning and losing. Strategy – taking the position of the other persons.

Source: Good Toy Guide in *Play Matters*, The National Toy Libraries Association

Although this chart is entitled 'Toy Guide', many of the suggestions for play opportunities and playthings can be met from things you have around the house or could make quickly and simply, or with some forward planning,

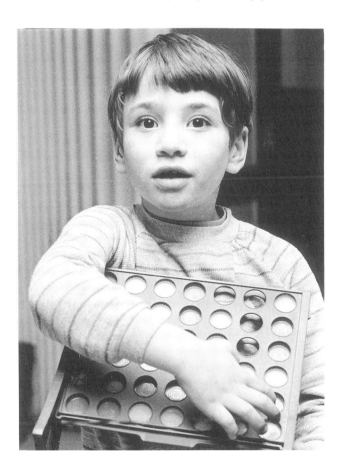

Courtesy: John Birdsall Photography

179

lay your hands on for free. Your task here is to think about opportunities and activities, not so much about toys.

1   Copy the guide and add a fourth column to each sheet, entitled 'We would use'. With a partner, work through the toy guide, and aim to enter at least one suitable plaything that costs little or nothing in each space. Where you can genuinely think of no home-found alternative, leave a blank. Compare your suggestions with another group's.

2   Go back and look at the blanks. Agree on at least one item for each blank that you consider to be good play value.

3   Cost your choices, from a catalogue or from local shops.

4   Identify an age group (a spread of up to two years) to buy equipment for and prioritise. Check with the suggestions you made in Task 1, Assignment 9. What items would you buy if you had (a) £50, (b) £100 to spend?

**TASK 2:
A safety check**

Everyday objects offer important play opportunities, particularly for children in full-time day care who need a homely atmosphere. You must, however, check that your alternatives to toys that have met stringent safety checks are also safe.

1   Work with a different partner for this, or with another pair. Your task is to go through your sets of suggestions for home-based alternatives, and to consider whether they would be safe to use in a day care setting. The best way to do this is to handle the object yourselves.

2   Design a simple leaflet, suitable for parents, childminders or day care workers (or all three but think carefully), with practical suggestions for beating the budget. Make sure your suggestions are not only cheap but that you show how to make them safe. They must be quick and easy to do. Further suggestions can be found in *A Practical Approach to Caring* (Pitman Publishing, 1991), p 127, by Kate Williams.

**TASK 3:
Make a toy**

Children love toys that are made specially for them. It's fun for the adult too. Often the simplest ideas give both of you the greatest pleasure. But simple must not mean dangerous, however well intentioned.

1   Before you make a toy for a child, read RoSPA's guidelines.
    (a) Why is it important to know about child development before you make a toy?
    (b) Why do you think RoSPA suggests you look at safety labels on toys?
    (c) Give an example of a 'non-pliable facial feature' that might be used in a toy.
    (d) How large would the smallest component have to be so as not to be dangerous to a small child that puts things in its mouth?

2   With this advice in mind, design and make your toy.

3   When you have finished, write a 'product label' for your toy. It should give information and advice on:

- the age of child the toy is designed for;
- the learning it stimulates;
- how to use, treat and maintain it.

Designing children's toys

Many of you choose to make a child's toy as part of a design project for an examination course. We cannot tell you how to design and make the toy but we can provide you with a set of guidelines.

Your guidelines

★ There are an estimated 50,000 accidents in U.K. homes each year involving toys, other playthings and sports equipment. You wouldn't want your toy to add to those figures, so 'SAFETY' is your key word. It is probably better, therefore, to make something that is relatively simple.

★ How old will the child be that uses your toy? Find out about the development and needs of children of that age. What are they likely to do with the toy? For example; a child up to two years may put everything and anything in its mouth. You may choose to make soft toys, bath toys or mobiles — things that are safe for such a child.

★ Look at existing toys for your chosen age group. Take note of any 'safety labels' or instruction/warning labels attached to the toys. Toys made to British Standards are preferable.

★ **DO NOT USE** — toxic paint, fragile or flammable materials. **AVOID** — sharp edges and points. **PLEASE MAKE SURE** — that any stuffing materials are clean; that ends of nails and screws, if used, are not accessible to the child; that non-pliable facial features are securely attached; that no toy component could block a child's windpipe if swallowed.

Reproduced by kind permission of RoSPA

**TASK 4:
Ordering from
a catalogue**

In the nursery where you have started work, music has not been a high priority. There is a box with a few tatty and broken instruments, but none of the present staff feel they have much expertise in it anyway. Yasmin, the new playleader, wants to change this and has asked you to draw up a provisional list of instruments to buy. You can spend £50.

I   Overleaf is an extract from a catalogue showing percussion instruments. Make a selection and cost your choice within your budget. You may, of course, decide to have more than one of a particular instrument.

181

making music

4 round carousel bells
Colourful & melodic bells that produce a pure clear tone when struck, can also be spun to make music.
MC8012   **each £13.95**

5 SbS chime bar set
EXCLUSIVE

A set of 8 individual chime bars covering a complete octave from C above middle C. Complete with eight beaters, each chime bar is a different colour for easy instruction and can be played separately or in the specially moulded tray. Accurately tuned to A440 they have a superb resonance.
MC8029   Complete set   **£39.95**

6 hand drum
18cm (7"). Supplied in assorted colours complete with a beater.
MC8009   **each £6.95**

7 hand drum with snares   NEW
18cm (7in) complete with a beater.
MC8031   **each £8.50**

8 bright ideas – music & movement
A really practical 96 page book full of dozens of new ideas. Sections include: developing listening skills; making sound and music; making instruments; and singing.
MC8011   "No VAT to add"   **each £5.95**

9 tambourine with head
Supplied in assorted colours, in two sizes:
MC8007   15cm (6")   **each £4.50**

MC8008   18cm (7")   **each £6.50**

10 tambourine without head   NEW
Supplied in assorted colours.
MC8030   15cm (6in)   **each £2.75**

11 mini maracas
15cm (6"). Designed for little hands. Supplied in assorted colours.
MC8006   **pair £3.50**

12 sleigh bells
MC8003   Assorted colours   **each £2.25**

13 triangle
12.5cm (5") complete with striker.
MC8005   **each £1.85**

14 cymbals
With easy grip solid handles – better for the early years.
12cm (5") diameter.
MC8002   **pair £6.50**

15 jingle bells
With extra large 25mm Bells.
MC8004   Assorted colours   **each £1.95**

16 castanet on handle
20cm (8") long, the handle will help little hands Colours may vary.
MC8000   **each £1.95**

17 round castanet
Special design for easy use. Supplied in assorted colours.
MC8001   **each £1.50**

Source: Catalogue of Step by Step 1992/3, suppliers to the PPA

cane rattles

Comfortable and easy to hold for all ages, these authentic African rattles are beautifully hand woven in natural cane.
Very pleasing percussion sounds and different in each case, depending on the shape and whether infilled with seeds or metal.

6 Bottle rattle – seed infill
MC8015 17cm (6½") **each £9.95**

7 Basket rattle – seed infill
MC8016 13cm (5") **each £9.95**

8 Horseshoe rattle – seed infill
MC8017 16cm (6") **each £15.95**

9 Dumbell rattle – metal infill
MC8019 33cm (13") **each £18.95**

10 Bulb rattle – metal infill
MC8018 16cm (6") **each £9.95**

11 indian bell   EXCLUSIVE

A copper brass bell with beater for adding a melodic percussion sound. 19cm (7½") high.
MC8023 **each £9.95**

12 claves   NEW

A pair made from either maple or rosewood for giving different sounds when hit together.
MC8026 MAPLE **pair £3.45**

MC8027 ROSEWOOD **pair £4.95**

13 bamboo rasp   EXCLUSIVE

A well made and attractive instrument that gives an intriguing sound. Complete with scraper that can be used by the smallest of hands! 28cm (11") long.
MC8020 **each £15.95**

14 pod shaped bell   NEW

A small hand held bell with beater that is easy to play and makes an unusual sound. The pod shaped bell comes from the Ashanti region of Ghana, West Africa. 19cm (7½") long
MC8025 **each £19.95**

ORDER FORM

Sbs

UNIT 4, BRUNEL WAY, THORNBURY INDUSTRIAL ESTATE,
THORNBURY, BRISTOL BS12 2MR.
TELEPHONE (0454) 281200 FAX (0454) 281677

NAME OF ESTABLISHMENT/GROUP: _____

ESTABLISHMENT/GROUP
ADDRESS: _____

DELIVERY ADDRESS: _____
(IF DIFFERENT)

PPA MEMBERSHIP No:
(if applicable)

_____ POSTCODE: _____

_____ POSTCODE: _____

DATE: _____ DAYTIME TELEPHONE No: _____ GOODS FOR ATTENTION OF: _____

Please quote the Education, Health OR
Social Service authority responsible for
the area in which your establishment/
group is located

ESTABLISHMENT/GROUP TYPE (PLEASE TICK BOX)

VOLUNTARY ☐   PRIVATE ☐   STATUTORY ☐

YOUR Sbs ACCOUNT No:

Catalogue number	Description	Colour/ Description	Quantity required	Price per unit	Total price excluding VAT

Please remember to add 17$\frac{1}{2}$% VAT

Special Delivery instructions:

_____
_____
_____

Total excuding VAT	
Carriage	**FREE**
VAT @ 17$\frac{1}{2}$%	
TOTAL PAYABLE	

Source: Order form from Step by Step, suppliers to the PPA

2 Compare your choice with someone else's. Your task is to agree on a final list, in the way you would have to agree a list with Yasmin.

3 Complete the order form opposite for the items you have chosen, following the instructions carefully.

TASK 5:
Getting it right

When your order arrives, there are three discrepancies. The wrong number of one item; the most expensive item you chose is out of stock and a substitution has been made; and one wrong item has been supplied (e.g. the wrong cane rattle, or hand drum/tambourine).

1 With your original partner, refer back to your order list, and decide where these errors might have arisen. Decide what outcomes you want.

2 Write to the suppliers to point out the discrepancies, and ask for your order to be corrected/amended in the way you agreed. Make sure you quote correct references etc. For advice on letter layout see *A Practical Approach to Caring* (Pitman Publishing, 1991), pp 276–8, by Kate Williams.

Assignment 11

Feeling good

TASK 1:
Your initiative

Children should . . . have opportunities to experiment, to use materials in new ways, to explore possibilities and to take pleasure in doing rather than in the end product. **No one should be under any illusion that tasks such as copying and the collective or individual making of identical objects are creative activities.**

Source: *Guidelines: Good practice for sessional/full daycare playgroups*, PPA, London

1   As you spend time with the children in your care, you will have formed ideas about their particular needs. The task here is to identify what you think would be a good activity for a particular child, or a small group of children. It may be something that tends to get squeezed out of the day (story telling? singing? talking with a quiet child, or a child learning English?); new possibilities with a familiar activity (baking playdough?) or a new activity. Discuss your ideas with your superviser.

2   Plan your activity: think through the timing, materials, relationships and conversation. Then carry it out at an appropriate time.

What is a family?
Courtesy: John Birdsall
Photography

3   Afterwards, write up your activity in report form, showing:
     (a)   the need you identified;
     (b)   what you did to meet this need;
     (c)   the outcome: how successful you think you were in your efforts.

TASK 2:
Self-assessment

In most courses and training schemes, you will be assessed on the skills you display in carrying out tasks in the workplace. Your tutors will discuss with you the particular skills they are looking for in your course of study. Fortunately, all the checklists of skills identified by the different assessment schemes have features in common and will increasingly correspond to the National Vocational Qualifications (NVQ) competences.

You will have to demonstrate two groups of competences: first the **specific tasks** you need to be able to carry out and the knowledge that underpins them; second, the **relationships** you form with your clients, the children, and the parents and other members of staff.

Below are some self-assessment questions to ask yourself about the activity you carried out in Task 1. They are not taken from any assessment checklist but are intended to encourage you to think critically about what you did and how you did it.

Self-assessment questions   **Describe what you did**

1   Was my choice of activity a good one?
     Did the child welcome my involvement?
2   Did I prepare adequately? Through
     discussion and negotiation? Did I have
     the things I needed?
3   Did I let the child go at his or her own
     pace? Offer opportunities for thinking
     aloud and conversation?
4   Did I give out the right signals to the
     child, verbally and non-verbally?
5   Did the child have the opportunity to
     create her or his own outcomes, or did
     I lead them to mine?
6   Did the child enjoy it? Did I?

TASK 3:
Equal
opportunities

Children have a right to grow up and learn in an environmnent free from prejudice and without discrimination. We know that without this freedom their development will be damaged:

- Children who grow up feeling that they are inferior – or that other people see them as inferior – because of their gender, skin colour, disability or family background will fail to achieve their full potential.
- Children who are allowed to assume superiority because of their colour,

their gender, their religion, their able-bodiedness, their class or for any other reason will have a false and damaging view of humanity.

- **All** children are damaged by attitudes and assumptions which fail to address in a positive way the differences which exist between us.

The playgroup can be the starting point in a child's journey towards self-esteem and an understanding of others.

Research shows that children as young as two years do notice differences in physical appearance, such as skin colour. Soon afterwards children are attributing values to these differences; a person with a dark skin is often seen as less important than someone with a light coloured skin, or as someone to be feared. These values are learnt; children are not born with them. They are learnt from the people close to them and absorbed from the evidence of their eyes and ears as they observe our unequal society.

Source: From 'Introduction' to *Equal Chances: Eliminating Discrimination and Ensuring Equality in Playgroups*, published by the PPA

In groups, small or large, consider this statement and discuss the following points.

1   'Children who grow up feeling that they are inferior . . . will fail to achieve their full potential.' Can you explain this statement? Do you agree with it?

2   'Children who are allowed to assume superiority . . . will have a false and damaging view of humanity.' What does 'assume superiority' mean in relation to (a) children, (b) adults? Give examples, actual or theoretical.

3   'All children are damaged . . .' How important do you think active policies to encourage equal opportunities are in the following playgroups? How would you set about it?
    (a)   In an affluent predominantly white area, with all white children.
    (b)   In which boys dominate the outside play area, on bikes or running around. Boys are in a majority in the group.
    (c)   In which the vast majority of children are black, in a predominantly black area.
    (d)   In which children show a fear of a child who has lost her hair through chemotherapy.
    (e)   A playgroup with 10% black children in a culturally diverse area in which the schools have about 40% ethnic minority children.
    (f)   In which the parents of a Down's syndrome child have applied for a place.
    (g)   In which the majority of children come from comfortable homes but a minority are funded by the local authority as having social priority.

4   When you have talked through these points, draft and agree your own statement about:
    (a)   why equal opportunities matter;
    (b)   what the term 'equal opportunities' should encompass;
    (c)   steps to take in early years work to encourage all children to realise their full potential.

TASK 4: Feeling good

Study the following sketches, mapping some of the things that make a child feel good.

1 Working in pairs, relate the 'I feel good' activities on p 190 to the 'I feel good' diagram below.

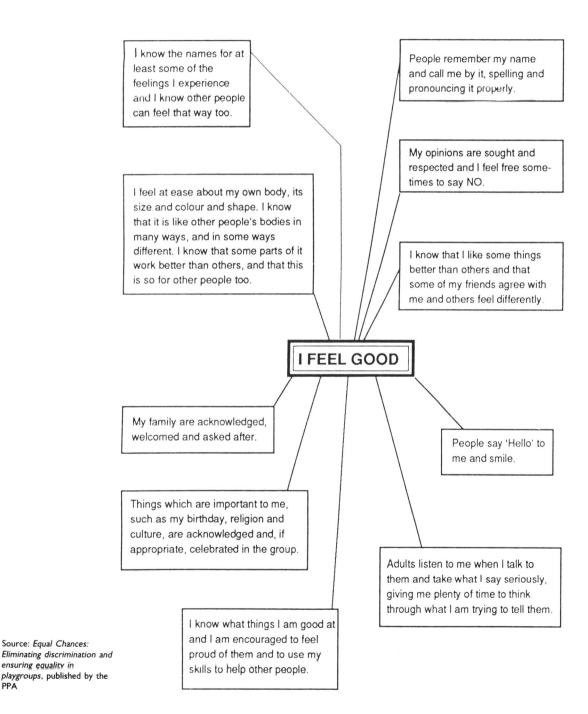

I know the names for at least some of the feelings I experience and I know other people can feel that way too.

People remember my name and call me by it, spelling and pronouncing it properly.

My opinions are sought and respected and I feel free sometimes to say NO.

I feel at ease about my own body, its size and colour and shape. I know that it is like other people's bodies in many ways, and in some ways different. I know that some parts of it work better than others, and that this is so for other people too.

I know that I like some things better than others and that some of my friends agree with me and others feel differently.

I FEEL GOOD

My family are acknowledged, welcomed and asked after.

People say 'Hello' to me and smile.

Things which are important to me, such as my birthday, religion and culture, are acknowledged and, if appropriate, celebrated in the group.

Adults listen to me when I talk to them and take what I say seriously, giving me plenty of time to think through what I am trying to tell them.

I know what things I am good at and I am encouraged to feel proud of them and to use my skills to help other people.

Source: *Equal Chances: Eliminating discrimination and ensuring equality in playgroups*, published by the PPA

CELEBRATE
Birthdays, seasons, religious festivals and observances – find out from families about traditions, decorations. Be careful not to make assumptions.

FEELINGS
Draw a happy or sad face on a paper plate. An adult can then write underneath: .... is happy when .... is sad when ....

BEING SPECIAL
Admire a child
'I do like ...'
'You have done that well ...'

THINGS I LIKE AND DISLIKE ... in a collage book, scrapbook; a bar chart made bit by bit; the whole group contributes

BODIES
Our body is our own. No one must intrude without permission. Our bodies are similar in some ways, and different in some. Some bits work well. Others less well.
● Look at yourself in a mirror and describe each other.
● Make life-size drawings of children with paints allowing the full range of skin colours with a positive statement under each.

I FEEL GOOD ACTIVITIES

NAMES
Know a child's full name and abbreviation. Display names correctly spelt in English and the child's language – on a paper plate, coat hook ... by a self portrait.

FOOD
Cut out pictures and stick on paper plates – show range of cultures – have different foods and fruit to taste, handle and smell – try different breads ... talk about foods at home.

FAMILIES
Photographs ... scrapbook ... talking about grandparents, relations, brothers and sisters ... animal families ... read stories about families which reflect the diversity of family patterns.

Ideas developed from *Equal Chances: Eliminating discrimination and ensuring equality in playgroups*, published by the PPA

2 Choose one activity, either from the ones suggested here (e.g. mirrors, paper plates, scrapbook) or from the PPA extract in Case Study 3, or of your own choice. Write this activity in the centre of a blank page, and draw out from it all the learning possibilities. Consider the six skill areas (*see* Assignment 9) and the 'I feel good' possibilities.

3   Plan your activity, with a view to carrying it out with a group of pre-school children. Set it out on a single side of A4. Use headings:

- **Objectives:** what you are trying to achieve;
- **Preparation:** steps you had to take, materials to collect, etc.;
- **Process:** what you did;

and include the heading **Review** to complete after you have had the chance to try out your activity.

Remember to allow each child time to talk and think at their own pace, and encourage plenty of talk, involvement and interaction throughout your activity.

TASK 5: Welcome to our playgroup

1   Consider these ways of administering a waiting list:

(a)   Each child's name is entered on the waiting list as parents approach you. When a vacancy arises, you phone the next on the list.

(b)   You arrange the names of the children on your waiting list according to date of birth, irrespective of when the parent approached you. You offer places on a strict next-by-age basis.

(c)   When a vacancy occurs, you check your list and offer places to maintain a balance of boys/girls, and take into account family circumstances when you know about them, e.g. if a new baby is expected.

Consider who would be advantaged and who would be disadvantaged by each method. What other methods for controlling admission can you think of? Decide on the method you would like to see in operation in your area. Give reasons.

2   Which playgroups in Task 3 (a)–(g) do you think should review their admissions policy? Why and how?

3   How would you ensure that **all** parents of pre-school children in your area know about a playgroup?

TASK 6: Find out

Find out about all the playgroups within easy access of where you live.

1   Find out the group name, address and telephone number, and show the exact location on a hand-drawn or photocopied map. Show bus routes and access. Make a note of how you found out about each one – word of mouth, libraries, Social Services, etc.

2   Pool your findings with others who live in your area. Divide the playgroups out between you. Arrange to visit at least one playgroup each. During your visit find out the following additional details where possible:

- Description of the group including: name, address and telephone number, registration, insurance details and access for those with disabilities

- Management and funding
- Fees, including any reductions available and systems regarding payment
- Settling-in procedure for new children
- Feeding and rest arrangements
- Policy regarding control and discipline
- Washing and toilet facilities
- An explanation of the role of the parents, volunteers, the key worker and other staff
- Names of playleaders, with details of experience and training, and of volunteer helpers
- Number of places
- Number of sessions per week, days and times of opening
- Admissions policy including usual starting age
- Activities and outings
- Arrangements for festivals and birthdays
- Attendance and health rules including exclusion periods for infectious diseases
- Complaints procedures
- Arrival and departure procedures.

Adapted from *Guidelines for Good Practice for Sessional Playgroups for 3–5 Year Olds*, published by the PPA

You may be able to combine this with an observation visit.

**TASK 7:
A leaflet**

Draw up a leaflet suitable for distribution to parents in your area, setting out this information and any other information you want to include to give a flavour of the playgroup, clearly and attractively. Show it to the playleaders (and parents) of the playgroup you visited and ask for their comments. Ask them where they think the best distribution spots are for a leaflet like this. Can you add any?

Assignment 12

Planning activities

Wherever you work, you need to know in advance what you will be doing with the children in your care. This is not to rule out spontaneous responses or events – a trip to the park on a nice day might be much better than any carefully planned activity – but you need to ensure that you have a balance and range of activities over a day and a longer period of time, and this needs planning. In this assignment you are asked to work through some of these processes.

TASK 1:
One day

E20 Time in the children's nursery day should be balanced to allow for activities that vary along such dimensions as:

- active/quiet;
- indoor/outdoor;
- child initiated/staff initiated;
- large muscle/small muscle movement; and
- individual/small group/large group play.

Such a variety in activities will enable children to develop their own rhythms for learning in accordance with variations in their energy patterns throughout the day.

Although children should not be made to go outside, if the outdoor area is attractive and offers a wide range of activities, few children will not want to avail themselves of this opportunity.

E21 Staff's planning of activities for children's outdoor playtime should be just as important as their planning of indoor activities.

Source: *Young Children in Group Day Care – Guidelines for Good Practice*, published by the National Children's Bureau, February 1990

Draw up an outline plan and suggested timing for activities for one day at:
(a) a sessional day care group, such as Manor Court Playgroup (*see* Case Study 3) (hours 9.30–12.00);
(b) a full day care group, such as in Case Study 2 (hours 8.00 a.m.–6.00 p.m.). Use the index to locate suggestions for activities in this book, and draw on your own observation and research. You should use a library for this and Task 2.

Be careful not to be tempted simply to repeat the pattern of the morning in the afternoon. The needs of chidlren in full day care are quite different to those who go to their own or to a minder's home after a play session.

Meal times and snacks are very important for these children as relaxing, sociable times. All children will need a quiet time, and many will need a sleep. The keyworker system is much more important in full day care, and time must be found for individual care and cuddles, and for the sorts of activities other children of their age will be part of at home.

**TASK 2:
One week**

1 Draw up an outline plan for these groups for one week. Again, this should not be a simple repetition for either group, and particularly not for the full day care group. You must, however, have a basic routine, which gives a sense of security and structure to the children's lives. Present your week in a timetable format.

2 Consider your outline from the perspective of two children in full day care:
(a) Lucetta, 11 months;
(b) Tyrone, 3½.
For these children write an individual timetable of the options available to them over a full week.

This activity is a little artificial because a child cannot, and must not, be made to follow a timetable. It is intended, however, to focus on what the day care offer looks like from an individual child's perspective.

Identify times when each child's keyworker would make special time for them – for example, to invite Tyrone to come out to the shop to buy some ingredients for cooking, have a cuddle and a story.

3 Compare your schedules with someone else's. Feel free to share your ideas and make changes.

**TASK 3:
One activity,
lots of learning,
lots of fun**

Study carefully:
(a) the 'Technology' diagram and all the activities that feed into this;
(b) the 'Cookery' page which shows the learning opportunities that can be developed from a single activity.

1 With a partner, agree a heading for each of the three groups of activities/learning shown in the 'Cookery' extract.

2 With a partner, choose one of the other boxes in the 'Technology' diagram, and develop its learning and language possibilities. Model your work on 'Cookery' using the headings you agreed on above. If you have a spread of choices in your group, you will have a very well developed curriculum in this area.

**TASK 4:
Make a
curriculum?**

Mount a display on a classroom wall or an exhibition stand of the group's work in developing the technology curriculum for young children.

Your display should be professional and attractive; decide what can be hand drawn and what would look better in large, display typeface. Consider how

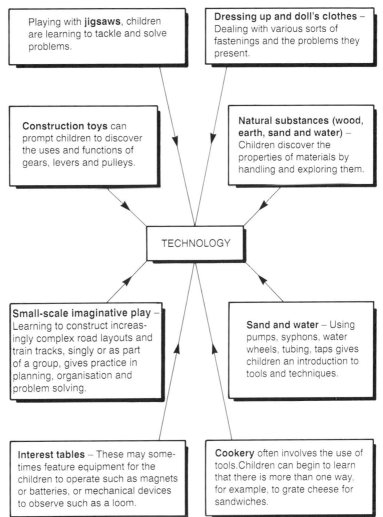

Playing with **jigsaws**, children are learning to tackle and solve problems.

Dressing up and doll's clothes – Dealing with various sorts of fastenings and the problems they present.

Construction toys can prompt children to discover the uses and functions of gears, levers and pulleys.

Natural substances (wood, earth, sand and water) – Children discover the properties of materials by handling and exploring them.

TECHNOLOGY

Small-scale imaginative play – Learning to construct increasingly complex road layouts and train tracks, singly or as part of a group, gives practice in planning, organisation and problem solving.

Sand and water – Using pumps, syphons, water wheels, tubing, taps gives children an introduction to tools and techniques.

Interest tables – These may sometimes feature equipment for the children to operate such as magnets or batteries, or mechanical devices to observe such as a loom.

Cookery often involves the use of tools. Children can begin to learn that there is more than one way, for example, to grate cheese for sandwiches.

Source: *What children learn in playgroups*, published by the PPA. This excellent publication presents a sequence of diagrams to illustrate areas of learning and experience, and reveals the learning opportunities of most play activities.

to make use of photographs and pictures and how to protect your display from marauding fingers, while encouraging people to take an active interest in it.

TASK 5: Permission

Your aim is to get your display to a wider audience. As a group, decide where you would like to display it, and set about securing the necessary permission(s) to do so.

If the person whose permission you are seeking is internal to the organisation, write a **memo**. If you would like to take it to an outside organisation (such as a library or or workplace) write a **letter** to the person concerned. (Advice on writing letters and memos can be found in *A Practical Approach to Caring* (Pitman Publishing, 1991), pp 274–7, by Kate Williams.)

COOKERY

Cookery is a familiar activity with a clearly recognisable purpose. This helps children and adults to work together and carry through a project. They will:

- talk about what they are going to do and prepare a plan of action
- perhaps compile a shopping list and shop for ingredients to match it
- unpack a shopping basket and check ingredients against the list
- assemble necessary utensils
- check arrangements for handwashing and aprons
- talk together about the tasks as they do them.

In the process, they will:

- use written symbols to create a shopping list and follow a recipe
- observe safety rules and understand the need for them
- learn about hygiene
- learn to follow through a sequence in the correct order as they use a recipe
- use the techniques of science as they observe changes made by mixing, beating, adding liquids, heating, cooling
- extend their mathematical skills as they estimate quantities, match them to the numbers being cooked for, weigh, measure and count ingredients.

Through experiments and discussion, the children can discover that food:

- tastes salt, sweet, sour, bitter, bland
- comes from different countries
- is grown or manufactured from a range of living materials
- is necessary to sustain life
- has to be stored properly
- can go bad
- can be sorted into different classes (e.g. fruit, vegetables) which can then be divided into various subsets.

Recipes and cooking utensils from different cultures give everyone a chance to identify and name what is familiar and to try what is different. This also ensures that all of the children see their 'home' food and equipment recognised and acknowledged in the group.

Cooking is especially successful in daycare playgroups, where the children can feel that they are making a real contribution to the functioning of the group by being involved sometimes in preparations for meals.

Language

Apart from all the sensory pleasure of cookery, this activity also gives children the chance to deal with language used for very specific practical purposes:

- to agree plans
- to lay down rules (e.g. about hygiene and safety)
- to communicate instructions
- to arrange activities in the right sequence.

In addition, as they discuss and compare notes on what they have done, children acquire the language of tastes, textures, smells and colours as well as the names of the necessary ingredients and techniques.

Source: *What children learn in playgroups*, published by the PPA

Assignment 13

Children's health and welfare

It would be helpful, but not essential, to have worked on Assignment 6 ('Milestones in child development') before you undertake Tasks 1 and 2.

TASK 1:
Observe a child
Observe a child over a period of half an hour. Draw up an observation chart such as the one below, noting down every five minutes what the child is doing. You can do this task during a visit to a playgroup or nursery, or by observing your own or a friend's child at home. Leave the last column blank until you have finished.

Make sure you know the child's name, age and first language.

Observation chart					
	What is s/he doing now?	What is s/he playing with?	Is s/he alone? With others? Who?	Is s/he quiet? Noisy? Talking?	Comments and review
start					
after 5 mins					
after 10 mins					
after 15 mins					
after 20 mins					
after 25 mins					
after 30 mins					

TASK 2: **A child's** **development**	Turn to Appendix I at the back of the book to find out more about the developmental stage of the child you have studied. Draw a grid using the same four headings as this chart and think back to your observation to see which of the skills in the Mary Sheridan chart you saw your child demonstrate. Add details about the context, materials, people your child was with. Look back to the age before the one you are focusing on, and ahead to the next stage where appropriate.

TASK 3:
Know your
children

People working in day care must keep accurate records of the children in their care. The essentials are stipulated in the Children Act. These are:

- child's name, address and phone number;
- age and date of birth;
- name by which the child is known and birth name (if different);
- surname and name of parents;
- emergency telephone numbers;
- information about any health problems or conditions and any medication the child takes.

Local authorities have discretionary powers to require additional information to be kept on record. This will usually include most of the following:

- child's sex;
- child's ethnic origins, first language, religion (if any);
- details of parents' home address(es) and workplace, and persons with parental responsibility;
- names, addresses, phone numbers of any person authorised to collect the child;
- consent for outings;
- name, address and phone number of child's doctor and health visitor;
- specific medical information: illnesses, dietary needs, allergies, record of immunisation;
- consent for medical attention in an emergency;
- space for details of any accidents. Details of all accidents requiring medical or first aid treatment should be entered and countersigned by the parent and staff member and action to contact the parent recorded. This is in addition to the mandatory Accident Book entry.

Design a form entitled 'Child's Personal Record' to make the recording of this information as simple as possible. Aim to keep essential information to one side of A4. Use the other side for details, and any additional information you think would be helpful to record.

You may wish to include information from the schedule of immunisation below.

WHEN TO PROTECT YOUR CHILD

At 2 months

Diphtheria		
Whooping cough	}	DPT one injection
Tetanus		
Polio		by mouth

At 3 months

Diphtheria		
Whooping cough	}	DPT one injection
Tetanus		
Polio		by mouth

At 4 months

Diphtheria		
Whooping cough	}	DPT one injection
Tetanus		
Polio		by mouth

At 12 - 18 months (usually before 15 months)

Measles		
Mumps	}	MMR one injection
Rubella		

3-5 years (around school entry)

Diphtheria		
Tetanus		booster injections
Polio		booster by mouth

Girls 10 -14 years

| Rubella | one injection |

Girls/boys 13 years

| Tuberculosis | one injection (BCG) |

School leavers

| Tetanus | one injection |

15-19 years

| Polio | booster by mouth |

Source: *Childhood diseases haven't died. Children have.*, published by the Health Education Authority

If your child has missed any of these immunisations, or started them late, don't worry. Your doctor will tell you how to fit them in so that your child is fully protected.

The Children Act suggests that people working with young children should share with parents their observations and assessments of their children, and records of the child's activities. Most local authorities consider this to be good practice. Should this be entered on the form? If not, how should it be shared?

TASK 4:
First Aid

If you work with young children, you should take a full first aid course run by the Red Cross or St John's Ambulance. This task if a taster or reminder.

Opposite is a table of first aid procedures. The condition on the left and brief description of it and the **Never** sections are correctly placed. Your task is to fill in the **Action** column by inserting the correct action in the slot from the scrambled procedures given on p 202.

Check your answers in Appendix 2 at the back of the book.

TASK 5:
The First Aid box

FIRST AID BOX

This should be a strong container impervious to dust and damp, clearly labelled with a white cross on a green background.

The following contents are recommended by the Health and Safety Executive, amounts varying with numbers involved:

ITEM	NUMBERS IN GROUPS		
	1–5	6–10	11–50
Guidance card	1	1	1
Individually wrapped sterile adhesive dressings	10	20	40
Sterile eye-pads with attachment	1	2	4
Triangular bandages	1	2	4
Sterile coverings for serious wounds	1	2	4
Safety pins	6	6	12
Medium size sterile unmedicated dressings	3	6	8
Large sterile unmedicated dressings	1	2	4
Extra large sterile unmedicated dressings	1	2	4

For children other useful items are:
A pair of sharp scissors
A pair of tweezers
A roll of non-allergic adhesive tape (micropore)
Packs of sterile gauze
Crepe bandage
Cotton wool
Finger stall
A container of cooled boiled water
Surgical or other waterproof gloves to be worn when dealing with bleeding, vomiting and incontinence
Mask for wearing when giving expired air resuscitation.

It is useful to stock some items for adult use only, e.g. sanitary protection wear.

It may also be more appropriate to have recommended contents in differing quantities for children (e.g. fewer extra large dressings but more triangular bandages).

Whenever an item is used it must be replaced as soon as possible.

FIRST AID PROCEDURES

	SYMPTOMS	ACTION	NEVER
BREATHING STOPPED	Unconsciousness, blue lips and finger nails, no movement of chest wall, child is silent – no sound of breathing.		NEVER . . . Panic or waste time.
HEART STOPPED	As above plus no carotid pulse felt.		NEVER . . . panic or waste time.
SEVERE BLEEDING	May be obvious site of bleeding. Feeling faint, general weakness. Nausea, pallor, especially face. Thirst. Increase in pulse rate but weak.		NEVER . . . leave the child alone or give drinks. Never apply a tourniquet.
UNCONSCIOUS	The child is lying silent. Does not respond to questions, may not respond to pain.		NEVER . . . give drinks or leave the child alone.
BURNS & SCALDS	Pain, usually with redness and swelling at the injury site. Blisters later.		NEVER . . . apply butter or lard, cream or ointments. Never burst any blisters.
CHOKING	Caused by obstruction to airway, e.g. food. Violent coughing. Difficulty breathing. Congestion of face. Eventual unconsciousness.		
CONVULSIONS OR FITS	May be twitching of face and limbs, upward eyes, rigidity of body, frothing at mouth, breath holding, unconsciousness plus high temperature in children.		NEVER . . . lie the child flat on his back. Never leave the child alone. Never forcibly restrain the child.
FALLS AND FRACTURES	Could range from bruising to fracture to unconsciousness.		NEVER . . . move the child unnecessarily if you suspect a fracture.
HEAD INJURIES	May be loss of consciousness, nausea and vomiting, amnesia, bruising, bleeding. May be no obvious symptoms.		NEVER . . . rule out damage to the brain even if no signs or symptoms.
POISONING (household articles)	Range from stomach ache and vomiting to obvious burning of lips to unconsciousness.		NEVER . . . leave the child alone. Never make the child vomit.
EYES (foreign body)	Visible redness and watering of eye. Pain and itching.		NEVER . . . leave an eye injury. If you are unhappy take the child to hospital.
EARS	Crying and holding ear. Perhaps foreign object sticking out of ear.		NEVER . . . press on the object – you may damage the ear.
NOSE BLEED	Bleeding from the nose.		NEVER . . . lie the child on his back or put his head back.
BITES	Punctured skin or just teeth marks at the site of the injury.		NEVER . . . approach the animal if it is frothing at the mouth.
CUTS/GRAZES	Blood at the site of the injury.		NEVER . . . cover without cleaning.
STINGS	Swelling and redness where the child has been stung. Sting may still be present.		NEVER . . . leave the child alone until the swelling disappears.
SPRAINS & STRAINS	Severe swelling and bruising which is painful.		NEVER . . . bathe the injury in hot water.

Source: *Guidelines for Good Practice for Sessional Playgroups for 3–5 Year Olds,* published by the PPA

Clear the airway of debris or obstructions. Open the airway by extending the head. Give mouth to mouth (or mouth to nose) ventilation. Action in the first 3 minutes is vital.

Try to prevent child rubbing eye. Natural watering of eye will remove small pieces of sand. Continue by irrigating eye with cold water. Other foreign bodies need medical attention

Swelling in the throat, on the tongue or near the eyes can be dangerous. Take to the hospital. If you can see the sting remove with tweezers.

Press gently at the site of the cut or graze. Clean with soap and water and cover with dry dressing or plaster.

Take the child, and the cause of the poison, to the hospital immediately. Check breathing. Begin resuscitation if breathing stops. Give child drink of water if lips burnt and child conscious.

If minor fall, tender loving care is best. If the bruising/ swelling is extensive, ease with a cold compress. If you suspect a fracture, do not move the injured part unless absolutely necessary.

Place the child over your knee, head down, slap between the shoulder blades up to 4 times. Check in mouth for dislodged foreign body. If unsuccessful, perform abdominal thrust up to 4 times.

Check breathing. Try to establish the cause. Loosen tight clothing. If breathing turn the child to the recovery position unless fracture of spine suspected.

Immerse in cold water for at least 10 minutes. Cover with a dry sterile dressing and bandage. Any burn greater than 1 cm square should be seen by a Doctor. For large burns dial 999.

Apply a cold compress. Support the injury with a pad and crepe bandage.

Make sure he can breathe, and that he does not injure himself by striking hard objects. Loosen constricting clothing. Make sure the child sees his doctor. Cool the child with tepid sponging if temperature high.

Mouth to mouth ventilation plus external chest compression. This should only be attempted by people who are experienced with external cardiac compression.

Clean with soap and water and check with parents that the child is immunised against tetanus, if bitten by an animal.

Lie the child down in the recovery position, keep him warm and calm. Get help immediately and move as little as possible. Keep under observation. Remember to tell a parent even if injury was only slight.

Earache. Contact a parent and advise that the child sees a doctor. Foreign body. Prevent child from touching ear. Foreign body needs to be removed at hospital.

Apply direct pressure on the wound using fingers and thumb, over a sterile dressing is possible. Use a ring pad if foreign body present. Lie the child down. Raise the uninjured part (unless you suspect a fracture). Apply sterile pad and bandage.

1 If you have the opportunity to check the contents of a day care setting's first aid box, do so. Check the contents of the box against the recommended list.

2 Go to a chemist and price the items on the HSE's list. How much would it cost to make up a first aid box for your home or workplace? (Note the recommended numbers.)

TASK 6: Common complaints

Can you recognise everyday childhood complaints? Find out the following details about the ailments below:

- signs and symptoms;
- incubation and infectious periods;
- action staff should take;
- treatment.

Ailments: head lice (nits); worms; measles; mumps; rubella; chicken pox; any other complaints and illnesses common in your area. Present your findings as a quick reference guide for staff working with children.

Assignment 14

Telling a story

TASK 1:
Storytelling

Read the article 'Tell me how a story goes' below and answer the questions that follow.

Tell me how a story goes

With puppets, props and storytelling aids, the book nook becomes a story corner.

Storytelling is a knack which develops through practice and compromise. Knowing that whatever you talk about with under-fives is either teaching them or consolidating their knowledge, your confidence as a storyteller – without a book to read from – will flourish.

The 'real books' movement, or 'whole language' philosophy reflects the belief that learning to be a fluent reader and writer happens in ways other than through reading schemes. But there is more to literacy than just books. Children are influenced dramatically by the *company they keep*, including the authors of the books they enjoy, the tellers of the stories they hear (even gossip), and the reactions of the personalities who talk to them. This is shown in the vocabulary a child uses – straight from the mouths of family, friends and relatives.

The elements of a story

Life is made up of stories. They are not often clear-cut and don't always produce the kind of ending we would like. Deciphering the elements of any story helps us see a pattern and to imagine within it an even better combination of experiences. If the children can feel *part of* this improved 'slice of life' it can influence their perception of themselves and help to teach them the enormous potential of stringing words together to relate fact or fiction.

The elements of a story are, very briefly: *Character, Conflict, Crisis, Climax*, and *Conclusion*.
Eg:

Little Bo Peep (*character*)
has lost her sheep (*conflict*)
and doesn't know where to find them (*crisis*)
"Leave them alone, and they'll come home, (*climax*)
bringing their tails behind them." (*conclusion*)

Usually all these elements revolve around a theme or proverb.

The conflict, which is at the centre of the story, is usually illustrated in several ways – resulting in repetition of an action or dialogue. In adult fiction the repetition is masked, but children love to hear repetition for the immediacy of something familiar.

The story of the Gingerbread Man illustrates this well. The conflict is his determination to get away from the old woman and man. He has several crises where he is beset by problems – he is chased by more and more characters. The final crisis is the climax where the 'kind' fox deceitfully offers him a lift across the river – only to swallow him up before he reaches across the other side. The conclusion is not particularly happy, but it is satisfying, which is what matters.

Where do I start?

This is easy. Be led by the children, or your own intuition. Sometimes it makes a change to have a *real* bowl of porridge for the children to stir while you read *The Magic Porridge Pot*. Supervising the stirring as well as holding the book is cumbersome so you abandon the book and tell the story you know off by heart. Try telling stories you know well, and provide a 'prop' as a focal point instead of a book.

Having practised this you'll be ready to make up a simple story, again using a 'prop'. It may be a hand puppet. It may be a teddy or a doll. It could be a handkerchief, or a bunch of flowers. Any object can be chosen for your story to focus upon. Remember, the story needs a character with a conflict; make it one the children can sympathise with.

What sort of crisis and climax?

The children may have suggested a name for your central character; now you can ask them how they think the character tries to get what it wants. Start them off with an idea. The little boy searches for the teddy – in the garden where he played (it's not there so this is crisis number one); under the bed where he slept (crisis two); in the bath (crisis three); at the post office (crisis four); outside the school (crisis five). Each attempt is met with a phrase like '*No teddy here*'. If the children contribute suggestions it ensures they are familiar with the situations in the story.

If you don't want the story to fizzle out you need to inject a climax. 'The very last place the little boy could look was . . . .' The children may come up with the ultimate crisis – but it's a good idea to have something up your sleeve just in case. '*In the washing machine!*' someone may suggest, or '*at the police station*,' or '*in the playgroup cupboard*'. If you want to turn the story in a certain direction, perhaps to illustrate a moral, you can always say 'Oh no, he didn't go to playgroup that day. I know where he tried looking last . . . .'

Where do I finish?

Whatever the result, teddy was definitely found. There has to be a satisfying conclusion. It would be disastrous if the story ended with the little boy (and the children) still wondering where teddy had got to. The children would be left feeling uneasy, as bad as if the story was interrupted and abandoned half way through.

Improvised props

On a day when none of the usual books, puppets, or props inspire you to construct an exciting story line, there may just be a few items you could slip into a carrier bag, from which the story will grow. There may be spare clothes in the cupboard – your central character (played by you or a willing child), perhaps from outer space, tries on each article in turn – in the wrong place. He might try knickers on his head, gloves on his feet, trousers on his arms, and socks on his ears. The children will be in stitches, and in the end, of course, everything has to go in its proper place – you (or your actor) wear the articles on top of normal clothes. If no clothing is available a story could revolve around a character trying a 'Lucky Dip' – finding the very last item in the bag is just what he wanted.

You are giving them part of your 'whole language'

The children may have contributed a large part of the story, and by the nature of most human groups it is likely that certain personalities have given more than others. But the result is that their ideas, combined with the vocabulary with which you were able to bind them together, have broadened their knowledge of life and the use of language. This, in itself, helps build the foundations for children to understand the written word and to communicate their own 'whole language' on paper.

Source: Bernie Ross, *Contact* magazine, published by the PPA, April 1992

1 'There is more to literacy than just books.' What are these other elements?

2 Why are stories important in children's lives?

3 What are the five elements of a story? Explain what each word means.

4 Why does the author suggest you retell traditional stories?

5 Should children's stories have happy endings? What is important about endings?

6 What suggestions for using props in storytelling are given here?

7 How does storytelling link with reading and writing?

8 Write a paragraph on your own views on the ideas about storytelling in this passage.

**TASK 2:
Tell a story**

1 Following the advice about the five elements in a story, retell a traditional story in your own words, and in your own way. Think about how you can use different voices for different characters; whether dialect and accents help to make the story come alive; at which points you would ask children for suggestions, and how you would include them. Consider whether and how you would use props, such as a hand puppet or story bag.

You could take as your basis a traditional European story (such as Aesop's fables), a West Indian folk tale (such as Anansi stories), an English nursery rhyme or traditional story, or a traditional tale from around the world.

2   Practise telling your story and when you are ready, tape record yourself. Listen to your recording, and consider what came across well and what you want to change.

3   Tell your story to a child, or small group of children.

4   How did it go? Now prepare another one . . .

TASK 3: Choosing children's books

Note to the tutor: If you decide to do this task as a whole group, bring in a box of 40–50 children's books, selected at random, and include books appropriate for the age ranges your course participants are considering. Students are welcome to bring in books – but ensure they are clearly identified for safe return.

1   Hand the books out to individuals at random. Spend about 15 minutes reviewing them. As people finish with some books move them around so everybody has seen about 10.

2   Take it in turns to show a book to the group, and briefly comment on:
   (a)   the age group you think it is suitable for;
   (b)   who it is by, and what it shows or its storyline;
   (c)   what you think of it, whether you enjoyed it;
   (d)   whether you think it is dated or will date;

(e)   whether you think children will enjoy it.
Continue this until you think you have shared a broad range of books.

3   Make your selection. Choose three books you like and would want to use with children of a particular age group, and one you did not. Again, explain your reasons to the group.

4   Write up brief book reviews of the books you have considered today. Include the information above, plus the following: publisher, date of publication, ISBN number, cost. Agree how many reviews you should write.

5   Type up and collate your reviews. You may wish to display the group's work in the library for a period of time.

TASK 4: Images in books

Books are powerful in conveying images of people. Books can encourage children to have a positive view of themselves, their capabilities and their futures. Equally, children can be led to see themselves as inferior or superior to others by reason of their sex, race, cultural origins and degrees of physical ability by the way people like themselves are or are not shown in books. (*See* the newspaper extract in Chapter 4, Part I for one nursery's steps to change children's self-image through a thoughtful selection of materials and activities.)

Below are some points to look for in a critical evaluation of images of themselves in books for children:

ILLUSTRATIONS
●   Are women and girls, boys and men shown both in domestic settings and in the world of work?
●   Are boys shown doing artistic/creative work or only girls?
●   Are people with disabilities presented at all, or only in such a way that they invoke pity? Is disability presented as a frightening deformity?
●   Are black people shown at all or only in certain roles – as athletes or transport workers, for example? Are doctors and lawyers shown as black?
●   Are black people and features of other cultures such as clothes shown in illustrations, perhaps as background, where they are absent from the text?
●   Look at the pictures in a book through the eyes of different children in your care. Are all children shown in satisfying and effective roles?

CHARACTERS
●   Who has the power? Who makes the decisions? Who is doing what? Who is active? Who is passive? Who is having fun?
●   Do some, e.g. girls/women, black, disabled, go along with decisions made by others, e.g. white people/boys/men?

LANGUAGE

- Is 'he' used where it need not be? To refer to 'she' and 'he'? Or for animals and things?
- Is 'man' used where there is an acceptable alternative – 'policeman' for 'police officer' for example?
- Are girls and women described with adjectives that reflect looks or passive qualities, e.g. 'pretty', 'good'?
- Does the language give out subtle messages about superiority or inferiority?

THE FACTS

- How accurate are the lifestyles shown? Will the children recognise real situations, dilemmas, experiences, or are they filtered through the writer's value system?
- Do jokey presentations encourage caricature – exaggerated or inappropriate sexual or racial features?

IMPLICATIONS

- If you were a boy/girl or black/white child looking at this book/reading this story, would you feel good about your own abilities?
- What messages does the book give about the relationships between men and women, black and white, and role in an able bodied world?
- Are all children shown doing things all children like doing? Or do only some have fun?

Use this checklist as a basis for an evaluation of the images of themselves portrayed to children in three books. Write a review of each book, and present your findings to the group.

**TASK 5:
Setting criteria**

Work in small groups. You are the staff group responsible for buying books for the nursery where you work. Establish the criteria by which you will judge what books to get or keep.

In your discussion you need to consider:

- What makes a good book?
- Can a book be 'good' and worth stocking if it fares badly on some of the points of positive images listed above?
- What would cause you to throw a book away?
- How will you judge the value of a factual/information book?
- How will you judge a fictional/imaginative book?

When you have agreed your criteria, present them to the whole group in turns, and expect discussion. Make sure you listen to other people's views, and discuss rather than argue.

At some point in the discussion, try the following for about five minutes. Before each person speaks, they have to summarise what the previous speaker said, to that person's satisfaction: 'You said that . . ., agreed? The point I would like to make is . . .'

Before you write up your criteria in a form suitable to present to the person responsible in your workplace, consider if the discussion has caused you to change your views. Then write up or type your criteria.

TASK 6:
A books
budget

Gisela, your boss, is taking two days' holiday, but leaves you this note

> 5.30 Monday
> They've just rung to say we can have the £75 for books, but the order has to go in quick or we'll lose it to another budget. Could you make out a list of books you think we should get, with publisher's details and price, and set it out neatly? It would be a good idea to write a few words about the books you choose on a separate sheet of paper to give to Mrs Chaudhury with the order when she comes on Thursday morning. See you then. Thanks, Gisela.

Decide on the age group you have in mind, and visit libraries and, with permission, a bookshop, to look at books. Write out a list of books you would like to buy. Since Gisela has not given you any guidance, go for a balance between factual and fiction.

Assignment 15

Safe or sorry?

> On average, 4 children are killed by accidents **every day**.
>
> Accidents are **the commonest cause of death** among toddlers and older children.
>
> For children between the ages of 10 and 15, **nearly half** of all deaths are due to accidents.
>
> Each year, **one child in every six** goes to a hospital accident and emergency department.
>
> **One in every three** of all patients going to a hospital accident and emergency department is a child.
>
> **One in every six** children in hospital is there because of an accident.

(Source: *Play it Safe! A guide to preventing children's accidents*, published by Health Education Authority and Scottish Health Education Group in association with BBC Play it Safe!)

**TASK 1:
The tip of the iceberg**

Figures for deaths show the pattern of accidents – they are the tip of the iceberg. For every death, there are scores of serious accidents requiring hospital treatment, and hundreds of minor accidents in and out of the home.

Deaths age 1–4 years 1989

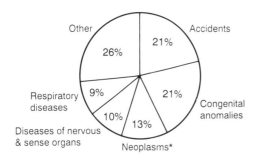

Deaths age 5–14 years 1989

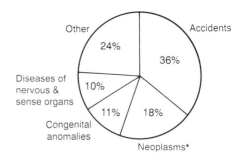

*Neoplasm = cancer   (Total = 1,078)

(Total = 1,175)

Distribution of major causes of death in children (England and Wales)
Source: *The Health of the Nation. A consultative document for health in England and Wales*, Cm 1523. Reproduced by kind permission of HMSO. Crown copyright 1992

1 (a) Which major causes of death cause fewer deaths in the 5–14 age group than in the 1–4 age group? Why do you think this is?
   (b) Which causes of death cause more deaths in the older age group? Why do you think this is?
   (c) Comment on the proportion of deaths caused by accidents in both age groups.

Fatal accidents in the home: by sex and age, 1989

England and Wales   Percentages and numbers

	Males					Females					All
	0–4	5–14	15–64	65–74	75 and over	0–4	5–14	15–64	65–74	75 and over	persons
Type of accident (percentages)											
Poisonings by drugs and biologicals	2	3	12	3	1	–	5	13	6	1	6
Other poisonings	–	3	8	3	2	1	–	6	3	1	4
Falls	4	13	18	55	69	7	5	15	51	75	44
Fire and flames	36	40	12	15	12	36	64	12	10	10	13
Natural and environmental factors	–	–	–	1	2	1	–	1	4	2	2
Submersion, suffocation and foreign bodies	38	27	10	5	5	28	9	8	9	4	8
Other accidents	8	3	3	2	3	10	–	2	2	2	3
Undetermined whether or not accident	11	10	37	16	6	17	18	43	15	3	21
Total (=100%) (numbers)	99	30	1,079	246	536	72	22	601	299	1,093	4,077

Social Trends 22. Reproduced by kind permission of HMSO. Crown Copyright.

2 Using the figures in this chart, draw four pie charts to show causes of fatal accidents in
   • males aged 0–4, females aged 0–4;
   • males aged 5–14, females aged 5–14.
   You may wish to draw these by hand, or use a computer. Include a key, and show the exact percentages for each group. Show the total number of deaths under each chart.

   Write a paragraph commenting on each pair of pie charts. Include the following: the total number of deaths in each group; how these are distributed; major causes of death; differences between the sexes; your suggestions as to causes for these differences.

   Discussion point: Discuss your findings in your group. Look carefully at the 'Undetermined whether or not accident' category across all age groups. What circumstances might prompt this doubt (a) in adults (age 15 and over), (b) in children (14 and under)? About which group do you feel greater concern?

TYPE OF ACCIDENT

Estimate = 1,143,000 injuries

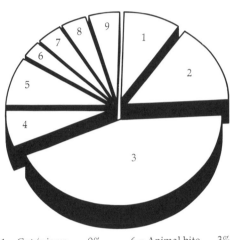

Children injured in the home (hospital cases, UK 1989)
Source: *Child Safety in the Home*, published by RoSPA

1 = Cut / pierce	9%	6 = Animal bite	3%
2 = Struck	15%	7 = Poison / inhalation	4%
3 = Falls	44%	8 = Hot liquid / object	4%
4 = Unknown	7%	9 = Foreign body	5%
5 = Others	9%		

3 The total number of children whose injuries required hospital treatment in 1989 is estimated at 1,143,000. Work out *how many* children required treatment for each type of accident.

TASK 2: Check it out! Take each statement in the extract from *Play It Safe!* at the head of this assignment and check out its accuracy. Some of the information is contained in the data in Task 1. Others, such as road accident figures for children and young people and hospital admissions, you will have to research yourself. You may prefer to use information available locally – road traffic and hospital admission figures in your area, for example.

Write up our research. Take each statement you have researched as a heading, and present your data and comments below.

TASK 3: Dangerous possibilities Work in groups of three for this task. Your task is to identify accident risks at different points in a young child's development. You will need:
- to copy the 'Developmental phases chart' (opposite) on to a large sheet of paper;
- a copy of the 'Developmental phases sheet' photocopied and cut up, or alternatively you could copy the entries on to yellow 'Post-it' labels.

I In groups, take each developmental phase slip and decide at what age **most children** develop that skill. Add to the slip examples of the activities

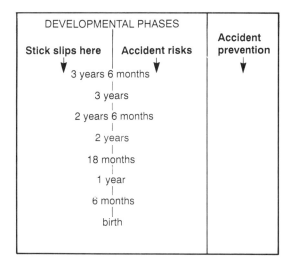

DEVELOPMENTAL PHASES		Accident prevention
Stick slips here	Accident risks	
	3 years 6 months	
	3 years	
	2 years 6 months	
	2 years	
	18 months	
	1 year	
	6 months	
	birth	

Developmental phases sheet

crawls upstairs	enjoys water play	turns knobs, dials and switches
rolls over	actively puts objects in mouth	wriggles and kicks
reaches out to grab things	crawls	moves objects – open and shut; push and pull
grips things between fingers and thumb	says single words	able to tell different tastes apart
pulls self up to stand	walks holding on to furniture	looks for hidden objects
walks without help	empties and fills containers	actively explores surroundings
copies other people	explores taste, smell and feel of things	screws and unscrews caps completely
lifts and moves head	talks in simple sentences	rides a bike with stabilisers
climbs – up furniture, trees	jumps from one or two steps	

Source: *Preventing Accidents to Children. A training resource for health visitors*, published by the Child Accident Prevention Trust, 1991

the child might now be able to do. Place the slips in the left-hand column, under the appropriate age. Refer to the chart showing the developmental phases in Appendix 1.

2 Then look at each six month interval and identify the related accident risks. When you have identified all the accident risks you can think of, agree on the three most significant risks for each age group. Write these in the middle column.

3 Compare your group's work with another's. Discuss similarities and differences.

4 Suggest safety and prevention tips for each of the accident risks you have identified. Enter these in the right-hand column.

TASK 4: Thinking safety

Each picture opposite shows a danger to children which could happen at home or in a day care setting. Taking each picture in turn state:

1 what accident might happen;
2 what action to take that instant to prevent the accident;
3 precautions to take to prevent the accident from happening again;
4 what to do if the accident does happen.

TASK 5: Children's concepts of accidents

One study of children, parents and accidents asked children to draw a picture of an accident – or to use fuzzy felt shapes and toys such as kettles and cups, and cars – to explore their experiences of accidents and their attitudes to them. Below are some of the accidents the children reported:

Falls indoors
- falling downstairs
- tripping over toys/objects
- bumping into furniture
- falling out of windows
- slipping on wet floor
- falling off furniture, such as beds
- falling as a result of fighting or pushing with brothers and sisters

Falls out of doors
- falling off walls
- tripping over toys
- falling out of trees
- tripping into water
- slipping on ice
- falling whilst playing
- fighting and messing around
- falling off bikes

- falling on broken glass
- falling while playing
- falling off playground equipment, such as swings or slides

Burns and scalds
- falling into a fire
- putting hand in fire
- being burnt by a too-hot shower/bath
- spilt tea/coffee
- cigarette burn
- spilling hot food
- touching hot iron
- eating too-hot food
- playing with fire
- grill pan and kitchen fires
- steam burn from saucepan
- clothes catching fire

Source: *Play It Safe! A guide to preventing children's accidents*, published by the Health Education Authority and the Scottish Education Group in association with the BBC

Roads
- being run over whilst crossing road
- running into the road
- chasing a ball
- falling off kerb/pavement
- car going on to pavement
- hurt as a car passenger
- being knocked off bike
- playing dares in the road
- playing in or near busyt roads

Other kinds of accident
- being bitten/scratched by a pet
- drowning in the sea
- being cut by a knife
- shutting fingers in doors or hinges
- getting stung by plants and insects
- swallowing small objects
- getting an object stuck in a mouth or ear
- being eaten by a shark
- seeing an aeroplane crash
- getting stuck in a life
- robbers in your house
- dares and deliberate risk-taking

Source: Gill Coombs, *You can't watch them twenty-four hours a day*, published by The Child Accident Prevention Trust, 1991

Some children included things which 'appeared to be somewhat different from the concept of accident used by professionals in accident prevention work, for example:

- making a mistake

  "This is me and my friend – she had an accident when we were dressing up – her cloak's the wrong colour."

- breaking something accidentally
- a domestic accident

  "Having a flood – our boiler burst." '

1 From your reading of the extracts above:
   (a) Which of the accidents listed above do you think might be based on the child's own experiences?
   (b) Would you class all the accidents described by children as 'accidents'?
   (c) In what ways do children's concepts of accidents differ from an adult's? Give examples.
2 Opposite are two extracts from the findings of this study:
   What are the implications of these findings for providers of:
   (a) pre-school day care;
   (b) after school and holiday day care for children aged 5–11?
3 Write a set of ten guidelines for providers of *either* pre-school day care *or* after school and holiday day care to increase their vigilance and safety awareness for these age groups of children. Set these out in an eye-catching way, so that the organiser could pin your page on the notice board for the attention of all.

Children aged three and four

At these ages many children did not appear to have a concept of 'accident' or 'danger'. The research suggests that those who do have such concepts have usually had some personal experience, but may not generalise from this to accidents in other settings. Lacking an 'accident' concept, most children appeared also to have no concept of cause or prevention.

Children aged five and six

At these ages, the majority of children (95%) did have some notion of 'accident' or 'danger'. Personal experience or observation of accidents seemed to be important factors in shaping these concepts, since the majority of children drew pictures of real accidents they knew about. However, they were also able to generalise from these to talk about other possible accidents. By this age most children seemed to have a sufficiently developed concept of 'accident' to allow them to speculate about imagined situations (the scenarios). They were also able to respond to general questions about causes and prevention, although many children's ideas remained quite specific, being related to a particular incident they had experienced.

(Source: Gill Coombs, *You can't watch them twenty-four hours a day*, published by The Child Accident Prevention Trust 1991)

TASK 6:
True or false?

Working with a partner, decide on whether you think each of the following is true or false. Check your answers in Appendix 2.

Questionnaire

True or false?

		True	False
1	Children aged 13 or over can legally buy and use fireworks.	☐	☐
2	Most children cannot cross a busy road safely until they are 11 or 12 years old.	☐	☐
3	If a child swallows a button-size battery, it will pass through them without causing harm.	☐	☐
4	The best way to make windows safe for toddlers is to have window locks fitted.	☐	☐
5	Baby-walkers are a safe and stimulating way to help babies learn to walk.	☐	☐
6	Most 3 year olds can be taught to recognise a warning symbol on a bottle.	☐	☐
7	It doesn't matter if children sit in the back or front of a car, as long as they are suitably restrained.	☐	☐
8	Children should not eat peanuts until they are at least 6 years old.	☐	☐
9	The special caps on medicines and cleaning fluid bottles are child proof.	☐	☐
10	The safest place to store bleaches and medicines is generally the kitchen.	☐	☐
11	Cooker guards create more hazards than they prevent.	☐	☐
12	As laburnum seeds are highly toxic, gardens and play areas should be cleared of all laburnum trees.	☐	☐
13	Most toy accidents are caused by dangerous toy design.	☐	☐
14	Children are not safe to go up or downstairs unsupervised until they are at least 3 years old.	☐	☐
15	Strip packaging of pills helps to stop children investigating and experimenting with pills.	☐	☐
16	Although funfairs are much safer now than they used to be, they are still a significant cause of child injury.	☐	☐
17	If a young child is particularly bright or developmentally advanced, the age recommendations on toys can be disregarded.	☐	☐

Source: *Preventing accidents to children. A training resource for health visitors*, published by the Child Accident Prevention Trust, 1991

Assignment 16

Happy eating

The traditional peasant diets of peoples all over the world – including the UK – are based on simple healthy foods, the sort we are now being urged to adopt. Traditional diets have a staple food based on crops grown in that country – rice, pasta, yams, bread, chapatis, potatoes. These are rich in starch, high in fibre, and are eaten with sauces made of fresh local vegetables, sometimes with meat. Plant oils are used for cooking, and nuts, seeds and pulses give all year round food value, from one harvest to another.

While eggs, fish and meat are important from a nutritional point of view, many cultures and individuals have perfectly healthy diets without all these elements. Until recently, meat was a luxury in this country too. In the lifetime of many now elderly people, the Sunday roast was cooked in the local bakehouse, because many families did not have an oven. Yorkshire pudding, eaten before the meat to fill the hungry mouths – 'Who eats most pudding will have most meat' – was cooked underneath the joint to catch the juices. Weekday recipes made use of the leftovers.

From this perspective, our present diet can be seen as an unfortunate blip in history. The affluence of the West has enabled us to eat as if every day is Sunday, and to make the mistake of thinking that the recipes for high days and holidays from around the world are for eating every day. Add to this the technology for preserving food (frozen meals, five minutes from carrier bag to table via microwave), the obvious attractions of convenience food (crisps, chips, sweet puddings, busy mum) and a less active lifestyle, and we have a recipe for an unfit, unhealthy population.

The upside of this is that we have choice. If we have lost the balance in the traditional diet of the UK, the diets of many people who have come to this country more recently offer models of how to change the balance – as well as lots of delicious recipes.

Assignment 19 in *A Practical Approach to Caring* (Pitman Publishing, 1991) by Kate Williams considers the elements of a good diet in some detail.

TASK 1:
Good food

The advice on what constitutes a healthy diet is now widely agreed. Sometimes it is expressed in terms of particular foods to eat more or less of, and sometimes it is expressed as guiding principles:

Checklist for a balanced diet

The 8 guidelines:
- enjoy your food
- eat a variety of different foods
- eat the right amount to be a healthy weight
- eat plenty of foods rich in starch and fibre
- don't eat too much fat
- don't eat sugary foods too often
- look after the vitamins and minerals in your food
- if you drink, keep within sensible limits

(Source: *Healthy Eating*, Food Sense Series published by MAFF. Crown Copyright 1991)

Study the two menus for nursery children below.

Menu A

Monday	Fish cakes Mashed potatoes Baked beans	Rice pudding Tinned fruit salad
Tuesday	Roast potatoes Sweetcorn Sausages	Apple crumble Custard
Wednesday	Roast beef Boiled potatoes Mixed diced vegetables	Iced sponge Custard
Thursday	Beefburgers Peas Chips	Fruit yoghurt
Friday	Fish fingers Mashed potato Tinned ravioli	Instant whip Fruit sponge

---

Menu B

Monday	Lasagne (vegetable) Lettuce and tomato salad	Yoghurt and banana
Tuesday	Fish pie Carrots	Baked apples (with sultanas) Custard
Wednesday	Macaroni cheese Broccoli	Fresh fruit salad Yoghurt
Thursday	Chicken casserole (West Indian) Rice and peas	Fresh fruit
Friday	Leek and bacon quiche Rice salad (with diced peppers etc.)	Rhubarb crumble (wholewheat) Ice cream

220

1 How well does each meal in each menu score for the 'healthy eating' points in the checklist – variety, fresh fruit and vegetables, starch and fibre, fat, sugar?

2 Identify the elements of each meal that are likely to be from a tin, or be bought in ready prepared. Does this make the food less healthy?

3 Identify dishes that originally came to the UK from countries around the world.

4 Identify traditional British food, and say whether you think it is healthy or unhealthy.

5 Identify any dishes you think are too fiddly to be practical.

6 Identify the meals where alternative food should be offered to children who do not eat meat, and from particular religious groups (see p 223). Suggest alternatives.

7 Draw up a healthy, tasty, attractive and practical week's menu for a school or nursery. To keep it simple, follow this pattern, rather than a cafeteria style. You may take elements but not whole meals from these menus if you wish.

TASK 2:
'Eat it up, it's good for you'

Has this approach *ever* worked?

1 In groups, list the rules about eating, 'encouragements' to eat, the points about the presentation of food served in a group setting (school, canteen, hospital) that most put you off eating. Aim for at least ten.

2 Make a list of about ten points that you think would make food and meal times attractive and encourage children in your care to eat healthier foods.

What is a family?
Courtesy: John Birdsall
Photography

3 Make a list of at least ten reasons why a child may not want to eat. What would you do about each one?

4 Identify the key messages you would like to convey to people responsible for planning menus and supervising children's meals.

**TASK 3:
A training
session**

Imagine you are responsible for an hour's training session with a group of cooks and lunchtime supervisors. Draw up a detailed plan for how you would structure the hour to get across your key messages (from Task 2). Design and draw up any handouts you would like them to take away.

**TASK 4:
Dietary
customs**

Many people have beliefs or views which determine the foods they eat. Some people take the view that it is wrong to eat meat (vegetarians), a few also avoid all foods deriving from animals (vegans). Food is an integral part of many religions and cultures; Jewish people, for example, only eat 'kosher' meat, from animals which were sent instantly unconscious at slaughter, the carcasses then being salted and steeped in water to remove all blood. To Hindus, the cow is a sacred animal and must never be eaten, but some Hindus eat other meats. Sikhs consider the pig to be 'unclean' and so pork is never eaten. Particular foods are part of many festivals – the traditional Christmas dinner is one of many.

Facing is a chart which summarises the food laws of some of the world's religions.

1 Research the diet and foods of one religious or cultural group. Include at least one ordinary weekday recipe, and one special recipe. You may wish to link this with your research on religions in Assignment 1.

2 Note down three countries from which the families of children in your area have come. Find out what the major religion(s) is (are) in those countries. Look back at your proposed menu for the week in Task 1. For which meals would you need to offer an alternative for children from these cultures? What would you offer?

3 For which meals would you have to offer an alternative for vegetarian children? What would you offer?

4 Present your revised menu, with your alternatives as options. Collate the group's menus.

5 Find out who is responsible for catering for either nurseries or schools in your area. Write to this person; explain the work you have undertaken on diet and cultural eating patterns and ask if he or she would be interested in receiving a copy of the group's work.

Note to tutor: Make sure only one agreed version gets sent!

A SUMMARY GUIDE TO THE FOOD LAWS OF SOME OF THE WORLD'S RELIGIONS

Please note that religions and culture are always changing, and individuals will adhere to none, some or all of the food laws according to their personal beliefs. What is important is that a food choice is available, which allows individuals to follow their beliefs.

Food	Buddhist	Christian	Hindu	Jewish	Muslim	Sikh
Eggs	some people	yes	some people (1)	yes but not with blood spots	yes not not with blood spots (2)	yes
Dairy foods: milk, butter	yes	yes	yes	yes	yes	yes
cheese	yes	yes	not if made with rennet (2)	not if made with rennet (3)	not if made with rennet (2)	yes
Chicken	no	some people do not eat any meat except fish during Lent and some people will eat only fish on Fridays	some people	kosher	halal	yes but not if it is kosher or halal
Lamb	no		no (2)	kosher	halal	
Beef	no		no	kosher	halal	no (2)
Pork	no		rarely/no	no	no	no
Fish	some people	yes	some people (with fins and scales)	with fins, scales and a backbone	with fins, scales and a backbone	some types
Shell-fish	no	yes	some people	no	some people	some types
Animal fat (4)	no	yes	rarely/no	no	halal	rarely/no
Margarine	no (5)	yes	some people	kosher	halal or kosher	some people
Alcohol	no	some people	no/rarely	yes – using kosher wine	no	yes
Tea/Coffee	yes	yes	yes	yes	yes	no
Nuts, pulses, vegetables	yes	yes	yes	yes	yes	yes
Fruit	yes	yes	yes	yes	yes	yes
Fasting	some people	some people	some people	yes – during Yom Kippur	yes – during Ramadan	some people

Notes (1) Strict Hindus do not eat eggs. (2) Some people may. (3) Orthodox Jewish people do not have milk dishes with meat dishes or within three hours of eating meat. (4) This refers to lard and suet and excludes dairy products. (5) Some people may eat it regularly.

Source: Appendix 5 in Sara E Hill, More Than Rice and Peas. Guidelines to improve food provision for black and ethnic minorities in Britain, published by the Food Commission, 1990

TASK 5:
Special diets

Some health conditions require special diets. These are known as 'therapeutic diets'. The person is not ill, but needs a special diet without which they would become ill.

I   Below is some advice for people working with a diabetic child:

AT SCHOOL

Children with diabetes are faced with challenges and problems in daily life that require special care and understanding. However, the child with diabetes does not want or need to be singled out. He or she can participate in all activities and can be expected to do what every other child can do. With a little attention to some simple guidelines and a little knowledge, no one should be anxious about taking care of such a child at school.

It is important for teachers, nurses, lunch-room personnel, playground and hall supervisors to be notified that a student has diabetes. A special diet, regular meals and snack times, and the possibility of an insulin reaction must be taken into account by all supervisory personnel who are in contact with the diabetic child. It is also advisable for teachers to meet with the parents of a child with diabetes.

In general, if a diabetic child is under your supervision:

- Watch his or her performance just before meal times.
- Do not assign physical exercise just before lunch.
- Help the child to eat the mid-morning (and possibly mid-afternoon) snack as inconspicuously as possible.
- Keep sugar readily available, and encourage the youngster to carry some form of sugar with him or her at all times – diabetic children soon learn to recognise and treat their own insulin reactions.
- Make sure that extra nourishment (carbohydrates) is taken before planned strenuous exercise to avoid a reaction.
- Any child suspected of being 'in reaction' must always remain in the company of an adult. Following an insulin reaction, do not send the child home alone.

(Source: *Your Child has Diabetes*, published by The Diabetes Foundation)

(a)   Does a diabetic child need to be treated differently to other children?
(b)   What precautions should responsible adults regularly take with diabetic children?
(c)   At what times should responsible adults be extra careful?
(d)   Find out what an 'insulin reaction' is. What signs do responsible adults need to watch out for?
(e)   Here are some other terms associated with diabetes. Find out what they mean and what responsible adults should watch out for: blood sugar level; hypoglycaemia; coma.

People with diabetes need to control calorie and carbohydrate intake. a diabetic child will have a diet sheet provided by the hospital, and the parents will be knowledgeable about what the child can eat, likes and dislikes. The child will probably know a lot too. Adults responsible for a child with diabetes should have an understanding of the principles behind the diet.

INTRODUCTION

Diet is a very important part of the treatment of diabetes. The aim is to try and control blood sugar levels to within normal limits and to prevent long-term complications of the diabetes.

The main aims of the diet are:

1 Eat regular meals.
   Distribute your food evenly through the day.
   Do not miss meals.

2 Control your weight.
   Your ideal body weight is . . . . kg.

3 Cut out sugary foods.
   Control the amount of total carbohydrate.
   Use artificial sweetener, e.g. saccharine, instead of sugar.

4 Include high fibre carbohydrate foods as part of your diet.

5 Eat moderate amounts of protein, e.g. meat, fish, cheese and eggs.
   Decrease your fat intake.

(Source: *The Diabetic Diet*, published by the Diabetes Foundation)

2 Find out the reason for each of the five pieces of advice above. Copy out the five points and show the reasons beside them.

TASK 6: Research

There are other conditions requiring a therapeutic diet. Find out what some of these are and research **one** condition. Include:

- a brief description of the condition, signs and symptoms;
- recommended diet, eating pattern and foods to avoid;
- key points for care workers to look out for;
- action to take in an emergency.

Present your research in a suitable format for a quick reference source for child care workers.

Assignment 17

Setting up a crèche

The tasks below are designed to bring together in a single practical assignment many of the strands of day care organisation explored in this book. The best outcome would, of course, be for the group to set up a half-term or holiday crèche or play scheme.

A definition:

'A crèche is a place where young children are cared for so that their parents/carers may take part in another activity on the same premises or at least within call.'

(Source: *Running a creche*, published by the PPA)

TASK 1: Who needs a crèche?

In this task you are asked to carry out a survey using a questionnaire to find out what the demand for a crèche in a number of different settings might be. You might consider a crèche in a:

- college, ongoing, term time only;
- college, half terms;
- sports centre, for particular sessions;
- all day conference or event (one off);
- workplace, ongoing;
- workplace, half terms and school holidays;
- any other?

1   As a whole group, decide which of these you think there may be a demand for.
2   Study the advice on the wording of questions below. Take it in turns to explain the reasons for the advice given in bold and the differences between the 'Don't ask' and the 'Do ask' questions. (Further advice on drawing up questionnaires can be found in *A Practical Approach to Caring* (Pitman, 1991), p. 279, by the same author.
3   Draw up the questions you need to establish the demand for a crèche.
4   Try out your draft questionnaire on members of the other small groups. This is your *pilot*. Make any changes necessary before you design, type and print your questionnaire.
5   Decide as a group how you will carry out your questionnaire; size of

Courtesy: G A Clark ARPS

sample, who your target group(s) are; how to reach them; timescale and how and when you will collate your results.

6 And get going . . .

DRAWING UP A SURVEY FORM

WORDING
Stick to short direct questions.
Ask only one question at a time. Use straightforward language. Avoid ambiguous words.
Make sure that your questions are perfectly clear.

eg: 'Have you got a car?' could mean, 'Are you a car owning household?' or 'Have you (as an individual) got your own car?'

DON'T ASK	
Have you got a car?	Yes/No
DO ASK	
How many cars in your household?	. . . . . .
Have you got the use of a car?	Yes/No
Have you got a car which is permanently available for your own use?	Yes/No

---

▶

227

Avoid imprecise words like 'often' or 'regularly'.
eg: 'Do you use your local bus service regularly?' could be answered 'Yes' but the 'Yes' might mean, 'Yes, to go to work every day', 'Yes, to go shopping every week' or even 'Yes, to visit Gran every month'.

DON'T ASK
Do you use your local bus service regularly?   Yes/No

DO ASK
Do you use your local bus service

    at least once per day? ☐
    at least once per week? ☐
    at least once per month? ☐
    less than any of the above? ☐
    never? ☐

Don't oversimplify questions in order to save space as you may not get the precise information that you require.

DON'T ASK
Has your child ever been in hospital?   Yes/No
How satisfied were you with the facilities?   Very/Fairly/Not at all

DO ASK
Has your child ever been an in-patient in hospital?   Yes/No
How satisfied were you with
  the nursing care   Very/Fairly/Not at all
  the welcome for parents   Very/Fairly/Not at all
  the facilities for parents to stay?   Very/Fairly/Not at all
  the play provision for patients?   Very/Fairly/Not at all
Has your child attended an out-patient clinic?   Yes/No
How satisfied were you with
  the appointment system?   Very/Fairly/Not at all
  the toilet facilities?   Very/Fairly/Not at all
  the provision of refreshments?   Very/Fairly/Not at all
  the play facilities?   Very/Fairly/Not at all

Avoid overlapping categories.

18–20   18–20
20–30 should be 21–30
30–40   31–40

LAYOUT
Leave plenty of space for answers. Use boxes and ticks wherever possible.

e.g. Who handles publications in your branch?
     Publications Officer? ☐
     Branch Fieldworker? ☐
     Chair/sec/treasurer? ☐
     Other ....
     (please write in)

Start with the easiest and most interesting questions. Leave the difficult ones to the end. Keep the questionnaire brief. Don't ask unnecessary questions.

Source: *So you want to do a survey?*, published by the PPA

TASK 2:
Your plans and
the law

1 In small groups, work through your first thoughts on how you want your crèche to run. Consider: Who is it for? Ages of children? When will it run? How many sessions? Hours? Sources of funding? Possible rooms/space? Who will staff it? Make a note of the details you agree. Present your ideas to the rest of the group, and agree a single plan. Write a letter outlining your plans and asking permission to the person/body whose agreement you need to run the crèche.

2 Below is an extract from *The Children Act 1989 Guidance and Regulations*. Read it and work out the implications of this for your proposed crèche.

OCCASIONAL DAY CARE FACILITIES

7.30. Paragraph 5 of Schedule 9 provides for day care facilities which are used on less than six days in a year to be exempt from the registration requirement. This exemption is intended to cover day care facilities set up for conferences and other occasional events. In all cases, before using the premises to provide day care for the first time, the organiser has to notify the relevant local authority that a day care facility is being provided. He should give information about its location, the numbers and age range of the children, numbers of staff and opening hours. Local authorities should keep a record of such notifications. It is unnecessary to visit the premises on each occasion but this should be done from time to time so that local authorities may satisfy themselves about the suitability of the premises. Where different organisations use the same premises, the six days apply in respect of each organisation not in respect of the premises.

Time limit

7.31. Section 71(2) states that registration is required where the day care provider or childminder is offering a service for children aged under 8 for a period or total periods of *more than 2 hours in a day*. This applies irrespective of the time spent in a day care or supervised activity or with a childminder by an individual child. Therefore facilities such as day nurseries and crèches in shopping centres, or leisure centres or colleges which are open throughout the day *are registrable*, even though individual children are likely to attend for less than 2 hours.

(Source: *The Children Act 1989 Guidance and Regulations Vol. 2*
Family Support, Day Care and Educational Provision for Young Children, HMSO, 1991)

(a) Will your crèche be run on less than six days a year? Why is this important?

(b) Do you have to contact the local authority if it is run on less than six days?

(c) What is the difference in the nature of your contact with the local authority if your crèche runs on less than six days a year or six days and over?

(d) What information do you have to give the local authority?

(e) Is the local authority obliged to visit your crèche?

(f)   Why does it matter whether your crèche runs for more or less than two hours per day?

TASK 3: Are you insured?

Crèches, even if they only look after two or three children for less than an hour, need insurance. The points below need discussion and action:

- Why is it important to have insurance? What might be the consequences if your crèche is not covered by an insurance policy?
- Get hold of a copy of the insurance policy that covers the building or institution in which you plan to run your crèche. Read it carefully to see if the crèche would be covered.
- If you think it is, write a letter to the insurers to ask for written confirmation that you would be insured.
- If you are not covered, contact an insurance company such as the Sun Alliance and ask for written details of their scheme.

TASK 4: Space for a crèche

1   Make a scale drawing, on squared paper, of the room/space you intend to use for your crèche. Work out the approximate area of the space.
2   Refer to the Standards Checklist given in Case Study 3, p 82. Calculate the approximate number of children you can accommodate.
3   Read the following advice from the PPA:

Premises

The size of the premises limits the number of children you can take. Unless you have unlimited space and helpers, you will need to arrange some form of pre-booking system in order to avoid having to turn people away.

The following should be carefully checked to ensure safety and a good quality experience for the children:

- Heating – heaters must have guards
- Floor surfaces – should be free of splinters and be clean
- Electrical sockets – should be covered
- Low level glass – should be safety glass or covered with boarding or guards
- Sharp corners on heavy low level furniture – should be padded
- Fire exits – must be left accessible and unlocked
- Adults must know the Fire Drill

A separate area should be available for babies and toddlers.

Hygiene – toilets should be clean and within easy reach of the crèche area. Check that the water supply to the basins is not dangerously hot.

Find out what kitchen facilities are available. If there is no fridge available for storing babies' bottles, you may need to bring a cold box.

Comfort – a warm, light and welcoming atmosphere with rugs and cushions on the floor will help to lessen the impact of an unfamiliar room.

Access – is it easy for prams and pushchairs to get to the premises? Are there stairs to negotiate? If so, is there a safety gate? Are there parking facilities?

Storage – if the crèche is a regular one, it would be a help to store some equipment on the premises.

(Source: *Running a crèche*, published by the PPA)

Use these guidelines as a practical checklist for your premises, and inspect the room/space carefully to ensure that it meets these criteria. Identify any changes that you think will have to be made.

TASK 5: Staffing

1 Refer again to the Standards Checklist in Case Study 3, p 82, to work out how many staff you will need, their qualifications and experience. Then draw up a **person specification** for the person responsible for running the crèche (coordinator), following the procedure on p 280.

2 Draw up a **job description** for the coordinator.

3 Devise the wording of a small advertisement for the post, suitable for publication in an appropriate in-house newsletter or local newspaper. You may wish to design the ad if you have access to a suitable IT package.

Note: Check out your institution's practices on advertising posts such as this, taking into account equal opportunities policies.

4 You will also need other staff.
   (a) Who will you aim to recruit as additional workers?
   (b) What qualities and qualifications will you be looking for?
   (c) Will you be able to use volunteers?

TASK 6: Equipment and activities

Use material elsewhere in this book to help you with this task.

1 Refer to the headings under 'equipment' in the Standards Checklist in Case Study 3, p 82. List the essentials you must have. Find out exactly what is required if this summary leaves you in doubt.

2 By now you should know:
   - the age range of the children to be cared for;
   - numbers of children;
   - room(s) available;
   - funding and budget available to start up;
   - how many hours/days children will be cared for.

   Keeping it to a minimum list the essentials for **furniture, general equipment, play equipment**, and **materials**.

3 Find out what you can get free – does your institution have paper and card you can use? an old cupboard or typewriter? bins? cleaning materials?

Can you make use of a playgroup's equipment? If you are running at half term, a nearby playgroup might be closed ... When you have this information, cost your list of remaining essential items as accurately as you can, using catalogues or local suppliers.

TASK 7:
Shock tactics!

The total you came up with is bound to come as a shock to whoever gave you permission to set up the crèche. Write a memo to this person, to accompany your (well presented) list of required items, explaining your choices and justifying the cost. (For advice on memo layout, see *A Practical Approach to Caring* (Pitman Publishing, 1991), p. 274, by Kate Williams.)

TASK 8:
Advertising and marketing

How will you let people know that the crèche will be running? How will you encourage them to take up your provision?

1   In groups draw up a strategy to advertise your crèche. Pool your ideas with the whole group. Then divide up the tasks between the group.
2   One element of your strategy will be to produce a publicity leaflet. Design your leaflet, giving details of the creche and include a booking form so you know numbers in advance.
3   You will also be able to use the booking form to gain the essential details you will be required to record about each child. (*See* Assignment 13, Task 3, for a list of these.)

TASK 9:
Into action

And finally ...
   Draw up a plan of action, counting down to the day the crèche starts. Identify all the **tasks** that need doing, **who** is to carry each forward, and **deadlines**.
   It may be helpful, if your crèche is to become a regular feature, to devise a way of getting feedback from all concerned with the crèche – this may include other employees or users of your building as well as parents, children and staff of the crèche. These can be the basis for a report reviewing the scheme.

   Good luck!

Assignment 18

In the playground

In this assignment you are asked to think about what is involved in being a playground supervisor. The focus is on older primary children, but many of the issues will apply to working with older and younger pupils.

TASK 1:
Know your
space

Overleaf is a plan of a primary school. Work with a partner.

1   Which areas of the school, inside and out, do you think children should be allowed to be in during the lunch hour in (a) good weather, (b) wet weather? You may wish to mark this in colour code on a copy of the map.

2   There are normally three supervisors on duty in the juniors in a lunch hour. To ensure that they have a full picture of the children's activities in the lunch hour, where do you think the staff should be and what should they do? Mark on the plan areas and activities you think might need particular attention.

3   Draw a simplified plan of the school on a large sheet of paper. Each pair should focus on a particular circumstance: wet day, very cold day, good weather, all staff present, one member of staff short. Outline to the group your plan for supervising the lunch hour.

4   Draw a plan of a school you know, primary or secondary, showing areas to which pupils have access during the lunch hour. Identify the areas you think might present the supervisors with problems.

TASK 2:
Setting
standards

1   With a partner, role play the following situations. Take it in turns to be the supervisor and the pupil.

   ● There is a commotion – shouting and fighting – in one corner of the playground. A group of children is forming around several flailing figures. The supervisor goes over to sort it out.
   ● Several pupils run down the corridor – not allowed in the school – past the supervisor. The swing door swings back and catches the supervisor.
   ● The supervisor finds two pupils in a classroom quietly using a computer. They say they have permission. The supervisor is sure they do not.
   ● As the last pupil leaves a lunch table, the supervisor notices that

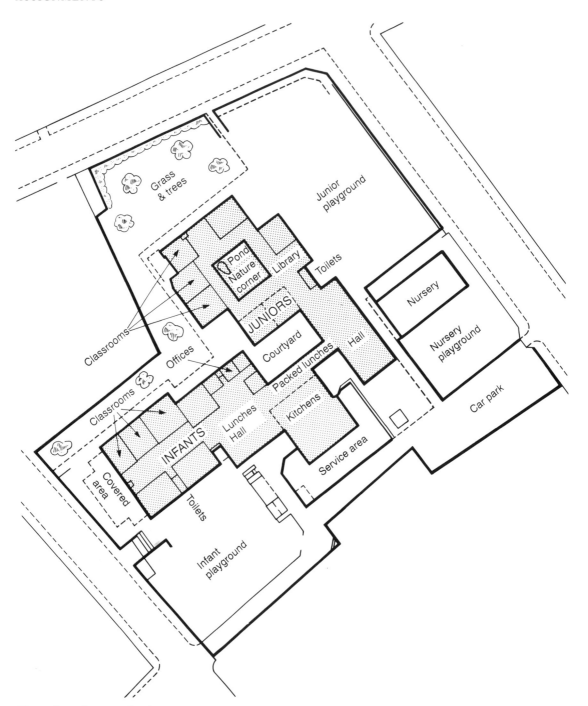

Plan of a primary school

several crisp packets have been left on the table and on the floor around it. The supervisor asks the pupil to clear them away.

- On a cold day the supervisor finds a group of pupils messing about noisily near the toilets. She asks them to go outside. Their response is surly and they swear at her under their breath.

2 **Never lose your temper.** For one experienced playground supervisor, this is the Number 1 rule

   With your partner, review the situations above and make a note of when you found yourselves getting angry, either as a pupil or as the supervisor. Compare your experiences with others in your group. Identify what it was that made you angry. Re-run the situations in which you got angry and **change the supervisor's responses** to reduce her own and the pupil's anger.

TASK 3: Golden rules

Listed below are some DOs and DON'Ts for you to consider. Rules, however, make much more sense if you know the reasons for them. Work out the reasons for each rule. You may make changes or add some suggestions of your own. Finally, present your rules and reasons as a poster suitable for display in the supervisors' room.

- DON'T ever lose your temper.
- DO give pupils the chance to take back what they said or apologise.
- DON'T shout at pupils.
- DO be polite even when you are feeling furious.
- DON'T threaten disciplinary action too soon.
- DO find out the facts before you jump to conclusions.
- DON'T touch an angry child.
- DO avoid being drawn into an argument.
- DON'T make sarcastic remarks.
- DO treat each pupil fairly.

Courtesy: John Birdsall Photography

- DON'T show favouritism or dislike.
- DO take a child to one side if you need to tell them off or to offer a listening ear.

**TASK 4:
Lunch hour
activities**

In some schools pupils have a number of lunchtime activities and clubs to take part in. Where this happens, the supervisor's job is made easier – there are fewer pupils to supervise and boredom is less of a problem. In other schools, there are few organised activities. What simple steps can staff take to encourage a range of activities?

1 You have noticed that the junior playground in Task 1 is dominated by older boys playing football at all break times. This does not allow younger children to play nor does it allow space for children to play other games. You also feel it encourages an aggressive attitude on the part of the dominant group. What could the school do about this? Discuss the options and agree a single plan of action.

2 Below are some games and activities played in schools and youth groups. Decide which you think would be worth trying in:

(a) an infant playground (age 5–7);

(b) a junior playground (age 7–11, or age groups within this).

*A word about
games*

'You can't teach kids to read before they're ready;

And you can't teach kids to compete before they're ready.

Children can't learn to compete before they learn to cooperate.'

Make it More Fun

■ Play simple games with simple rules! ■ Keep active! ■ De-emphasize scoring; use different kinds of scoring. ■ Spend more time playing than explaining or disciplining. ■ Give short, clear, simple instructions.

The 'Traditional' Version:

'Okay everybody, we're going to play dodge ball. Now listen up. Jerry and Janice will be captains and they'll pick two teams . . . (10 minutes later) Are we nearly ready? Right, Leanne you take Shaheen and Josh, you take Adrian. (Groans) And now we're already to play. Adrian, you get the ball; hurry now; and Josh's team will be in. Throw the ball, Adrian and try to hit someone. Shaheen, you're supposed to try and *dodge* the ball. Okay, you're out; go sit on the red line . . .'

The 'Fair Play' Version:

'Okay everybody, we're going to play dodge ball. Number off, '1, 2, 1, 2 . . .' 1s on the south side and 2s on the north side. Here are the three balls. Remember, if you get hit by a ball from the other team you switch sides. Everybody ready? Let's go.'

Safety Tip: Balls must be thrown below waist level.

TABLE TENNIS PASS Needs table tennis table, ball and two bats. In two lines, one at each end. First player hits the ball, puts the bat down and goes to back of line. Other side hits it back and does the same. Second person has to return it and so on.

ONE AT A TIME TAG Pick half a dozen safe bases. Only one person can hold/occupy this at a time. When someone else wants to use the safe place, original occupier must move to another base, avoiding the catcher.

PEBBLE DASH Usable in small groups. Stand in a line and hold out hands, palms together leaving small hole in top.

Secretly drop a small stone into someone's hand. On a command the person with the pebble has to get to a home base without being caught.

VOLLEY BALL A variation is for every member of the team to touch the ball at least once before it goes back over the net.

CHAIN TAG Normal tag but as players are caught, they hold hand of catcher. Eventually you get a long chain – chain can split into twos, threes, or fours. In the long chain version, fugitives can only be caught by two ends so are able to try and break through the middle.

Cat and Rat (West Indies)

Players again stand in a circle, holding hands and moving round. One player, the *rat*, is in the centre, and another player, the *cat*, is outside. The cat must try to break through the moving circle to capture the rat. Again, players in the circle must try to prevent the cat from entering, without letting go of their hands, but this time they may help the rat to dodge in and out of the circle in his efforts to avoid the cat.

Tin Can Football (Ghana)

For this game 20 empty tins are needed; baked bean size is ideal. Yoghourt or cream cartons are also suitable. Remove the labels from half the tins, and leave them on the rest, or colour half the cartons, making two teams of 10 players each. Goalposts can be made from 4 more tins, or from 4 sticks fixed in the ground. A football pitch is scratched on the ground, and each player arranges his team as he wishes; after this the tins are not moved. Two empty sardine cans may be laid on their sides between the goalposts to act as goalkeepers.

The first player starts by flicking the ball – a pebble, bean or marble – between thumb and forefinger towards his opponent's goal. If the ball hits one of his own players, he flicks again; if it hits one of his opponent's players, his opponent flicks next, and so on. Football rules apply for corners, offside, etc. The winner is the highest goal scorer.

Taken from: *Fair Play for Kids*, Commission for Fair Play Canada; *The Great Play Times Kit*, produced by the National Playing Fields Association; *Games Children Play*, collected by Susan Adams for John Adams Toys Limited, Wargrave, Berks

3   Think up, or find out, at least *three* additional activities for each age group, and present your suggestions in booklet form, for easy reference for staff. Be sure to include rules, and a list of essential materials or equipment where these are needed.

TASK 5: What do you do?

In each of the following situations decide what, if anything, the supervisor should do.

I   Ricky's mum has always taken him home for lunch. Now in the 2nd year juniors he has started to stay at school for the lunch hour.

2   Mandy appears much younger than other girls in her class. She wears old-fashioned clothes and seems to like helping – tidying up, running errands. She doesn't seem to have friends.

3   A bubbly little girl, who always seemed to have lots of friends, was cheery and friendly with the supervisors, Florrie in particular, but became tearful and quiet. Florrie took her aside and she admitted being beaten at home.

4   A group of girls teased Shiraz. They made her run errands, giving messages to older children. This brought her thumps from both older boys and girls. You noticed this.

5   You think Yvette is spoilt. She wants everything first, she's noisy and pushy, and wants to be the centre of attention. She constantly comes to you with complaints about other children.

Assignment 19

No bullies in this school

There is a belief among adults that if bullies are ignored they will stop bullying; others think that bullying is an inevitable phase of childhood that will pass without their intervention. Still others think that all children must learn to 'stand up for themselves', so that adult intervention to protect victims of bullies would merely inhibit a valuable social lesson. The material presented here throws serious doubts on these beliefs . . .

(Valerie Howarth, in the Introduction to *Bullying, the Child's View*, an analysis of telephone calls to ChildLine)

TASK 1:
What is
bullying?

1   Do you think 'bullying' is the right word for each of the following situations?

   (a)   Some boys laugh at Laura because she wears buckle shoes not trainers. She is upset.

   (b)   Jessica's best friend, Cleo, has become best friends with Mia, and a group of girls who hang around with her. These girls tease Jessica and won't play with her. Cleo does not say anything.

   (c)   Older boys pick on first-year junior boys new to the playground. Two trip them up, and a third thumps or kicks the child after he has fallen.

   (d)   A child moves to a different part of the country. Other children mimic his/her accent.

   (e)   A boy with a reputation for being 'hard' tells Duane, who was allocated the place next to him by the teacher, that no possession or school book of his must ever pass the mid line of their table. Duane makes sure nothing ever does.

   (f)   Mina does not dare go to the toilet at school, because a group of girls who hang around there make her feel uncomfortable.

   (g)   Kevin lives in the same street as Philip. They get on quite well and used to visit each other's houses. At school, Philip has become wary of Kevin. Sometimes he's nice; sometimes he joins the gang, and won't look at Philip or play with him. Philip gets the odd thump and elbow from these boys.

   (h)   Matthew, aged 4, tells his mother that some kids in the nursery bullied him when they kept knocking down his building. They wanted the bricks for their own construction.

   (i)   When David and his friends play football, an older boy asks if he can join them. They always agree, although they'd like to say no. He kicks the ball hard at them, kicks it out of play across the playground, and always spoils the game. Now they stop playing when they see him approach.

2   Working in small groups, agree a definition or description of what bullying is. Compare your definition with that of other groups. Draft a version the whole group can agree on.

3   What do you think each of the following should do about situations (a)–(i) above? You may wish to divide the situations between small working groups:
   (a)   the child;
   (b)   the parent;
   (c)   the supervisor (where relevant);
   (d)   the teacher;
   (e)   the school as a whole.
   Identify one problem each of these would have in taking action.

TASK 2: ChildLine

Below is a table analysing calls made to ChildLine's 'Bullying Line' in the spring of 1990.

Types of bullying reported by gender of victim

Behaviour	Girls affected % (n=1,156)	Boys affected % (n=483)
1. Teasing:		
picked on for no reason	19	20
called names/unspecific	6	5
called names/physical differences	14	19
personal problems	7	5
Total teasing	46	49
2. Disturbances in relationships		
ex-friends calling names	10	3
rivalry for friends	8	3
pressure to conform	3	3
Total peer problems	21	9
3. Physical assault	22	31
4. Extortion/theft	12	9

(Adapted from Jean La Fontaine, *Bullying, The Child's View*, published by Calouste/Gulbenkian Foundation)

1   Draw two pie charts, using these figures, to show the pattern of bullying reported by (a) girls and (b) boys. Use appropriate colouring or shading to show the four major categories.

2   Comment on what your charts show. Note the numbers in each case. What are the main findings? Does anything stand out? Does anything surprise you?

TASK 3:
Bullying at this
school?

To do this task, you need to work with a group of school children, preferably within school. If this is not possible, you may be able to agree another way of surveying a group of children. Aim for a reasonably large sample of 100 or more. (For advice on drawing up questionnaires refer to the index and see *A Practical Approach to Caring* (Pitman, 1991), p. 279, by the same author.)

Draw up a questionnaire designed to find out about children's experiences of bullying. First decide what you want to find out, then work out the wording of the 10–12 questions. Areas to include: whether they have been bullied – details of when, where, in what way, who by; effects of bullying; what should be done about bullying; attitudes to bullies; some personal details.

TASK 4:
Report back

1   Compile the results of your survey. You may find it easier to make sense of the results if the group divides into pairs, each analysing the replies to one or two questions. Present your findings as effectively as you can – as tables of figures, or in chart form. If you have access to a computer, you may wish to use it.

2   Write a short formal report on bullying in school. (For how to write a report see *A Practical Approach to Caring* (Pitman 1991), p. 281, by the same author.)

(a)   Your **Terms of Reference** are '... to find out about children's experiences of bullying in ... (school or area)' as in 1 above.

(b   Under **Procedure** describe how you set about finding out.

(c)   You have already compiled your **Findings** in 2 above. Incorporate these here.

(d)   What **Conclusions** can you draw?

(e)   What **Recommendations** do you feel you can make?

TASK 5:
Tackling
bullying

1   **What can an individual child do?** The chart 'Are you being bullied?' overleaf shows a thinking process a child who feels bullied might work through, preferably with an adult, to minimise their chances of being bullied.

Work through it with a partner. Make any alterations or additional suggestions you think might be helpful. Redraw it to include your suggestions.

2   **What can the whole school do?** Study the Code of Conduct below:

CONTRACT
1.   We will not tolerate bullying or harrassing of any kind.
2.   We will be tolerant of others regardless of race, religion, culture or disabilities.
3.   We will not pass by if we see anyone being bullied – we will either try to stop it or go for help.
4.   We will not allow bullying or harrassing going to or from school, either on the school bus or public transport or walking.

241

ARE YOU BEING BULLIED?

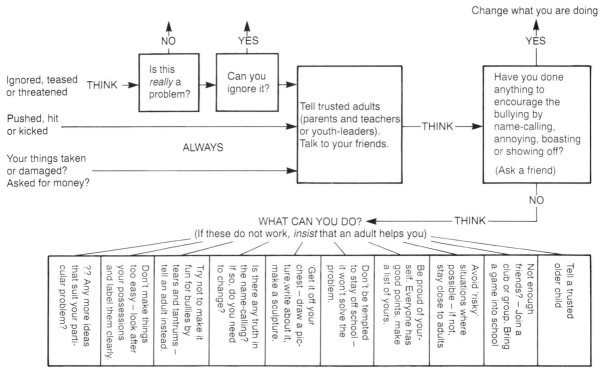

A Higgins and S Priest 1988

Source: Erling Roland and Elaine Munthe (eds), *Bullying, An International Perspective*, David Fulton Publishers, 1989

5. We will allow a quiet area in the playground for those who do not want to run around or be in games.

6. We will use our 'time out' room if we feel angry, or under pressure or just need time to calm down or work out what is wrong.

7. We will not litter or draw on school property (walls, toilets, books, etc.).

8. We will be kind to others, even if they are not our friends and will make new students feel welcome.

9. On school journeys we will act in a way which brings credit to our school.

10. We will have a discussion group once a week in class to talk about any problems that are bothering us.

11. We will be honest when asked about anything that we have done or are supposed to have done.

12. We will co-operate with and abide by the findings of the school court.

(Source: Michelle Elliott, *A Whole-School Approach to Bullying*, Longman, 1991)

242

(a) In small groups work through the Code of Conduct to decide which points you would want to keep in a policy for your school. Make any changes or additions you think necessary. Compare your points and wording with other groups, and finalise a version the whole group can agree on.

(b) **Principles into practice.** Your task here is to identify what the school as a whole and staff, students and parents need to do to implement these principles.

   As a group, complete the action plan for the first principle, shown below.

Principle   **Action plan**

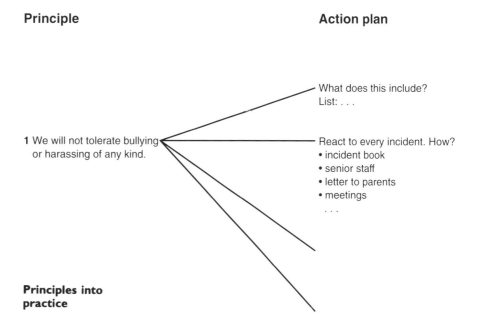

1 We will not tolerate bullying or harassing of any kind.

What does this include?
List: . . .

React to every incident. How?
• incident book
• senior staff
• letter to parents
• meetings
   . . .

Principles into practice

Divide the rest of the principles between the group, working in pairs. Take a whole sheet of paper for each principle. Write the principle on the left of the page and the 'action plan' on the right. Under this heading, list the actions that need to be taken to implement the principle.

TASK 6:
A whole school
policy

Make sure you have copies of all the action plans. Go through them, making changes to avoid duplication and omissions. You now have the basis for writing a complete whole-school policy for dealing with bullying.

Either

1 Draft and design a booklet, suitable for distribution to pupils, parents, all staff and visitors to the school, showing your principles and action plan.

or

2 Design a poster, suitable for display in and around the school, giving a clear anti-bullying message.

Assignment 20

Dis/Ability

TASK 1:
A busy life

Tanni Grey, a politics graduate from Loughborough University, won four gold medals in the 100, 200, 400 and 800 metres at the 1992 Paralympic Games in Barcelona. This was all the more remarkable since, as with Olympic events, athletes increasingly tend to specialise in particular events – yet she won over sprint as well as middle distance.

Judy Watson is Head of the English Department at a school in Ashford, Kent. She had some sight as a child, and finally lost her sight when she was 21.

> Kids forget that I can smell chewing gum in their mouths and that crisps make a tremendous noise. In my lessons, I always ask that everyone sits in the same place and it is easy to identify who is tapping a pen or talking when they shouldn't be.
>
> I use Braille books in the classroom and plan lessons, mark work and complete various administrative tasks with the help of readers. Whilst at college and in the early years of my career, my readers were volunteers but now the training agency gives me money to pay someone. It's much better this way. My present reader is called Ruth and she comes to my home in the evenings at seven o'clock so that she can read to me. When we are doing marking, she reads out the work and corrects spelling and punctuation, then she tells me what it was she had to correct and I tell her what mark and comment to write at the bottom.
>
> Having successfully passed my teaching course, I started work in September 1974 at the Sheppey School in Kent, a mixed comprehensive school of 1800 pupils. I was very happy there even though I found it hard work. Teaching requires a great deal of energy and everyone finds it exhausting, particularly when they are new to it. I used to get fed up with working all day and then coming home to readers and having to work every evening as well. I still have to do that and still get fed up with it at times, but most teachers work in the evenings so it isn't that unusual.

Source: Richard Reiser and Micheline Mason, *Disability Equality in the Classroom: A Human Rights Issue*, available from 78 Mildmay Grove, London N1 4PJ

1   Below are points from 'Good manners towards people who are blind or partially blind', p 195 from *'Disability Equality in the Classroom: A Human Rights Issue'* by Richard Reiser and Micheline Mason. Nineteen points are listed but the explanations and exmaples have been omitted. Your task is to add these in one or two sentences to support each point. Work with a partner or in small groups.

245

1. Notice who they are.
2. Introduce yourself *by name* before starting a conversation.
3. Say a blind person's name when you are starting a conversation.
4. Speak before touching someone.
5. Be ready to describe things to give basic information.
6. Don't move off without telling the person 'I'm going now'.
7. Do not avoid the words see, look, etc.
8. Ask a blind person if they need help **before** giving it.
9. Tell a person where a chair or bed or whatever is, and put their hand on the chairback.
10. Some blind people like to have food arranged on a plate like a clock.
11. Allow blind people, particularly young children, to touch things and get in a mess.
12. Allow blind people, particularly young children, to touch you.
13. If anything is changed in an environment that a person with little or no sight uses regularly, tell the person.
14. Warn a blind person about possible dangers in a new environment.
15. Remember that blind people and people with little sight are excluded from all information given in printed form.
16. Don't pat or distract a guide dog while he or she has her harness on.
17. Move out of the way of a person feeling their way along by use of a long cane.
18. Don't make assumptions about what a blind or partially sighted person can or can't do.
19. Explain to a blind child (or adult) any special needs of other children or adults with whom he or she may come into contact.

When you have completed your explanations, you may like to compare them with those given in the original. This excellent folder of materials on disability by people with disabilities is an essential resource for work in this area.

2   How accessible is your workplace? Go round the premises in which you work and the local streets in small groups with one group member using a wheelchair. Draw a plan or diagram of your route and mark in all the obstacles to access. Note the attitudes of people you encounter. (Specific itineraries and points to consider are suggested on p. 96 of *A Practical Approach to Caring* (Pitman Publishing, 1991) by Kate Williams. If you need to borrow a wheelchair from a hospital or day centre you need to arrange this well in advance.)

3   Write a set of 'Good manners' towards people with physical disabilities, equivalent to the 'Good Manners' in 1 above.

**TASK 2:
Different
abilities**

Note to the tutor: For this task you need copies of a quick crossword from a newspaper in 1 and to anticipate materials required for 2.

1   Working on your own, see how long you take to complete the crossword. Agree a maximum time before you start – five minutes?

What is a family?
Courtesy: G A Clark ARPS

Review

The purpose of this activity is to consider how our particular abilities – or lack of them – show in relation to a standard task. How quickly did each person complete the crossword? How did you feel about doing the task?

2   Find out what specialist skills members of the group have. Each person must identify one skill they have, and describe it to the group.

Ask those group members with skills that could be demonstrated in the room to demonstrate their skills and to teach them to others in small

247

groups. Stick with it, helping where necessary, until you are satisfied that everyone in your group is competent.

Write a clear set of instructions to enable a new learner to do the skill you have just taught (or learnt). Anticipate the difficulties they may have.

Review

How easy did you find it to learn a new skill? Were you concerned that other people seemed to find it easier/harder than you did? Have you learnt anything that would make you a better teacher for someone who found it harder than you did?

3   List the specialist skills held by different group members on the left of your page. On the right give yourself a mark between 1 and 10 for how good you think you are at this skill. You may wish to see what others think of your marking – you are more likely to undervalue your abilities than to overvalue them! Then write a concluding paragraph 'Different abilities' in which you consider how you view the lines between ability, less ability and disability.

**TASK 3:
Can do**

1   Divide your page into three columns, headed 'Can do well', 'Can just do', 'Cannot do' and enter the following in the appropriate column:

- Draw using a computer.
- Ride a bike.
- Swim 20 lengths.
- Put on socks.
- Operate a video.
- Explain how a hoover works.
- Place knives and forks correctly on a table.
- Read in braille.
- Spread butter/margarine on bread.
- Drive a car.
- Get dressed unaided.
- Cook and decorate a birthday cake.
- Turn pages accurately.
- Climb a ladder and paint guttering.
- Draw a circle.
- Recite multiplication tables.
- Explain why it rains.
- Do up buttons.
- Operate a hoover.
- Take a person's blood pressure.

Add a brief explanation as to why you cannot do those things you have listed in your 'Cannot do' column.

2   Mark with an asterisk (*) those activities you would expect a child of
    3 to be able to do. What explanation would you give for why you would
    not expect a child of 3 to be able to do those activities not asterisked?

3   (a)   What can a child do? Observe a child – with or without a disability
          – and make ten statements about what this child can do. Do not
          include unconscious activities (breathing, sleeping, etc.) but include
          skills you think represent an achievement for the child.
    (b)   What is the child still learning to do? Try and identify ten actions
          or activities you think the child is trying to achieve. What difficulties
          is the child trying to overcome?
    (c)   How does this process of identifying skills and difficulties in learning
          relate to working with children with disabilities?

TASK 4:
What's the
problem?

1   What is cerebral palsy? Find out some of the causes and effects of cerebral
    palsy and the disabilities a child with cerebral palsy may experience. Start
    with library research. Find the addresses of voluntary and self-help groups
    locally and nationally; within the group agree on no more than one person
    to write or phone each group to ask for information.

2   Read the following extract about the difficulties a child with cerebral palsy
    may have in dressing and, after discussion, answer the questions that follow:

We have only to watch a normal baby being dressed and undressed to
realise how a mother chatters spontaneously to him and how, even before
he can talk, he babbles in response. Many cerebral palsied children are
unable to respond even in this way and in time it is easy for a mother not
to bother to talk to her child and to dress him in silence.

A normal child also has the advantage of being able to ask questions when
he is puzzled; to learn by trial and error; to make use of and build up on
previous experiences, and to ask for help immediately he requires it. Yet
it still takes about five years before he is almost independent. One can
appreciate that the cerebral palsied child, with his many and varying
difficulties, cannot be proficient in his dressing and undressing unless he
is helped in all his problems.

As we dress the cerebral palsied child we can help him to get to know
and feel the various parts of his body, naming them as we do so. We can
explain that his socks go on his feet and why; that his jersey goes over his
head, and so on. We can point out the various openings in his clothes,
relating clothes to the parts of the body: for example, the head through
the neck opening; the arms through the sleeves. We can help him to relate
such phrases as 'push your foot into your shoe', 'pull your arm out of your
sleeve', as we perform the movement and, if he is beginning to talk, he
should be asked to say the words at the same time as he does the actions.
Later on colour can be included in the conversation, comparing the colour
of his clothes with other things around him. This can be followed, when
he has reached the stage of understanding such things, by showing him
which is the top and bottom, which is the right side and the left, which

the inside and which the outside. In this way he will not only be learning how to dress himself but also accumulating knowledge which he can use in other activities.

It is important, when finding out the difficulties the cerebral palsied child has when he starts to co-operate and take over his own dressing or undressing, that we try to understand *all* the problems involved, not merely those of manipulation.

Parents should understand why a child is unable to put on his socks. Perhaps he cannot distinguish the tops from the toes, or see the openings, or understand what is being asked of him. He may be unable to bend his hips sufficiently to enable him to bring his arms forward to reach his feet, or cannot bend one leg at a time, and his mother's attempts to bend his knee may result in his hips becoming straight, making him either fall backwards or, in some cases, collapse forwards. He may not be able to grasp when his arms are straight out in front of him, or to hold his socks and, at the same time, to pull them up; or he may drop the sock when he turns his head to look at his hand. His balance may not be secure enough in sitting, and he has to drop whatever he is holding to use one or both hands for support. These and many more problems may prevent him from putting on his socks – i.e. not one difficulty but a number of difficulties interacting on each other. We must analyse his problems carefully and help him with them before we can expect him to be independent.

(Source: Nancy R. Finnie, *Handling the young cerebral palsied child at home*, Heinemann Medical, 1968)

(a) What advantages do most children have over a child with cerebral palsy in learning to dress?

(b) What strategies for helping the child with cerebral palsy to dress are suggested in paragraph three? How do these suggestions help with other aspects of the child's development?

(c) What point is being made in paragraph four?

(d) Towards the end of this passage the author concludes that difficulties in putting on socks may be caused by '... not one difficulty but a number of difficulties interacting on each other.' What are these difficulties?

3 Extend your research into cerebral palsy to consider the problems a child with cerebral palsy may have with one of the following:

- gross motor movements (rolling, sitting, crawling, walking);
- feeding;
- manipulation (fine motor movements) as in bead threading, building, sticking, drawing/writing, etc.;
- communication.

Give detailed consideration to what the 'difficulties interacting with each other' might be and strategies to help the child overcome them. Consider how you can divide the areas between group members. You may also wish to include a consideration of different therapeutic approaches – of Bobath and Peto, for example.

TASK 5:
Language and
communication

1 How do we communicate? Brainstorm the different ways in which we convey meaning:

- face to face;
- in a foreign country;
- in silence;
- in the dark;
- to convey pictures in the mind;
- on paper;
- to convey emotion.

2 Below are some symbols of a non-verbal language, mostly Rebus. Children without speech can point to a symbol to communicate.

solution

swimming

book

food

telephone

supper

quiet

give

(a) Consider the symbols and discuss how appropriate and effective you think they are. Would you suggest any changes?

(b) Devise another ten symbols you think would be useful to a child of five. Ensure you have a spread of things, activities and qualities – concrete nouns, abstract nouns, verbs, adjectives and adverbs.

3 Find out more about *one* other language: braille, Makaton (or similar system), sign language, standard manual alphabet, signed number system. Get a copy of the language basics and try to learn to communicate some simple needs. Try it out on someone else learning the same language.

**TASK 6:
Images of
disability**

1   Below are three logos used by Mencap. At the top is the 'little Stephen' logo used until 1992; below are two of five images adopted in 1992.

MENCAP

mencap

making the most of life

mencap

making the most of life

Reproduced by kind
permission of Mencap

Discuss the differences between the old and new images.
(a)   What characteristics in a person with a mental handicap are suggested by (*i*) the 'little Stephen' image, and (*ii*) the 1992 images?
(b)   What emotions do (*i*) the 'little Stephen' image, and (*ii*) the 1992 images appeal to?
(c)   Comment on the effect of the typeface used in each image.
(d)   How do you think the following respond to the images:

   • people with learning difficulties?
   • the general public?
   • people likely to give money to Mencap?

2   Read the article below, and after discussion, answer the questions that follow:

No person is an island, entire of themselves. Apart from disabled people. Alone, single, on the hoardings of the traffic-islands, roadways and train-stations of this country. In black-and-white, grim realist Charities advertising shows The Truth. The 'andicapped Need Yo! Why else would charities portray disabled people in Black-and-White, when all else, the beautiful people of Coke and Benetton, are in Colour? The Creatures Time

Forgot, these products of tired, needy welfarism, need you – like a hole in the head!

But those images are not just myths, they are constructions too. The great constructions sites in our cities are not those inaccessible buildings but are those charities hoardings which construct lies. The photo-montaged hyper-reality sells a product, 'The Disabled' not so much to buy but to buy your distance from! Appearing now, Aliens From Inner Space!

But they are constructions. Not only does the content work against the long-term integration of disabled people into society on our own terms, the process itself works on a deeper level of oppression. The next time you pass one, take a closer look. Look at the Multiple Sclerosis posters of the woman with a ripped-paper back. Look at how warm and softly brown this Black-and-White poster is. Of course it is, because the Warm Thing (women in advertising) is being violated. Your hopes are being violated because, as you would think if you believed Charities advertising, disability is seen, and sold, as violence. Two oppressions, women, disabilities, or both, for the price of one! Look at the Spastics Society's offerings. Attitude Change they call them (middle-class fund-raising). Look at the picture of the wheelchair-using man as he reaches for the lift-buttons. Again, take a closer look. Look at the process that this image has been put through. It is really two images montaged together; the torso of the man onto the wheelchair. Look at the acute sharpness of the chair (particularly the wheels) and look at the blurry, soot-and-chalk retouching on the figure, the systematic exclusion of human detail, the slovenly, unkempt look of the wheelchair user. The message is clear – the wheelchair is more important, and more intelligent, than he is. Even in the liberal attitude-change poster, disabled people have to be seen to be dependent.

Dependency, of course, within the dynamics of the lives of disabled people, is supposed to mean stupidity and a burden. Within the work that I have done for this exhibition, this is clearly nonsense. But in trying to construct positive, empowering, campaigning imagery to fight against the negative campaigns against disabled people, I have tried to explore both the politics of the issue (and letting people speak for themselves) as well as the process of representation. The method and the morals are equally important.

David Hevey, Photographer.

From 'Beyond the Barriers: Disability, Sexuality and Personal Relationships' A Camerawork Touring Exhibition. 081-980 6256

(Source: Richard Reiser and Micheline Mason, *Disability Equality in the Classroom: A Human Rights Issue*, available from 78 Mildmay Grove, London N1 4PJ)

(a)   Explain the point David Hevey is making in paragraph 2.

(b)   What are the author's criticisms of the multiple sclerosis posters? Do you agree?

(c)   Explain David Hevey's criticisms of the Spastics Society posters with a wheelchair. Do you agree?

(d)   What do you think the author means by 'the politics of the issue' (last paragraph)?

3 Collect advertisements from newspapers for charities for children and other people with disabilities. Write an analysis of how one works on the paper's readership. Consider the overall impact, the typeface, wording, the picture/logo, strategies for encouraging contributions, the image of need or disability. Conclude with a comment about how effective you think the ad is and its impact on the three groups of people in 1 (*d*) above.

**TASK 7:
Campaign for
Real People**

This is the name of a campaign by the National Union of Journalists (NUJ) to promote equality of opportunity for all. Read the extract below from the leaflet *It's about disability*.

At least one in ten of the population has a severe disability. Most of us will have a temporary or permanent disability at some time in our lives.

- People with disabilities include those with physical, mental, sensory, learning and speech difficulties. Sometimes the disability is not recognisable. People with disabilities should not therefore be seen as a homogenous group.
- People with disabilities are not 'the problem' – it is society that handicaps people by its environments and attitudes. So how do the media contribute to the misrepresentation?

Invisible and marginalised

- The media tend to assume that their audience are able-bodied. If people with disabilities are seen at all, the focus is on the disability, even when the disability is irrelevant.
- Issues important to people with disabilities are often not seen as newsworthy, and are marginalised into specialist publications or programmes.
- News about disability is most often represented by able-bodied 'experts'. People with disabilities are the real experts on their own lives. The organised collective voice of people with disabilities is rarely consulted.

Stereotyped

Stereotypes are insulting and can be damaging. The most common of those which purport to describe people with disabilities are:
courageous – pathetic – helpless – tragic victim – recipient of charity – eternally cheerful – grateful – 'abnormal' – constantly searching for a cure or miracle aids – asexual. It is rarely acknowledged that they may also be black, lesbian or gay.

Stereotypes distort reality. They perpetuate false notions of 'normality', emphasising the difference between 'them' and 'us'. They lead people to fear that disability inevitably means a tragic end to a life of fulfilment. They focus on the personal aspects of disability that can be relieved by charity rather than the political and economic changes required to end discrimination.

Language

Language used to refer to disability is often inaccurate and offensive.

- People with disabilities are people first – 'the disabled' focuses only on the disability. Do not use words like 'cripple', 'deaf and dumb', 'abnormal'.
- Use the correct term for the disability, e.g. Down's Syndrome, not Mongol; cerebral palsy, not spastic. Misuse of language is unprofessional.
- Words associated with disability are frequently used perjoratively, e.g. lame duck, blind stupidity, deaf to reason. Avoid such usage.

Access

- Blind, partially-sighted and deaf people's right to information is hampered by the lack of materials on tape, in large print and braille, and sub-titles and signing on television.
- Complete access details should be given when publicising events.
- People with disabilities rarely get the opportunity to work in the media. Yet no-one can represent people with disabilities better than they themselves.

  The media has both created and perpetuated the negative representation of people with disabilities which has led to discrimination against them. It must now work towards showing the real picture and redressing the balance.
- Include more positive and varied images of people with disabilities, even when disability is not the focus.
- Responsible journalism demands accurate representation – contact representative groups.
- Avoid sensationalism which exploits individuals.
- Any audience will include people with disabilities – reflect their concerns too.

(All members of the NUJ are bound by the Code of Conduct which is part of the Union's rule book. Clause 10 says: 'A journalist shall only mention a person's race, colour, creed, illegitimacy, marital status (or lack of it;), gender, sexual orientation or disability if this information is strictly relevant. A journalist shall neither originate nor process material which encourages discrimination on any of the above-mentioned grounds.')

(Source: *It's about Disability . . .*, Campaign for Real People, Equality Council, NUJ)

Your task is to rewrite this extract to angle precisely the points made in the leaflet at people in your profession or occupation – people working with children, some of whom will have disabilities obvious or hidden. Use the same headings and feel free to use points and wording from the NUJ leaflet, but make enough changes, adding and changing examples to make the message crystal clear to your target audience.

Type and produce your leaflet, and, with your tutor, consider how you can give your leaflet wider circulation.

And finally

Stephen Wiltshire was 11 when he was shown drawing London buildings on the BBC's QED programme 'The Foolish Wise Ones' on the effects of autism. In the book of his drawings published afterwards, Sir Hugh Casson writes:

> Happily, every now and then, a rocket of young talent explodes and continues to shower us with its sparks. Stephen Wiltshire – who was born with severe speech difficulties – is one of those rockets. A natural gift for drawing was unearthed by his teachers and nourished until it became not so much the medium as the message itself – a passionate and personal form of communication.

(Reproduced courtesy of J.M. Dent & Sons Ltd 1987)

Drawing by Stephen Wiltshire
(© Stephen Wiltshire 1987)

S is for St Paul's Cathedral

Assignment 21

A sporting chance

This pie chart shows how children spend their time:

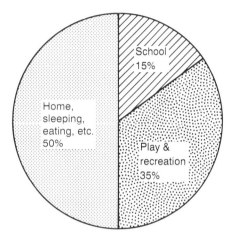

In the course of a year, the average 10 year old has about 35% of his or her time potentially free for play and recreation – twice as much as the time spent at school each year. Where and how children play is therefore an important issue.

('Make way for children's play', Playboard, 1985)

1 Does anything surprise you about this chart?
2 Do a double check, based either on the schedule of a child you know or can arrange to interview or on memories of yourself at about 10. How many hours does the child spend doing what? You may wish to show more specific categories (e.g. watching TV, eating, sport, sleeping, etc. shown separately). Do one analysis for term time and one for holidays.

   Draw two pie charts to show your findings, and then write two paragraphs, one in which you compare term time with holidays, and one in which you compare your findings with the pie chart above.
3 One holiday play scheme (PATCH, in Bradford) surveyed the children (aged 5–12) who attended and found that the hours in a child's day averaged out as follows: sleep, 11 hours; play scheme, 7.9 hours; home 5.1 hours.

   Draw a pie chart to illustrate these figures, and comment on the significance to providers of out-of-school and holiday play schemes.

What is a family?
Courtesy: John Birdsall
Photography

TASK 2:
Where do
children play?

Opposite are the results of a survey into where children play. The children were aged 9–16 from Rhyl, a seaside town in North Wales.

Imagine you are the author of this research and report. Your terms of reference were 'To find out where children play and the extent to which current provision in the area meets children's needs for play and recreation'. Write a formal investigative report using the information opposite as your findings. Pay particular attention to the conclusions you draw and make specific recommendations.

TASK 3:
Local options

What are the sport and leisure options in your area for children of school age? As a whole group brainstorm the options and divide up the research between you.

Be detailed – 'park' may include a playground, fishing, clubs, and open access (or booked) coaching, as well as opportunities for informal play. Find out the timetable of activities at the local leisure centre(s) and swimming pool(s).

Make sure you can supply the following information (where applicable):

Activity (e.g. football coaching)
Venue (e.g. Clissold Park)
Time/day (e.g. Saturdays 10 a.m.–12 noon)
Cost (e.g. £1)
Contact
Address

Tel.

Findings

General Summary

In response to the question "Where do you play when not in school" the following general details emerged.

All children were asked to indicate whether they played in the listed places, Regularly, Sometimes or Never; for the purpose of this summary we amalgamated all responses from all age groups.

All Children

	Regularly/ Sometimes	Never
a. In the house	62%	38%
b. In the garden	11.8%	60.3%
c. Outside in view of the house	44.8%	55.2%
d. Nearby streets	56.1%	43.9%
e. Friend's house	72.9%	27.1%
f. Play centre	18%	82%
g. Sports/leisure centre	71.7%	38.3%
h. Adventure playground	13.6%	86.4%
i. Youth centre	35.2%	64.8%
j. Local playground	20.2%	79.8%
k. Other places	76.4%	23.6%

Other places a high proportion of children used "other places" regularly in favour of conventional provision. Places which were highlighted frequently included:

i) Amusement Arcades
   (very high on the list)
ii Night/Social Club
   (older girls and boys)

Question 10 "What do you like about the playground?"

Note We received 664 answers to this question. Many children gave more than one answer, however, it is worth noting that 395 (59.5%) said they "didn't like anything about the playground".

There was no list for children to refer to in this question, they simply had to identify what they considered to be a favourite aspect of the playground. The following is therefore their list made up of things they said.

All children

		%
a.	Don't like anything	59.5
b.	Swings	8.7
c.	Interesting	6
d.	Plenty of space	5.4
e.	Tennis courts	4.3
f.	Socialising/meeting friends	4
g.	Facilities	2.7
h.	Football pitch	2.2
i.	Climbing frame	2.2
j.	Roundabout	1.3
k.	Barrels	1
l.	Seesaw	.8
m.	Slide	.7
n.	Flowers	.5
o.	Assault course	.4
p.	Close by	.3

Question 11 "What don't you like about the playground?"

Note 624 responses were recorded and it is highly probable that a number of children gave more than one answer. As in question 10, no pre-made list was used, the children's responses were therefore un-prompted.

All children

		%
a.	Boring	34.8%
b.	Dislike everything	17.6%
c.	Childish	14
d.	Dog dirt	4.3
e.	Unsafe	4.2
f.	Dirtiness	3.9
g.	Vandalism	3.2
h.	Bullying/intimidation	2.7
i.	Being moved on	2.5
j.	Old equipment	2.5
k.	No separate areas for older children	2
l.	Broken glass	1.3
m.	Lack of facilities	1.2
n.	Too crowded	1.2
o.	Bars	1
p.	Other - no sand grass too high slide swings climbing frame junkies no litter bins toadstools	3.6

Source: Tony Chilton, *Where Can Children Play? A study into out-of-school play provision and play characteristics of children living in Rhyl, North Wales*, on behalf of the Rhyl Adventure Playground Association, published by Rhyl Community Agency, 1989

TASK 4:
Database

1 In the whole group, agree the method you will use to organise and store the information. Consider the pros and cons of:

- a directory;
- a card index;
- a computer-held database;
- any other ... annotated map?

Choose the method and format you think will best meet your needs – it must be available to you as of now. Consider also the benefits of cross referencing, listing by venue. So the example above would be one activity (with times/day, costs, etc.) listed under 'Clissold Park'. Others would include fishing (note closed season dates) roller blades/sucker ball (e.g. Sunday morning, by the bandstand, free), tennis coaching (e.g. Sunday morning, pre-booked).

Then get storing ...

2 Test your system. In pairs, take turns to be the inquirer and the responder. If you can use an internal phone link, so much the better. As the inquirer, decide on information you would like, and ask questions until you have all the information you would need in order to turn up in the right place at the right time with the right equipment ... As the responder, locate the information, pass it on, and be prepared for questions. If you find gaps in your information, review and complete it.

TASK 5:
Have a go!

This is where you, with a partner, set off to try an activity you have always fancied doing but never got round to – and write a report on it! Plan your trip – a real check on your database. Where appropriate:

- phone to check details – times, days, booking, kit, cost etc;
- find out how to get there, bus routes, etc.;
- make notes for your report. Decide in advance what points to cover: impressions (age and upkeep of buildings); opening hours (are they convenient?); facilities (what's on offer? showers? coffee bar?). Is it user-friendly? How does it cater for the whole community? Can wheelchair users get to the cafe? Is it good value? Did you enjoy your session? Will you go back?

You may decide to organise a sheet to prompt you on your visit, or to note your impressions and organise them afterwards. Make sure you have the essential information.

TASK 6:
A holiday play scheme

1 Opposite is a holiday play scheme programme. Discuss it in small groups or with a partner and within an agreed time limit give your views as to how good it is. Consider – Is it varied? Is there a balance between different activities? Between trips and centre-based activities? Are children 5–8

Holiday Playscheme

SUMMER '87 PROGRAMME

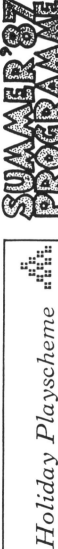

	Week 1	Week 2	Week 3	Week 4	Week 5	Week 6	Week 7
Mon		Mon 27 Jul — Clay Models / Papiermaché Masks / Rounders (Sch. Playing Field)	Mon 3 Aug — Mural Painting / Rounders	Mon 10 Aug — Outing by Minibus to SEA LIFE (Southsea) 08.45 Start, Packed Lunch & Bathers, Return 16:30 [COST £3·25]	Mon 17 Aug — Outing by Minibus to PAULTON'S PARK 09·50 Start, Packed Lunch, Return 16:30 [COST £3·50]	Mon 24 Aug — Outing by Minibus to SANDBANKS 09·00 Start, Packed Lunch & Bathers, Return 16:30 [COST £1·00]	Mon 31 Aug — SCHEME CLOSED FOR BANK HOLIDAY
Tue		Tue 28 Jul — Cricket in the Park / Painting & Woodwork	Tue 4 Aug — Cookery / Unusual Nature Finds (with Prize)	Tue 11 Aug — Food Pictures / Play-dough Models	Tue 18 Aug — Rounders (Sch. Playing Field) / String Pictures	Tue 25 Aug — Wool & String Pictures / To the Park	Tue 1 Sep — Sorting-out & Packing-up / To the Park
Wed		Wed 29 Jul — All-day Outing MAYFLOWER PARK, Packed Lunch 09·30 Start – 16:00 [COST £0·50]	Wed 5 Aug — All-day Outing SPORTS CENTRE, Packed Lunch 09·30 Start – 16:00 [COST £1·50]	Wed 12 Aug — Finger-painting / Games (Sch. Playing Field)	Wed 19 Aug — Cookery / Book-marks & Woodwork	Wed 26 Aug — Tooth-pick Pictures / Swimming (Oaklands) [COST £0·50]	Wed 2 Sep — All round to JENNY'S STATELY ROMSEY HOME (No admission charges!) Packed Lunch [COST £0·75]
Thu	Thu 23 Jul — Paper Folding & Painting / To the Park	Thu 30 Jul — Swimming (Oaklands) [COST £0·50] / Races in the Park	Thu 6 Aug — Craft Activities / Swimming (Oaklands) [COST £0·50]	Thu 13 Aug — Park & Swings / Paper Folding	Thu 20 Aug — Paper Folding & Badge Making / Team Games & Big Fun-ball	Thu 27 Aug — Nature Walk for Stones then painting 'em / Games (Sch. Playing Field)	
Fri	Fri 24 Jul — Treasure Hunt / Sewing & Model Making	Fri 31 Jul — Painting Clay Models & Sticky Pictures / Nature Walk	Fri 7 Aug — Cricket in the Park / Team Games (Sch. Playing Field)	Fri 14 Aug — Bubble & Blow Pictures / Clay Pots	Fri 21 Aug — Keep Fit / Play-dough	Fri 28 Aug — To the Park / Keep Fit	

WE HAVE LIFT-OFF!! 3····▷2····▷1

BACK TO SKOOL!

Source: Running a Holiday Playscheme. A Manager's Guide, published by the Cabinet Office, Equal Opportunities Division. Crown copyright

and 9–12 equally well catered for? Would you have liked to do it/like your kids to?

2 With your partner/group, draw up a possible holiday play scheme programme for your area, and present it like the example overleaf.

Note to tutor: This activity could be extended to include detailed work on setting up a play scheme, locations, costings, record keeping, recruitment, etc. *See* Assignment 17.

**TASK 7:
Stranger
danger**

1 As children gain independence and go places on their own, they need to know how to deal with approaches by strangers. Below is a simple strategy for encouraging young children to say no to strangers:

SAY 'NO!' WITH TOM AND JOANNE

(Child and adult to speak alternate lines.)

If someone offers you a treat.
Say 'NO!'

If someone wants you to keep secrets:
Say 'NO!'

If someone asks you into their house:
Say 'NO!'

If someone offers to take you home from school:
Say 'NO!'

If you get lost and someone asks you to go with them:
Say 'NO!'

If someone tries to touch you:
Say 'NO!'

If someone offers you a lift:
Say 'NO!'

If someone says they'll buy you something:
Say 'NO!'

If you're not sure, don't say 'yes':
Say 'NO!'

BE STRONG!   BE CLEVER!   BE CAREFUL!   BE SAFE!

Source: D Pithers and S Greene, *We Can Say No. A Child's Guide*, published by the NCH, 1986

With a partner or in small groups discuss:
(a) What you think the stranger dangers might be in the programme you suggested in Task 6.

    (b)   What strategies playworkers might adopt to encourage older children to recognise, avoid and report frightening or unwelcome approaches by adults.

    (c)   Playworkers also need to be aware of the experiences children bring with them to play schemes, to recognise these, and to know what to do if abuse is suspected. Look at the material in Assignment 7 and see how this might be relevant to playworkers.

3   Present your ideas as a quick-reference 'Guidelines' for out-of-school and holiday playworkers.

Assignment 22

Going solo

TASK 1:
Leaving home

1 Devise a questionnaire designed to find out:

- at what age people left home;
- how much contact people have/had with their families after they 'left home'.

You could take a small sample – the members of your group, for example – or a larger sample – each person in the group asks ten people.

Design your questionnaire, type it up, print it, and pilot it before you carry out the survey. (See index for surveys and questionnaires. *A Practical Approach to Caring* (Pitman Publishing, 1991), pp 279–80, by Kate Williams gives further advice.)

2 Present your findings in chart form with written comments.

TASK 2:
Leaving care

Read the extracts on pp 265–6 on the experiences of young people leaving local authority accommodation.

Under the Children Act (s. 24) local authorities have a duty to 'advise, assist and befriend' young people in preparation for leaving and after they have left local authority accommodation.

1 In groups, discuss the situations and problems shown by the extracts. Agree a policy for the age at which you think young people should leave and the support they should receive, comparing it with the support other people get. Draw up a practical programme for preparing young people for independence.

2 Present this as a well argued set of proposals. Use each proposal as a heading, and give your reasons in a paragraph below.

TASK 3:
Starting out

Work with a partner.

1 Imagine you are moving into a furnished bedsit. It has a bed, table, two chairs, an easy chair, gas cooker, sink, kitchen cupboard/work surface, two well used saucepans, four odd plates and a collection of odd bits of cutlery, a two-bar electric fire, grotty carpet and curtains. Make a list of the items you would need if you were to move into this bedsit. When you have your list, rework it into 'essential' and 'desirable'.

Only 1 in 5 authorities had a telephone helpline

77% paid cash to care leavers

Several authorities said their attempts to set up independent living units had been frustrated by opposition from local residents. Even where independent living training has been established, social workers have found that it cannot prepare young people for the dire poverty they will face trying to support themselves on a youth training allowance or lower benefit rate paid to under-25s.

"How able were you to do all the cooking, cleaning, washing, ironing, budgeting, pay bills, be responsible for a tenancy, live with maximum parental support of two hours per week, know how to claim benefits and know how to use the NHS system?" And they add: "Who at this age was even interested in all this?"

This question was put to a small group of youngsters who had either moved out into the community or were preparing to do so. The answer to the question was an unsurprising "no". Even for a well balanced young person, the sudden assumption of all these necessary, if unexciting, responsibilities would be crushing. Yet, as Bob Foster, assistant centre manager at Parklands, a social services-run residential centre in Gloucestershire, points out, a number of youngsters in care are anything but. "We are talking about a group of youngsters who are increasingly more damaged and disturbed and dependent than most and who are leaving care without any specific qualifications and a poor history in education," he says. "Yet, our society and social workers traditionally have high expectations of what these youngsters can achieve at the age of 16. It's quite unrealistic."

I FEEL SO LONELY
I've just left care after being with foster parents for the last year. I've got a nice flat and some money to do it up. But I feel very lonely and can't seem to make any friends. I don't like to keep going round to the foster parents all the time. Please can you help?
DARREN (18) Manchester

One London authority had no leaving care scheme, no advice service, no key workers, no independent living units, no grants to voluntary organisations and no support to former foster carers

No wonder that so many of these young people end up as casualties. As Bill Grieve in Edinburgh says, too many non-offending youngsters who go into care end up in custody, or as psychiatric admissions or statistics on the suicide files.

Loneliness and practical survival
Much of the moving was a result of loneliness in single person accommodation. By the end of the first year of the study all the young people wanted to leave single person accommodation despite its satisfactory physical standards. Feelings of loneliness and isolation were accentuated for those who were unemployed and had nowhere to go. The contrast between living alone and the communal life, particularly of residential care, where privacy and solitude are rarely available, was more than some young people could tolerate.

Indeed, using the nuclear family as the yardstick, some social workers in the field are even challenging the notion of achieving sudden independence for young people at all.

"We prefer to talk of encouraging 'appropriate dependency,'" Bill Grieve, principal officer with Save the Children in Edinburgh, remarks. "The whole business of expecting a 16- or 17-year-old in the space of a single year to become independent is a rather crazy concept."

And he adds pertinently: "The majority of people not in care don't leave home on average until they're about 23. We think this is very discriminatory. Why shouldn't we be offering long term support to those young people in the same way as others living in families enjoy?"

The fact that most people receive support from relatives throughout their lives is not irrelevant. "At the age of 43 I still have close family relations on whom I am dependent or have a relationship with."

75% of authorities used B+Bs

Sources: *Social Work Today*, 24 September 1992, 8 October 1992, 22 October 1992; *Who Cares?*; 'Leaving care', *Highlight*, NCB

43%
made no special provision for pregnant young women

Here is how Jon, a graduate of the Parklands Centre, articulated the need for the changes drawing upon his own experience.

"I had been in Parklands for around 10 months before I moved out into board and lodgings. The reason why I moved out was because I felt that Parklands wasn't geared to people of over 16 living in residential care. While I was in Cedar Unit (a long term unit) I was doing independence training, buying food, cooking and so on. But other aspects of being 'independent' were not catered for.

"Bedtimes and pick-ups were still at the same time for us as for everyone else. When most of my friends were not even thinking of going out until 9pm or later, it was difficult for me to hold down a reasonable social life.

"Another problem was the fact that a lot of staff don't really take a lot of notice of what you say. They are asking you to be 'independent' and an 'adult' by doing more things yourself yet they treat you and your views as if you were a child."

Homelessness

Surveys have consistently found that young people who have been in care are vastly over represented among samples of single homeless people. Recent studies by Centrepoint Soho show that the link between homelessness and leaving care persists. In 1987 23 per cent of young people referring themselves to the nightshelter had lived in children's homes, but in a repeat survey in 1989, the figure had risen to 41 per cent.

While some authorities give one-off payments ranging from a few hundred to up to £2,000, others make intermittent means-tested contributions which vary dramatically. Naypic feels a national policy of leaving care grants and a more integrated system of preparation for leaving care is essential.

The safety net that most young people get from their families for as long as they need it is what young care leavers lack — the knowledge that in a crisis, financial, emotional or even physical, there is a place they can go, and stay, for as long as they need.

66% of authorities have established supported lodgings

HOW WILL I MANAGE AFTER CARE?

I'm just coming up to leaving care and I feel scared, even though I look forward to my freedom. I don't seem to know much about money or how to get a place to live. My friends here feel the same. I don't often see my social worker – he's too busy.
SARAH (16) Hampshire

Sixty-nine per cent of authorities said they has preferential access to council flats for housing people leaving care, but this caters for only a fraction of the need. For example, one county with up to 250 over-16s leaving care each year had managed to negotiate nominations for care leavers with only one of the seven district housing authorities in the country – a total of three tenancies a year.

Bearing in mind the present high levels of youth unemployment, and the consequent demand by employers for higher educational qualifications, it is predictable that care leavers will have difficulty competing for jobs because their education has been frequently disrupted. Indeed being in care has been authoritatively described as an 'educational hazard'. One study of 135 care leavers found 75 per cent had no educational qualifications compared to an average of eleven per cent of all school leavers in the three authorities studied.

Then cost your list (from a catalogue or local shops), and total it.

2   On the food front, there is nothing but an empty cupboard in the bedsit. Draw up a list of essential cupboard items you would need to start out. Cost it.

3   As this is a subject actively under consideration by professionals at present, your local social services department might be interested in your views. Discuss with your tutor what you could do to share your proposals with them.

TASK 4: **Surviving on a budget**	Turn to p 23 and check the weekly rate of income support for a young person under 25. Assume that the 16–17 year old would qualify for benefit under the 'hardship' rules.

I   Find out the current rates of income support.

2   Out of this you have to pay for electricity, gas, food, clothes, travel, personal items.

Work out how much you would have to pay each week in gas and electricity in November, and how much you have left for other living expenses. You need to agree the assumptions that underpin your budgeting – are you basing the profile around yourself? Is the person at college/work during the day? or at home? (There are several practical exercises in budgeting and fuel costs in *A Practical Approach to Caring* (Pitman, 1991) by the same author.)

TASK 5: **Cooking in a bedsit**	(Assignments 19 and 20 in *A Practical Approach to Caring* (Pitman, 1991) by the same author explore many aspects of healthy eating, with lots of practical activities.)

I   In small groups, draw up a suggested menu for a week's food in a bedsit. Include breakfast and evening meal, and suggestions for snacks. Your suggestions must be cheap, easy to shop for, easy to cook, easy on the washing-up and reasonably healthy.

2   Pass your suggestions round the other groups for their comments. Take out any item that over half your group do not like. Negotiate this!

3   Examine the recipe overleaf. Does it meet the criteria in I?

4   Write out full instructions for how to cook the meals on your revised menu. Be precise about:

●   equipment;
●   quantities for one;
●   cooking times and methods.

5   Cost the shopping you would have had to do for this week's food, excluding items already in your cupboard from Task 3. 2 above.

Is this in line with the amount you had allowed for food in Task 3? If not, what will you do about it?

Simply take . . .

1 tablespoon olive oil
2 cloves garlic, crushed
375g (12oz) unsmoked rindless bacon, cut into strips
2 × 250g (8oz) packs fresh egg tagliatelle
142ml (5fl oz) carton double cream
25g (1oz) freshly grated parmesan cheese
1 jar green pesto
salt and freshly ground black pepper
fresh basil and pitted black olives to garnish

1. Heat the oil in a saucepan, add the garlic and bacon and cook over a medium heat for 5–6 minutes, stirring occasionally.
2. Meanwhile, cook the pasta, following the pack instructions.
3. Drain the pasta, add to the bacon mixture, and stir in the cream, pesto, cheese and seasoning to taste.
4. Cook for 1–2 minutes and transfer to a warmed serving dish. Garnish with the basil and olives and serve immediately.

Cooking time: Approximately 15 minutes
Serves: 4

There are lots of delicious alternative ingredients for this recipe:
- *Substitute dried egg and spinach tagliatelle instead of fresh.*
- *Use sunflower oil or extra virgin olive oil instead of olive oil.*
- *Substitute red pesto for green pesto.*
- *Use half the quantity of dried grated parmesan instead of fresh.*
- *Use crème fraîche, single cream or Greek style natural yogurt as an option to double cream.*
- *Add a few chopped mushrooms or salad onions.*
Wine suggestion: (2) JS Bianco di Custoza 75cl

(Source: Sainsbury's)

TASK 6: A cookery book

1 Come round to my place . . .
    Decide on a meal you would cook for another member of your group. Then 'invite' them round – for real if you want the excuse – and check their likes and dislikes. Make any changes necessary to your planned menu. Work out quantities for two (or three, or four . . .).
2 Gather all the suggestions for cooking in a bedsit in a single cookery book, attractively presented. Include only essentials: equipment, basic measurements, essential terms and language, and advice on healthy eating on a tight budget.

TASK 7:
Back at home

After you have left home — wherever your last home was — it can be hard to accept that life back at home goes on without you. Other people's lives change too, and so home changes.

Below are some changes at home that might happen while you are away. The list was drawn up from the perspective of a young person leaving care, but many points apply to us all.

You've been away in care and now you're . . .
Going Home

WHAT YOU MIGHT EXPECT TO BE THE SAME	WHAT MIGHT BE DIFFERENT
the flat or house	they could have moved house or
your room	redecorated or moved the furniture or
the people	given your room to someone else.
■ parents	■ parents could have split up there could be new step-parent(s)
■ brothers and sisters	■ step-brothers and sisters
■ grandparents	■ grandparents could have moved
■ the pets	■ pets might have died
■ neighbours	■ neighbours change
■ friends	■ friends could have gone or lost interest
■ your school	■ your school might not be able to have you back
■ your hobbies or sport	■ it may not be so easy to do them now
■ your favourite food or music	■ your family might not know what your tastes are now

---

(Source: *Who Cares?*, Issue 16, Summer 1991)

1 In groups, consider how you would feel if you found each of these changes when you went back home. What would help you feel better about it?
2 Working on your own, draw the diagram overleaf in relation to you and your family. Draw about eight houses, and write in each the members of your household at 3–5 year intervals (or a different time span by agreement). By each, allow space for those 'lost' to the household and those 'gained'. Circle the house where you found the changes most difficult.

You may wish to share your thoughts on the difficulties different members of the household might have experienced with the changes you have telescoped on the page.

Alternatively, you may wish to keep your thoughts to yourself. Depending on the time span taken, every family will have major changes

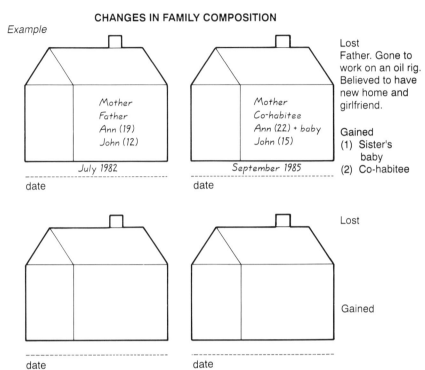

CHANGES IN FAMILY COMPOSITION

Example

Mother
Father
Ann (19)
John (12)

July 1982

date

Mother
Co-habitee
Ann (22) + baby
John (15)

September 1985

date

Lost
Father. Gone to
work on an oil rig.
Believed to have
new home and
girlfriend.

Gained
(1) Sister's
    baby
(2) Co-habitee

Lost

Gained

date

date

Adapted from Chart B,
*Decisions in Childcare: Recent
research findings and their
implications*, reproduced by
kind permission of HMSO.
Crown copyright 1985

in household composition to record as children grow up, move away, move back and move off, as parents grow old, and as crises come and go.

Change is stressful. A final activity might be to pool your group's tips on how to deal with stress in family relationships – and compile them under a DO and DON'T checklist.

Assignment 23

At work

In this assignment you are asked to do various tasks in which you build up a picture of your workplace or work experience placement – day nursery, nursery, playgroup, after school or holiday play scheme, whatever – and to record it in a way that may be helpful to another student or trainee going to work in the same place.

TASK 1: Getting the picture

1 Give a brief outline of your workplace. Include:

- its name, address, phone number, location;
- a brief description of the premises;
- first impressions of the building and environment – how big, how old, how well maintained it is;
- how many children are cared for there, age range of children;
- hours and type of care offered (sessional, full time, extended day).

2 Make a scale drawing of the unit, the whole premises where this stands alone, or the part of the building used by this group. Show the location of:

- main area(s);
- outdoor area(s);
- staff/office area;
- parents area (if any);
- storage areas;
- fire escapes, alarms, equipment;
- toilets, sinks and wash areas;
- kitchen/food preparation areas.

TASK 2: Who works there?

1 Make a list of the different people who work in your workplace in the course of the day or week, and outline briefly what they do. There may be several – manager, assistants, social worker, cook, caretaker, health visitor, cleaner – or very few – perhaps two paid workers and volunteers.

2 With a partner, draw up a questionnaire which will enable you to find out more precisely what responsibilities people have. Include questions on training/qualifications, skills and personal qualities. Pay may be a sensitive issue.

3 Type your questionnaire, preferably on a word processor, leaving enough space for you to write the answers.

4   Try out your questionnaire on your mentor or superviser and ask them for comments on your questions, and the way you conduct the interview. Make any changes necessary before you interview one or two members of staff at your workplace.

TASK 3:
The children

Find out some basic information about the children, their ages, numbers of boys/girls, ethnic origins. Present some of this information in a bar chart.

TASK 4:
Your job

1   Give an outline of what happens in a typical day or session; note the basic structure of the day – the times at which particular activities happen, and the range of activities on offer at any one time.
2   Describe what you do through the day.
3   Describe in greater detail two activities you undertook in the past week. Describe what you did, how you did it, how you felt, how the children responded to you and how other staff members reacted.

TASK 5:
A record

Design a booklet you could give another person from your group going to your workplace, giving them essential information. Include selected information from your work on this assignment so far and practical information:

- who is in charge while you are there;
- what to do if you are sick, absent or late;
- the shape of the day;
- relationships with parents and carers;
- tips on working with other members of staff (and volunteers if any);
- hours, breaks and conditions;
- essential health and safety, record keeping;
- confidentiality and tact;
- any dos and don'ts about working there you think it would have been helpful to know before you started.

TASK 6:
A talk

Give a talk to your group about your workplace or placement. This may be the first time you have formally talked to the whole group about your placement so think carefully about what to include from the following suggestions:

- selected work from this assignment so far;
- examples of things you have done with the children;
- a description of the children and their needs – an outline of the range of backgrounds may be appropriate;
- your impressions of the quality of the child care your setting offers;
- your first impressions and your feelings now;
- what you have learnt from the placement;
- what you have enjoyed most and least.

Be prepared for questions and honest answers.

Assignment 24

Report for court

The law affects our daily lives in many ways, from how we park a car to how we look after children. Many aspects of the law are familiar. Much of this book has been written around the law, but courts and courtrooms remain unfamiliar territory, if only because we rarely go near one.

The work in this assignment involves writing reports, and a visit to a court. In this way, the two ways in which people have contact with a court – a written statement and an appearance in person – should become more familiar.

TASK 1:
An accident report

There are many contexts in which you might be asked to write an accurate factual report of an event – such as a car accident, or as here, a personal accident report. Under health and safety legislation, every workplace is required to maintain a record of accidents, and this is a registration requirement for every child care setting.

Interview a member of your group about an accident they have had. Imagine you were required as a witness to record what happened and what action was taken. Complete the accident report form overleaf with details you gain from your partner.

TASK 2:
A report on a child

Write a report on a child you have come to know from your workplace. Use the following headings:

- name, age and other details you know about the child and family;
- how you came to know the child and for how long;
- health;
- development;
- play;
- relationships with other children, with adults.

Keep your report factual, avoiding opinions and judgements. This is a useful format for taking stock and thinking about any child. It is similar to the format of a court report when they want to build up a picture of a child and the family. Your report would be one piece in the jigsaw.

PLAYSCHEME – ACCIDENT REPORT FORM

Name of establishment

Child's surname   Child's first name(s)   Age

Parents' address and tel. no.

Date and time of accident

How did accident occur and where?

What were the nature of injuries and treatment given on site? Who gave treatment?

Was medical attention sought?   Yes [ ]   No [ ]

Was an ambulance called?   Yes [ ]   No [ ]

Was the injured party admitted into hospital?   Yes [ ]   No [ ]

If 'Yes', who escorted the child to which hospital?

Did the injured party remain at the playscheme?   Yes [ ]   No [ ]

Were the parents informed of accident?   Yes [ ]   No [ ]   If 'Yes', when?

Name and address of witness to accident

Date and time reported to Chairman/Secretary/Day Care Organiser

Has the insurance company been informed?   Yes [ ]   No [ ]

Signature of playleader   Signature of Assistant Playleader   Signature of Scheme's Chairman

TASK 3:
Arranging a
visit

1 Look up 'Courts' in the phone book, and note the addresses and phone numbers of the various courts in your area.

2 Draft a letter to the Clerk of the Court asking if, in principle, you/your group can visit as an observer. Explain briefly why you want to visit and suggest dates and times. Only one letter from the group should be sent – check with your tutor.

Note to tutor: A visit to the Family Proceedings Court would be ideal but harder to arrange as the Clerk has to ask the parties if they agree. A visit to any court in action – even traffic offences – gives a flavour of the law.

3 Find out which local solicitors are on the Law Society Child Care Panel. Note their details. You may be able to arrange an interview to find out about their work.

TASK 4:
The visit

Make notes on:

- The courtroom: the layout; who sits/stands where.
- The proceedings: who starts the proceedings off? Who is everybody? How many magistrates are there? How do they deal with the case? Is the language easy to follow? Is it intimidating? Do people speak for themselves or do solicitors speak for them?
- The outcome: how was the case summed up? Did you understand what was going on? Did the people involved? Were they satisfied with the outcome?

On your return, discuss your visit and write up your notes.

TASK 5:
Research

Research one topic within the broad subject of the law relating to children, young people and families. Here are some suggestions:

- an aspect of the Children Act – look back at Part 1 to help you identify areas to research;
- the Criminal Justice Act 1991 and young offenders;
- the workings of the Family Proceedings Court;
- young people's rights in relation to the law;
- jobs in the law.

Agree an outline and length with your tutor.

Assignment 25

Finding a new playworker

Manor Court Playgroup (*see* Case Study 3) needs to recruit a new playworker to work with Roisin, the playgroup leader. In this assignment, you are asked to think through the processes, and take the parts of the people involved. Before you start this assignment, re-read the text of Case Study 3.

This assignment considers the process of job application from both sides of the table. In this it is complementary to Assignments 34 and 35 in *A Practical Approach to Caring* (Pitman 1991) by the same author which take a step-by-step approach to applying for jobs, starting from self-assessment and writing a CV, through reading and replying to ads, to completing forms, going to interviews and after. At the end of this assignment is a page of ads in the child care field which can be used in conjunction with these two assignments in *A Practical Approach to Caring*.)

Facing is a summary of the stages in recruiting a new playworker. The tasks relate to these stages.

TASK 1: **Advertise**	1 In small groups, draft the advertisement for the post. Consider what wording you will use in the ad to encourage people from a wide range of backgrounds to apply. When you have agreed the wording, design and lay out your ad. Find out the rates of pay for playgroup work, include this, and give a closing date 4 weeks from the appearance of the ad. 2 Where do you think Manor Court should advertise? Agree on the most effective place(s) to advertise to reach the sort of applicants you want in your area, then find out how much it would cost to place your ad.
TASK 2: **Job description and person specification**	This task is an extended role play in which issues are thrashed out in groups of people taking specific perspectives. (See also Task 5 in Assignment 17.) You need to allow enough time to see it through. Your tasks are: • Read the **job description** carefully, and agree any changes you want to make (*see* p 278). • Draw up a **person specification** for the post. Decide what **experiences, qualifications** and **personal qualities** you agree are **essential** for the job, and those that you think are **desirable**. Draw up a simple grid and enter the qualities in the relevant box.

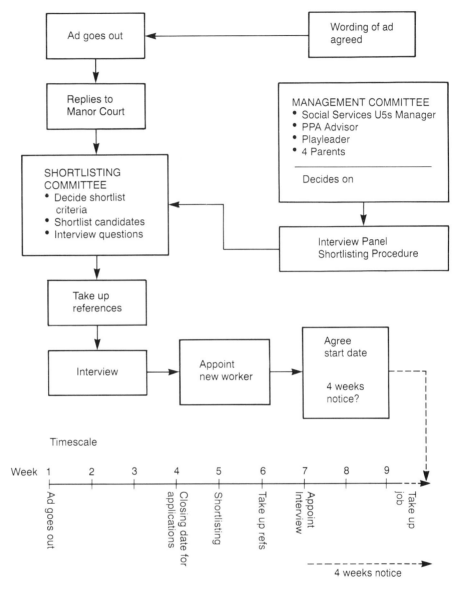

Finding a new playworker

- Propose the shortlisting procedure. Should applicants be invited to visit the playgroup? Meet the playleader? Should visits be part of the selection procedure, or entirely informal? Should only shortlisted applicants be invited to visit?

Arrange to type these up. and print copies.

   Do these tasks in groups, taking the parts of the Manor Court Management Committee/Interview Panel. Each group should consist of the following three people plus parents:

- The **Social Services Unders 5s manager.** She is experienced in appointing staff. She has a good knowledge of the requirements for staff under the Children Act and feels that anyone applying for a job in child

MANOR COURT PLAYGROUP
Assistant Play Leader Job Description

Note: Manor Court Playgroup expects all its employees to have a full commitment to the Playgroup's Equal Opportunities Policy and acceptance of personal responsibility for its practical application. All staff are required to comply with and promote the policy and to ensure that discrimination is eliminated in the service of the Playgroup.

JOB PURPOSE
To assist the Playleader in the running of the Playgroup.

MAJOR TASKS
1. To understand and comply with the Playgroup's Equal Opportunities Policy.
2. To encourage and participate in the provision of a high standard of play to meet the developmental and physical needs of the children.
3. To be responsible for the Health and Safety of the Playgroup and the well-being of the children at all times.
4. To be responsible for such administrative duties as keeping accurate records, e.g. register of children, accident reports, Health and Safety procedures.
5. To be responsible for maintaining equipment in a safe and hygienic manner and advising ongoing needs for equipment to meet the changing needs of the group.
6. To deputise for the Playleader in their absence.

JOB ACTIVITIES
1. To provide multicultural play experience and equipment which reflects the needs of all the children.
2. To assist in the provision of a safe environment and maintain high standards of hygiene in accordance with with statutory requirements and to make these known to parents/carers.
3. To ensure all equipment is safely set up, maintained and stored after use.
4. To liaise with and involve the Management Committee in the organisation and operation of the group.

5. To ensure that there is an adequate staff ratio on a sessional basis advising management of any change.
6. To ensure sensitive support to parents and carers at all times.
7. To communicate with parents/carers in a positive constructive manner and to encourage parental involvement in the sessions and support them in managing the group.
8. To work as part of a team.
9. To make time available on a regular basis to discuss the day-to-day running of the group with other staff.
10. To attend Management Committee meetings as and when invited.
11. To attend relevant meetings.
12. To ensure that all visitors to the Playgroup are welcomed and students in the group supported.
13. To ensure that all records of children are accurate and kept up to date and children registered in accordance with the Children Act 1989 regulations.
14. To be familiar with and operate emergency procedures and make staff, parents and carers aware of these procedures, e.g. fire drill, accident reports.
15. To initiate and participate in cleaning of equipment and keep a record of this.
16. To ensure that the children's individual needs for care and welfare are met.
17. To keep up to date with relevant information and to attend appropriate in-service training including first aid refresher courses.
18. To keep up to date with the latest ideas in the Under Fives field through courses and publications.
19. Any other duties relevant to the position in negotiation with the Management Committee.

Responsible to: Management Committee

care should by now have an understanding of the key elements of the Act and know what is required of playgroups. She is personally committed to equal opportunities in employment: people who use her authority's services – in this case children and parents – should see people of their own ethnic origins in positions of responsibility.

- A **PPA Adviser** who is interested in the attitudes of applicants to play and opportunities for development in the pre-school years. How would they strike a balance between bright creative ideas for activities and children's need to talk and explore at their own pace? How will they deal with the professional isolation of a small community playgroup?
- The **Playgroup leader**, Roisin, who is looking for someone she thinks she will get on well with, who will relate well to the parents, be reliable and long term, and practical and caring with the children.
- The other members of the Management Committee are **parents**. You may choose to take the part of someone quite unlike yourself, perhaps someone from another ethnic or social group. Or you may choose to act yourself. In either case, you should decide what qualities you would want to see in the new playworker. You may wish to adopt one or more of the following perspectives: some parents would like to see more structured activities in playgroup; some would like the playgroup to extend its hours to tally with the school day; some like it as it is; some would like to see more children like their own in the group, others want to keep the present mix; some parents are keen to help in the playgroup, and get fully involved, others prefer to drop their kids and go.

| TASK 3: Both sides of the table | The group needs to agree on the organisation and timing for this. One possibility is for one 'Management Committee/Interview Panel' (the three key people plus two parents maximum) to take the part of the interviewing panel, and for another group to be the interviewees. However you arrange it, the process will be as follows:

- **Applicants** to receive job description and person specification drawn up in Task 2 and application forms (overleaf). Complete the forms, assuming that you have successfully completed the course you are currently taking. Take care to address the points in the job description and person specification. You want to be offered the job. Agree a closing date/time for receipt of applications.
- **Interview panel** to agree and draw up a list of topics and possible questions to ask, bearing in mind the particular professional interests of the three workers as outlined above, and the concerns of parents. Decide who will focus on which topics.

Agree a date and time for the interviews. You may wish to record or video the interviews, or appoint two of your group as observers to make notes on the *process* of the interview.

MANOR COURT PLAYGROUP
Southside Community Hall
Manor Road
Manchester

JOB APPLICATION FORM

JOB TITLE:

PERSONAL DETAILS

Full name: Date of birth:

Address: Telephone number:

---

1. RELEVANT WORK EXPERIENCE
Please give details including dates. This work can be paid or unpaid.

Title of organisation   **Job title/responsibilities**   **Dates**

2. EDUCATION AND TRAINING
Please give details. List any education and/or training including short courses you think is relevant to your application.

3. PLEASE GIVE YOUR REASONS FOR APPLYING FOR THIS POST.
What aspects of your skills, experience and training make you suitable for this post?
(Please use person specification when answering this question.)

4. PERSONAL EXPERIENCE
Are there any aspects of your personal experience which you consider relevant to this post?

5. STARTING DATE
If you are offered the job, how soon could you start?

6. REFERENCES
Please give the names, addresses and telephone numbers of two referees. We will contact them only if we offer you the job.

Name (1) .... (2) ....
Position held ....
Address ....
....
....
....
....
Tel no: ....

I declare the information given on this form is correct to the best of my knowledge

Signed .... Date ....

TASK 4:
The interview

The whole group should decide whether to interview all the 'applicants' or, as would happen in a real job application, a shortlist. If you decide to 'shortlist', the panel must be prepared to explain their choice – why they did not shortlist some candidates.

The panel must give the interviewees a time for their interview. Appoint a Chair, agree an order for questions, and decide how to assess the answers the interviewees give – and run to time... It can be helpful to have an outside person on the panel, perhaps taking the part of the Under 5s Manager, if this can be arranged.

Interviewees must arrive on time, be prepared to answer and ask questions, look the part...

TASK 5:
Feedback

In real life feedback from an interview tends to come in the form of an offer of a job or a rejection. Often you never learn why. The important part of this exercise is to gain as much feedback as you can about yourself. Each applicant should have the opportunity to make the first comments, then ask the panel and observers about how they thought they performed. If you were videoed, each 'interviewee' should make the first comments. You might like to:

- ask what the panel thought of your application form. What caught their attention? What might you work on another time?
- ask each member of the panel what they thought of your answers to their questions;
- tell the panel about what you thought of their questions: were they fair? hard to answer? did they give you the chance to do yourself justice?
- ask the panel how they thought you felt in interview. Tell them how you did feel. Ask them how they felt. Could either party have made changes that would have helped the interviewee?

If you re-run this exercise, swap roles. Both parties should be more skilled at it!

TASK 6:
Follow-up

1 **Plug those gaps!** Build on the feedback you got from the mock interview, and check the job description to identify any topics you do not know about: health and safety, first aid, hygiene, 'adequate staff ratios', registration, accident report procedures. There is something in this book on all of these...

2 **Starting work.** Find out what you have to do about tax when you start a new job.

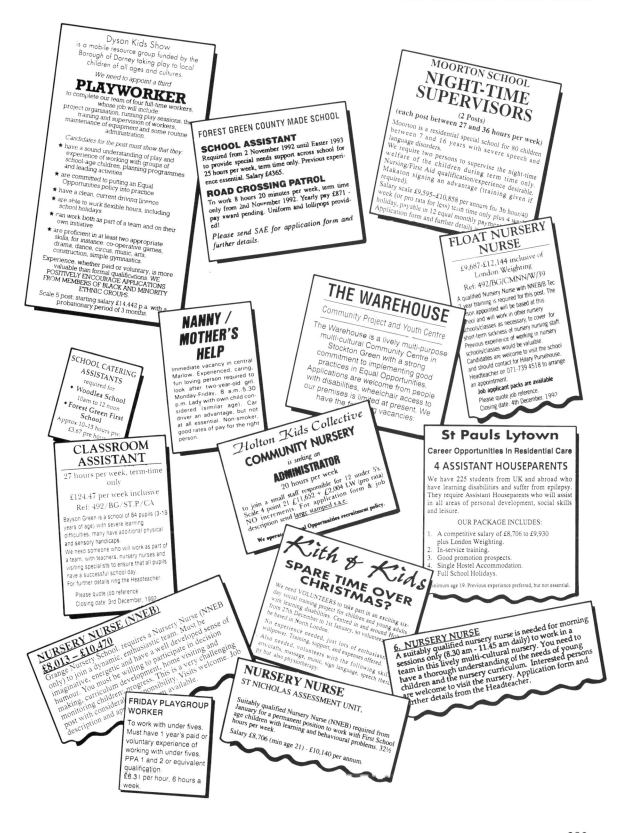

Part 4

APPENDICES

Appendix 1

The developmental progress of infants and young children

A word of warning! Dr Mary Sheridan, who first drew up the chart shown on pp 288–95 in 1960 to help her own observations, preferred the term 'stepping stones' of development to 'milestones'. The range of 'normal' development at any age is considerable, and it should not in itself be a cause of concern if a child does not reach a particular 'stepping stone' by a particular age. It is often more helpful to measure a child's development against his or her own achievements three or six months ago, than against other children of the same age. Some developmental stepping stones are dependent on previous experiences and opportunities rather than innate abilities. In our multicultural society of the 1990s, some children will not use a knife and fork at home (*see* age 5) and few 4 year olds will have to worry about tying a tie! It is helpful to talk to parents to find out what their expectations of their child are; this way you will gain an insight into children's different experiences and the abilities they show at home. However, it is very helpful to have a broad range of development presented in this way, and the more familiar you become with the stepping stones of child development, the quicker you will spot when a child needs further investigation or help.

Stepping stones of development chart

C=Child   M=Mother   E=Examiner

Age	Posture and large movements	Vision and fine movements
1 month	Lies on back with head to one side; arm and legs on same side outstretched, or both arms flexed; knees apart, soles of feet turned inwards. Large jerky movements of limbs, arms more active than legs. At rest, hands closed and thumb turned in. Fingers and toes fan out during extensor movements of limbs. When cheek touched, turns to same side; ear gently rubbed, turns away. When lifted head falls loosely. Held sitting, head falls forward, with back in one complete curve. Placed downwards on face, head immediately turns to side; arms and legs flexed under body, buttocks humped up. Held standing on hard surface, presses down feet, straightens body and often makes reflex 'stepping' movements.	Turns head and eyes towards light. Stares expressionlessly at brightness of window or blank wall. Follows pencil flash-lamp briefly with eyes at one foot. Shuts eyes tightly when pencil light shone directly into them at 1–2 inches. Notices dangling toy or rattle shaken in line of vision at 6–8 inches and follows its slow movement with eyes from side towards mid-line on level with face through approximately quarter circle, before head falls back to side. Beginning to watch mother's nearby face when she feeds or talks to him with increasingly alert facial expression.
3 months	Now prefers to lie on back with head in mid-line. Limbs more pliable, movements smoother and more continuous. Waves arms symmetrically. Hands now loosely open. Brings hands from side into mid-line over chest or chin. Kicks vigorously, legs alternating or occasionally together. Held sitting, holds back straight, except in lumbar region, with head erect and steady for several seconds before bobbing forwards. Place downwards on face lifts head and upper chest well up in mid-line, using forearms as support, and often scratching at table surface; legs straight, buttocks flat. Held standing with feet on hard surface, sags at knees.	Visually very alert, particularly preoccupied by nearby human face. Moves head deliberately to look around him. Follows adult's movements near cot. Follows rattle or dangling toy at 6–10 inches above face through half circle from side to side, and usually also vertically from chest to brow. Watches movements of own hands before face and beginning to clasp and unclasp hands together in finger play. Recognises feeding bottle and makes eager welcoming movements as it approaches his face. Regards still objects within 6–10 inches for more than a second or two, but seldom fixates continuously. Comerges eyes as dangling toy is moved towards face. Defensive blink shown.
6 months	Lying on back, raises head from pillow. Lifts legs into vertical and grasps foot. Sits with support in cot or pram and turns head from side to side to look around him. Moves arms in brisk purposeful fashion and holds them up to be lifted. When hands grasped braces shoulders and pulls himself up. Kicks strongly, legs alternating. Can roll over, front to back. Held sitting, head is firmly erect, and back straight. May sit alone momentarily. Placed downwards on face lifts head and chest well up supporting himself on extended arms.	Visually insatiable: moves head and eyes eagerly in every direction. Eyes move in unison: squint now abnormal. Follows adult's movements across room. Immediately fixates interesting small objects within 6–12 inches (e.g. toy, bell, wooden cube, spoon, sweet) and stretches out both hands to grasp them. Uses whole hand in palmar grasp. When toys fall from hand forgets them or searches only vaguely round cot with eyes and patting hands.

Age	Hearing and speech	Social behaviour and play
1 month	Startled by sudden loud noises, stiffens, quivers, blinks, screws eyes up, extends limbs, fans out fingers and toes, and may cry. Movements momentarily 'frozen', when small bell rung gently 3–5 inches from ear for 3–5 secs. with 5 secs. pauses: may move eyes towards sound. Stops whimpering to sound of nearby soothing human voice, but not when screaming or feeding. Cries lustily when hungry or uncomfortable. Utters little guttural noises when content. (Note–Deaf babies also cry and vocalise in this reflex way, but if very deaf do not usually show startle reflex to sudden noise. Blind babies may also move eyes towards a sound-making toy. Vision should always be checked separately.)	Sucks well. Sleeps most of the time when not being fed or handled. Expression still vague, but becoming more alert, progressing to smiling at about 5–6 weeks. Hands normally closed, but if opened, grasps examiner's finger when palm is touched. Stops crying when picked up and spoken to. Mother supports head when carrying, dressing and bathing.
3 months	Sudden loud noises still distress, provoking blinking, screwing up of eyes, cry and turning away. Definite quietening or smiling to sound of mother's voice before she touches him, but not when screaming. Vocalises when spoken to or pleased. Cries when uncomfortable or annoyed. Quietens to rattle of spoon in cup or to bell rung gently out of sight for 3–5 secs. at 6–12 inches from ear. May turn eyes towards sound: brows may wrinkle and eyes dilate. May move head from side to side as if searching vaguely for sound. Often licks lips in response to sounds of preparation for feeding. Shows excitement at sound of approaching footsteps, running bath water, etc. (Note–Deaf baby, instead, may be obviously startled by M's sudden appearance beside cot.)	Fixes eyes unblinkingly on mother's face when feeding. Beginning to react to familiar situations – showing by smiles, coos, and excited movements that he recognises preparation for feeds, baths, etc. Responds with obvious pleasure to friendly handling, especially when accompanied by playful tickling and vocal sounds. Holds rattle for few moments when placed in hand, but seldom capable of regarding it at same time. Mother supports at shoulders when dressing and bathing.
6 months	Turns immediately to mother's voice across room. Vocalises tunefully, using single and double syllables, e.g. ka, muh, goo, der, adah, er-leh. Laughs, chuckles and squeals aloud in play. Screams with annoyance. Shows evidence of response to different emotional tones of mother's voice. Responds to baby hearing tests at 1½ feet from each ear by correct visual localisation, but may show slightly brisker response on one side.	Hands competent to reach for and grasp small toys. Most often uses a two handed, scooping-in approach, but occasionally a single hand. Takes everything to mouth. Beginning to find feet interesting and even useful in grasping. Puts hands to bottle and pats it when feeding. Shakes rattle deliberately to make it sound, often regarding it closely at same time. Still friendly with strangers but occasionally shows some shyness or even slight anxiety, especially if M is out of sight.

Age	Posture and large movement	Vision and fine movements
9 months	Sits alone for 10–15 minutes on floor. Can turn body to look sideways while stretching out to grasp dangling toy or to pick up toy from floor. Arms and legs very active in cot, pram and bath. Progresses on floor by rolling or squirming. Attempts to crawl on all fours. Can stand holding on to support for a few moments, but cannot lower himself. Held standing, steps purposefully on alternate feet.	Very observant. Stretches out, one hand leading, to grasp small objects immediately on catching sight of them. Manipulates objects with lively interest, passing from hand to hand, turning over, etc. Pokes at small sweet with index finger. Grasps between finger and thumb in scissor fashion. Can release toy by pressing against firm surface, but cannot yet put down voluntarily. Searches in correct place for toys dropped within reach of hands. Looks after toys falling over edge of pram or table. Watches activities of adults, children and animals within 10–12 feet with eager interest for several seconds at a time.
12 months	Sits well and for indefinite time. Can rise to sitting position from lying down. Crawls rapidly on all fours. Pulls to standing and lets himself down again holding on to furniture. Walks round furniture stepping sideways. Walks with one or both hands held. May stand alone for few moments.	Picks up small objects, e.g. blocks, string, sweets and crumbs, with precise pincer grasp of thumb and index finger. Drops toys deliberately and watches them fall to ground. Looks in correct place for toys which roll out of sight. Points with index finger at objects he wants to handle or which interest him. Watches small toy pulled along floor across room 10 feet away. Out of doors watches movements of people, animals, motor cars, etc., with prolonged intent regard. Recognises familiars approaching from 20 feet or more away. Uses both hands freely, but may show preference for one. Clicks two bricks together in imitation.
15 months	Walks unsteadily with feet wide apart, arms slightly flexed and held above head or at shoulder level to balance. Starts alone, but frequently stopped by falling or bumping into furniture. Lets himself down from standing to sitting by collapsing backwards with bump, or occasionally by falling forward on hands and then back to sitting. Can get to feet alone. Crawls upstairs. Kneels unaided or with slight support on floor and in pram, cot and bath. May be able to stoop to pick up toys from floor.	Picks up string, small sweets and crumbs neatly between thumb and finger. Builds tower of two cubes after demonstration. Grasps crayon and imitates scribble after demonstration. Looks with interest at pictures in book and pats page. Follows with eyes path of cube or small toy swept vigorously from table. Watches small toy pulled across floor up to 12 feet. Points imperiously to objects he wishes to be given. Stands at window and watches events.

Age	Hearing and speech	Social behaviour and play
9 months	Vocalises deliberately as means of inter-personal communication. Shouts to attract attention, listens, then shouts again. Babbles tunefully, repeating syllables in strings (mam-mam, bab-bab, dad-dad, etc.) Understands 'No-No'; and 'Bye-Bye'. Tries to imitate adults' playful vocal sounds, e.g. smacking lips, cough, brr, etc.	Holds, bites and chews biscuits. Puts hands round bottle or cup when feeding. Tries to grasp spoon when being fed. Throws body back and stiffens in annoyance or resistance. Clearly distinguishes strangers from familiars, and requires reassurance before accepting their advances. Clings to known adult and hides face. Still takes everything to mouth. Seizes bell in one hand. Imitates ringing action, waving or banging it on table, pokes clapper or 'drinks' from bowl. Plays peek-a-boo. Holds out toy held in hand to adult, but cannot yet give. May find toy hidden under cup. Mother supports at lower spine when dressing.
12 months	Knows and immediately turns to own name. Babbles loudly, tunefully and incessantly. Shows by suitable movements and behaviour that he understands several words in usual context (e.g. own and family names, walk, dinner, pussy, cup, spoon, ball, car.) Comprehends simple commands associated with gesture (Give it to Daddy. Come to Mummy. Say bye-bye, clap hands, etc.) Imitates adult's playful vocalisations with gleeful enthusiasm. May hand E common objects on request, e.g. spoon, cup, ball, shoe.	Drinks from cup with little assistance. Chews. Holds spoon but cannot use it alone. Helps with dressing by holding out arm for sleeve and foot for shoe. Takes objects to mouth less often. Ceasing to drool. Puts wooden cubes in and out of cup or box. Rattles spoon in cup in imitation. Seizes bell by handle and pokes clapper, etc. Rings briskly in imitation. Listens with obvious pleasure to sounds and repeats activities to produce them. Gives toys to adult on request and sometimes spontaneously. Finds hidden toy. Likes to be constantly within sight and hearing of adult. Demonstrates affection to familiars. Waves 'bye-bye' and claps hands in imitation or spontaneously. Child sits, or sometimes stands without support, while Mother dresses.
15 months	Jabbers loudly and freely, using wide range of inflections and phonetic units. Speaks 2–6 recognisable words and understands many more. Vocalises wishes and needs at table. Points to familiar persons, animals, toys, etc. when requested. Understands and obeys simple commands (e.g. shut the door. Give me ball. Get your shoes).	Holds cup when adult gives and takes back. Holds spoon, brings it to mouth and licks it, but cannot prevent its turning over. Chews well. Helps more constructively with dressing. Indicates when he has wet pants. Pushes large wheeled toy with handle on level ground. Seldom takes toys to mouth. Repeatedly casts objects to floor in play or rejection usually without watching fall. Physically restless and intensely curious. Handles everything with reach Emotionally labile. Closely dependent upon adult's reassuring presence.

291

Age	Posture and large movements	Vision and fine movements
18 months	Walks well with feet only slightly apart, starts and stops safely. Runs stiffly upright, eyes fixed on ground 1–2 yards ahead, but cannot continue round obstacles. Pushes and pulls large toys, boxes, etc., round floor. Can carry large doll or teddy-bear while walking. Backs into small chair or slides in sideways. Climbs forward into adult's chair then turns round and sits. Walks upstairs with helping hand. Creeps backwards downstairs. Occasionally bumps down a few steps on buttocks facing forwards. Picks up toy from floor without falling.	Picks up small sweets, beads, pins, threads, etc., immediately on sight, with delicate pincer grasp. Spontaneous scribble when given pencil and paper, using preferred hand. Builds tower of three cubes after demonstration. Enjoys simple picture book, often recognising and putting finger on coloured items on page. Turns pages 2 or 3 at a time. Fixes eyes on small dangling toy at 10 feet. (May tolerate this test with each eye separately.) Points to distant interesting objects out of doors. Beginning to show definite preference for using one hand.
2 years	Runs safely on whole foot, stopping and starting with ease and avoiding obstacles. Squats to rest or to play with object on ground and rises to feet without using hands. Pulls wheeled toy by cord. Climbs on furniture to look out of window or open doors, etc., and can get down again. Walks upstairs and down holding on to rail or wall: two feet to a step. Throws small ball without falling. Walks into large ball when trying to kick it.	Picks up pins and thread, etc., neatly and quickly. Removes paper wrapping from small sweet. Builds tower of six cubes. Spontaneous circular scribble and dots when given paper and pencil. Imitates verticle line (and sometimes V). Enjoys picture books, recognising fine details in favourite pictures. Turns pages singly. Recognises familiar adults in photograph after once shown. Handedness usually well developed.
2½ years	Walks upstairs alone, but downstairs holding rail, two feet to a step. Runs well straight forward and climbs easy nursery apparatus. Pushes and pulls large toys skilfully, but has difficulty in steering them round obstacles. Jumps with two feet together. Can stand on tiptoe if shown. Kicks large ball.	Picks up pins, threads, etc., with each eye covered separately. Builds tower of seven cubes and lines blocks to form 'train'. Recognises minute details in picture books. Imitates horizontal line and circle (also usually T and V). Paints strokes, dots and circular shapes on easel. Recognises himself in photographs when once shown. Recognises miniature toys and retrieves balls 2–⅛ inches at 10 feet with each eye separately.

Age	Hearing and speech	Social behaviour and play
18 months	Continues to jabber tunefully to himself at play. Uses 6–20 recognisable words and understands many more. Echoes prominent or last word addressed to him. Demands desired objects by pointing accompanied by loud, urgent vocalisation or single words. Enjoys nursery rhymes and tries to join in. Attempts to sing. Shows his own or doll's hair, shoe, nose.	Lifts and holds cup between both hands. Drinks without much spilling. Chews well. Hands cup back to adult. Holds spoon and gets food to mouth. Takes off shoes, socks, hat. Indicates toilet needs by restlessness and vocalisation. Bowel control usually attained. Explores environment energetically. No longer takes toys to mouth. Remembers where objects belong. Casts objects to floor in play or anger less often. Briefly imitates simple actions, e.g. reading book, kissing doll, brushing floor. Plays contentedly alone, but likes to be near adult. Emotionally still very dependent upon familiar adult, especially M. Alternates between clinging and resistance.
2 years	Uses 50 or more recognisable words and understands many more. Puts 2 or more words together to form simple sentences. Refers to himself by name. Talks to himself continually as he plays. Echolalia almost constant, with one or more stressed words repeated. Constantly asking names of objects. Joins in nursery rhymes and songs. Shows correctly and repeats words for hair, hand, feet, nose, eyes, mouth, shoe on request.	Lifts and drinks from cup and replaces on table. Spoon-feeds without spilling. Asks for food and drink. Chews competently. Puts on hat and shoes. Verbalises toilet needs in reasonable time. Dry during day. Turns door handles. Often runs outside. Follows M round house and copies domestic activities in simultaneous play. Engages in simple make-believe activities. Constantly demanding M's attention. Clings tightly in affection, fatigue or fear. Tantrums when frustrated but attention easily distracted. Defends own possessions with determination. As yet no idea of sharing. Plays near other children but not with them. Resentful of attention shown to other children.
2½ years	Uses 200 or more recognisable words but speech shows numerous infantilisms. Knows full name. Talks intelligibly to himself at play concerning events happening here and now. Echolalia persists. Continually asking questions beginning 'What?', 'Where?'. Uses pronouns, I, me and you. Stuttering in eagerness common. Says a few nursery rhymes. Enjoys simple familiar stories read from picture book.	Eats skilfully with spoon and may use fork. Pulls down pants or knickers at toilet, but seldom able to replace. Dry through night if lifted. Very active, restless and rebellious. Throws violent tantrums when thwarted or unable to express urgent needs and less easily distracted. Emotionally still very dependent upon adults. Prolonged domestic make-believe play (putting dolls to bed, washing clothes, driving motorcars, etc.) but with frequent reference to friendly adult. Watches other children at play interestedly and occasionally joins in for a few minutes, but little notion of sharing playthings or adult's attention.

Age	Posture and large movements	Vision and fine movements
3 years	Walks alone upstairs with alternating feet and downstairs with two feet to step. Usually jumps from bottom step. Climbs nursery apparatus with agility. Can turn round obstacles and corners while running and also while pushing and pulling large toys. Rides tricycle and can turn wide corners on it. Can walk on tiptoe. Stands momentarily on one foot when shown. Sits with feet crossed at ankles.	Picks up pins, threads, etc., with each eye covered separately. Builds tower of nine cubes, and (3½) bridge of three from model. Can close fist and wiggle thumb in imitation. R and L Copies circle (also V, H, T). Imitates cross. Draws man with head and usually indication of one other part. Matches two or three primary colours (usually red and yellow correct, but may confuse blue and green). Paints 'pictures' with large brush on easel. Cuts with scissors.
4 years	Turns sharp corners running, pushing and pulling. Walks alone up and downstairs, one foot per step. Climbs ladders and trees. Can run on toptoe. Expert rider of tricycle. Hops on one foot. Stands on one foot 3–5 secs. Arranges or picks up objects from floor by bending from waist with knees extended.	Picks up pins, thread, crumbs, etc., with each eye covered separately. Builds tower of 10 or more cubes and several 'bridges' of three on request. Builds three steps with six cubes after demonstration. Imitates spreading of hand and bringing thumb into opposition with each finger in turn. R. and L. Copies cross (also V, H, T, O). Draws man with head and legs and also trunk or features. Draws very simple house. Matches and names four primary colours correctly.
5 years	Runs lightly on toes. Active and skilful in climbing, sliding, swinging, digging and various 'stunts'. Skips on alternate feet. Dances to music. Can stand on one foot 8–10 secs. Can hop 2–3 yards forwards on each foot separately. Grips strongly with either hand.	Picks up minute objects when each eye is covered separately. Builds three steps with six cubes from model. Copies square and triangle (also letters: V, T, H, O, X, L, A, C, U, Y). Writes a few letters spontaneously. Draws recognisable man with head, trunk, legs, arms and features. Draws simple house with door, windows, roof and chimney. Counts fingers on one hand with index finger of other. Names four primary colours and matches 10 or 12 colours.

(First drawn up by Dr Mary Sheridan)

Age	Hearing and speech	Social behaviour and play
3 years	Large intelligible vocabulary but speech still shows many infantile phonetic substitutions. Gives full name and sex, and (sometimes) age. Uses plurals and pronouns. Still talks to himself in long monologues mostly concerned with the immediate present, including make-believe activities. Carries on simple conversations, and verbalises past experiences. Asks many questions beginning 'What?', 'Where?', 'Who?'. Listens eagerly to stories and demands favourites over and over again. Knows several nursery rhymes.	Eats with fork and spoon. Washes hands, but needs supervision in drying. Can pull pants and knickers down and up, but needs help with buttons. Dry through night. General behaviour more amenable. Affectionate and confiding. Likes to help with adult's activities in house and garden. Makes effort to keep his surroundings tidy. Vividly realised make-believe play including invented people and objects. Enjoys floor play with bricks, boxes, toy trains and cars alone or with siblings. Joins in play with other children. Understands sharing playthings, sweets, etc. Shows affection for younger siblings. Shows some appreciation of past and present.
4 years	Speech completely intelligible. Shows only a few infantile substitutions usually p/t/th/f/s and r/l/w/y/ groups. Gives connected account of recent events and experiences. Gives home address and (usually) age. Eternally asking questions 'Why?', 'When?', 'How?' and meanings of words. Listens to and tells long stories sometimes confusing fact and fantasy.	Eats skilfully with spoon and fork. Washes and dries hands. Brushes teeth. Can undress and dress except for back buttons, laces and ties. General behaviour self-willed. Inclined to verbal impertinence when wishes crossed. Strongly dramatic play and dressing-up favoured. Constructive out-of-doors building with any large material to hand. Needs other children to play with and is alternately co-operative and aggressive with them as with adults. Understands taking turns. Shows concern for younger siblings and sympathy for playmates in distress. Appreciates past, present and future.
5 years	Speech fluent and correct except for confusions of s/f/th/. Loves stories and acts them out in detail later. Gives home address. Gives age and (usually) birthday. Defines concrete nouns by use. Asks meaning of abstract words.	Uses knife and fork. Washes and dries face and hands, but needs help and supervision for rest. Undresses and dresses alone. General behaviour more sensible, controlled and independent. Domestic and dramatic play continued from day to day. Plans and builds constructively. Floor games very complicated. Chooses own friends. Co-operative with companions and understands need for rules and fair play. Appreciates meaning of clocktime in relation to daily programme. Tender and protective towards younger children and pets. Comforts playmates in distress.

Appendix 2

Answers to selected assignment tasks

Assignment 13, Task 4

First aid procedures

	Symptoms	Action	Never
Breathing stopped	Unconsciousness, blue lips and finger nails, no movement of chest wall, child is silent – no sound of breathing.	Clear the airway of debris or obstructions. Open the airway by extending the head. Give mouth to mouth (or mouth to nose) ventilation. Action in the first 3 minutes is vital.	NEVER ... Panic or waste time.
Heart stopped	As above plus no carotid pulse felt.	Mouth to mouth ventilation plus external chest compression. This should only be attempted by people who are experienced with external cardiac compression.	NEVER ... Panic or waste time.
Severe bleeding	May be obvious site of bleeding. Feeling faint, general weakness. Nausea, pallor, especially face. Thirst. Increase in pulse rate but weak.	Apply direct pressure on the wound using fingers and thumb, over a sterile dressing if possible. Use a ring pad if foreign body present. Lie the child down. Raise the injured part (unless you suspect a fracture). Apply sterile pad and bandage.	NEVER ... leave the child alone or give drinks. Never apply a tourniquet.
Unconscious	The child is lying silent. Does not respond to questions, may not respond to pain.	Check breathing. Try to establish the cause. Loosen tight clothing. If breathing turn the child to the recovery position unless fracture of spine suspected.	NEVER ... give drinks or leave the child alone.
Burns and scalds	Pain, usually with redness and swelling at the injury site. Blisters later.	Immerse in cold water for at least 10 minutes. Cover with a dry sterile dressing and bandage. Any burn greater than 1 cm square should be seen by a Doctor. For large burns dial 999.	NEVER ... apply butter or lard, cream or ointments. Never burst any blisters.
Choking	Caused by obstruction to airway, eg food. Violent coughing. Difficulty breathing. Congestion of face. Eventual unconsciousness.	Place the child over your knee, head down, slap between the shoulder blades up to 4 times. Check in mouth for dislodged foreign body. If unsuccessful, perform abdominal thrust up to 4 times.	
Convulsions or fits	May be twitching of face and limbs, upward eyes,	Make sure he can breathe, and that he does not injure himself by striking hard	NEVER ... lie the child flat on his back. Never

	rigidity of body, frothing at mouth, breath holding, unconsciousness plus high temperature in children.	objects. Loosen constricting clothing. Make sure the child sees his doctor. Cool the child with tepid sponging if temperature high.	leave the child alone. Never forcibly restrain the child.
Falls and fractures	Could range from bruising to fracture to unconsciousness.	If minor fall, tender loving care is best. If the bruising/swelling is extensive, ease with a cold compress. If you suspect a fracture, do not move the injured part unless absolutely necessary.	NEVER ... move the child unnecessarily if you suspect a fracture.
Head injuries	May be loss of consciousness, nausea and vomiting, amnesia, bruising, bleeding. May be no obvious symptoms.	Lie the child down in the recovery position, keep him warm and calm. Get help immediately and move as little as possible. Keep under observation. Remember to tell a parent even if injury was only slight.	NEVER ... rule out damage to the brain even if no signs or symptoms.
Poisoning (household articles)	Range from stomach ache and vomiting to obvious burning of lips to unconsciousness.	Take the child, and the cause of the poison, to the hospital immediately. Check breathing. Begin resuscitation if breathing stops. Give child drink of water if lips burnt and child conscious.	NEVER ... leave the child alone. Never make the child vomit.
Eyes (foreign body)	Visible redness and watering of eye. Pain and itching.	Try to prevent child rubbing eye. Natural watering of eye will remove small pieces of sand. Continue by irrigating eye with cold water. Other foreign bodies need medical attention.	NEVER ... leave an eye injury. If you are unhappy take the child to hospital.
Ears	Crying and holding ear. Perhaps foreign object sticking out of ear.	Earache. Contact a parent and advise that the child sees a doctor. Foreign body. Prevent child from touching ear. Foreign body needs to be removed in hospital.	NEVER ... press on the object – you may damage the ear.
Nose bleed	Bleeding from the nose.	Sit the child down, head tilted forward, and pinch the end of his nostrils for 10 minutes. Try to prevent child blosing nose or picking it after bleeding stopped.	NEVER ... lie the child on his back or put his head back.
Bites	Punctured skin or just teeth marks at the site of the injury.	Clean with soap and water and check with parents that the child is immunised against tetanus, if bitten by an animal.	NEVER ... approach the animal if it is frothing at the mouth.
Cuts/grazes	Blood at the site of the injury.	Press gently at the site of the cut or graze. Clean with soap and water and cover with dry dressing or plaster.	NEVER ... cover without cleaning.
Stings	Swelling and redness where the child has been stung. Sting may still be present.	Swelling in the throat, on the tongue or near the eyes can be dangerous. Take to the hospital. If you can see the sting remove with tweezers.	NEVER ... leave the child alone until the swelling disappears.
Sprains and strains	Severe swelling and bruising which is painful.	Apply a cold compress. Support the injury with a pad and crepe bandage.	NEVER ... bathe the injury in hot water.

Assignment 15, Task 6

1 **Fireworks** – *False.* It is illegal for children to be supplied with fireworks until they are 16, under the Fireworks (Safety) Regulations 1986 and the Explosives (Control of Fireworks) Regulations (Northern Ireland) 1970. There is no law governing the **use** of fireworks, which can be dangerous regardless of age.

2 **Crossing roads** – *True.* Children find it hard to judge the speed and distance of vehicles on the road. By the time they are 8 or 9, most children can safely cross quiet back streets, by waiting for traffic to clear. On a busy main road where they need to judge the speed of vehicles, children cannot cross safely until they are 11 or 12.

3 **Swallowing batteries** – *Controversial!* Some studies suggest children come to no harm from swallowing small batteries. Other studies suggest that the battery can become trapped on its way through the body. The metal covering may then corrode and allow toxic mercury to leak out.

4 **Window safety** – *True.* Window locks help to stop children from opening windows. However, the key **must** be kept nearby in case of fire. From about two and a half most children can use a key to undo a lock. The alternative to locks are bars or grilles on windows, but these also need to be removable in case of fire.

5 **Babywalkers** – *False.* There is **no** evidence that babywalkers help babies learn to walk any sooner than they might otherwise do. Babies can move very fast in babywalkers, making them hard to supervise. Babywalkers are involved in more accidents to children than any other single item of baby equipment. During 1987 there were an estimated 6,000 accidents involving babywalkers in England and Wales.

6 **Warning symbols** – *False.* Most children cannot recognise warning symbols until the age of 4. By this age they can usually also identify different kinds of bottles, making the symbol superfluous. Symbols like the skull and crossbones have been found to be attractive to young children and to encourage rather than discourage them from investigating further.

7 **Car seats** – *False.* Children are marginally safer in the rear seat of a car. The main safety point is that, whether in front or rear seats, children need a restraint suitable for their age. It is much safer for a child to travel restrained in the front seat than unrestrained in the back. By law anyone travelling in the front of a car must use a seat belt or child restraint. Children under 14 in the back of a car must use rear seat belts (or a suitable restraint), where these are fitted and available (Road Traffic Act, 1988; Motor Vehicle (Wearing of Rear Seat Belts by Children) Regulations (Northern Ireland) 1989).

8 **Peanuts** – *True.* Peanuts contain arachis oil which is an irritant. If a peanut is inhaled, the arachis oil causes mucosal oedema – a small piece of peanut can then block a relatively large airway. Children of 6 and over chew food better and have bigger airways than young

children. They are therefore at less risk from peanuts.

9   **Safety caps** – *False*. No cap is child proof, only child resistant. Most children can undo safety caps from the age of 5, and some even before that. However, this is not significant as the peak ages for children putting things into their mouths indiscriminately is 1–3 years.

10 **Storing medicines** – *Variable!* This depends on people's own circumstances and housing. Lockable bathroom cabinets used to be very hard to come by, but recently several new models have become available. In the absence of a lockable cupboard or cabinet, the kitchen is usually a better storage place simply because there is generally more adult supervision here than in the bathroom.

11 **Cooker guards** – *True*. Cooker guards get very hot and can burn a child. They are also expensive and children can put their fingers through the guard and touch the hob. Lifting pans of food and liquids over the top of a guard can be an added danger.

12 **Laburnum seeds** – False. Although laburnum seeds are toxic, you have to eat *very* large quantities to feel any ill effects. The only reason for clearing laburnum from a garden or play area, is if it is likely to be used by any children with handicaps who are compulsive eaters. Common garden plants which *are* poisonous are foxglove, lily of the valley and larkspur.

13 **Toy design** – *False*. Accidents involving bad toy design, such as eyes coming off teddy bears or protruding metal spikes, are quite rare. More often children hurt themselves by falling over or on to toys. Young children may take small bits from toys and put them in their ear or nose or swallow them.

14 **Stairs** – *True*. Many people think children aged 18–24 months can manage safely on stairs unsupervised. However, most accidents involving stairs happen to 2–3 year olds. Regular checks of stairgates are essential as some accidents also happen when children lean against gates which give way.

15 **Strip packaging** – *True*. As strip packs are hard for a young child to open, it takes longer for a child to ingest dangerous quantities of pills from a pack than from a bottle. However, some sweets are sold in strip packs which may confuse some children.

16 **Funfairs** – *False*. Funfairs are safer today due to improved safety standards and health and safety regulations. The perceived risks of funfairs are much higher than the reality of accident rates. For the year April 1986 to March 1987, five hundred million rides were enjoyed, with forty accidents and only two fatalities. On the basis of these figures you are twenty-five times more likely to die from being struck by lightning than at a funfair.

17 **Toy age recommendations** – *False*. The age recommendations on toys are based on children's physical safety rather than on their ability or stage of development. However advanced a child is, they are still vulnerable to bits of toys or small toys lodging in their nose, ears or throat.

Appendix 3

Useful addresses

Many organisations are mentioned in the text which may be of use to you in follow-up work in conjunction with the case studies and assignments. These and other useful addresses are given below.

Child Accident Prevention Trust
4th Floor, Clerks Court
10–18 Farringdon Lane
London EC1R 3AU
Tel: 071-668 3828

Child Poverty Action Group
4th Floor, 1–5 Bath Street
London EC1V 9PY
Tel: 071-253 3406

Childline
Freeport 1111
London N1 0BR
Tel: Freephone Helpline 0800 1111

Children's Legal Centre
20 Compton Terrace
London N1 2UN
Tel: 071-359 6251 (Advice line)

Children's Rights Development Unit
235 Shaftesbury Avenue
London WC2H 8EL
Tel: 071-240 4449

Children's Society
Edward Rudolph House
Margery Street
London WC1X 9JL
Tel: 071-837 4299

Commission for Racial Equality
Elliot House, 10–12 Allington Street
London SW1E 5EH
Tel: 071-828 7022

End Physical Punishment of
Children (EPOCH)
77 Holloway Road
London N7 8JZ
Tel: 071-700 0627

Family Policy Studies Centre
231 Baker Street
London NW1X 6XT
Tel: 071-486 8179

Family Rights Group
The Print House
18 Ashwin Street
London E8 3DL
Tel: 071-923 2628

Family Welfare Association
501–505 Kingsland Road
Dalston
London E8 4AU

Food Commission
88 Old Street
London EC1V 9AR
Tel: 071-253 9513

Gingerbread
35 Wellington Street
London WC2E 7BN
Tel: 071-240 0953

Health Education Authority (HEA)
Hamilton House, Mabledon Place
London WC1H 9TX
Tel: 071-383 3833

Kids Clubs Networks
279–281 Whitechapel Road
London E1 1BY
Tel: 071-247 3009

Mencap
Mencap National Centre
123 Golden Lane
London EC1Y 0RT
Tel:071-454 0454

National Childminding Association
8 Mason's Hill
Bromley
Kent
Tel: 081-464 6164

National Children's Bureau (NCB)
8 Wakley Street
London EC1V 7QE
Tel: 071-278 9441

National Children's Homes
85 Highbury Park
London N5 1UD
Tel: 071-226 2033

National Council for One Parent
Families
255 Kentish Town Road
London NW5 2LX
Tel: 071-267 1361

National Society for the Prevention
of Cruelty to Children (NSPCC)
67 Saffron Hill
London EC1N 8RS
Tel: 071-242 1626
Advice line Freephone 0800 800500

National Playing Fields Association
25 Ovington Square
London SW3 1LQ
Tel: 071-581 2402

Play Matters/National Toy Libraries
Association
68 Churchway
London NW1 1LT
Tel: 071-387 9592

Pre-School Playgroups Association
(PPA)
61–63 Kings Cross Road
London WC1X 9LL
Tel: 071-837 4942

Royal Society for the Prevention of
Accidents (RoSPA)
Cannon House, Priory Queensway
Birmingham B4 6BS
Tel: 021-200 2461

Spastics Society (**NB:** Soon to
change its name)
12 Park Crescent
London W1N 4EQ
Tel: 071-636 5020

Voluntary Organisations Liaison
Council for Under Fives (VOLCUF)
77 Holloway Road
London N7 8JZ
Tel: 071-607 9573

Index

equipment 82, 171, 176–9, 231
European Community (EC) 110, 123, 134–41

facilities 125, 260
family
  centre 56, 69
  patterns 10, 12–13, 126–8, 129–31, 190
  proceedings 2, 15, 275
  services 19, 25, 52
  structures 15, 116–25, 126, 129–31, 269–70
father 13, 54, 70–1, 98–9, 120
First aid 200–2, 214, 296–7
fit person 64, 82
flowchart 56, 161
food 112, 113, 194–6, 219–25, 267–8
form 68, 102, 184, 198, 274, 289–91
foster care 4, 6, 10, 13, 16, 29, 43, 45–6, 47, 68, 127, 132, 265

games 236–7
good practice 58, 65–7, 175, 179, 186
GP 61, 80, 125
grandparents 3, 11, 71–3
guardian-ad-litem 5

harm 4, 43, 48–58, 69
health 9, 21, 22, 34, 56, 71, 80, 94, 197–202, 221
  visitor 58, 70, 80, 159, 160
homelessness 41, 61, 69, 266
hospital 9, 210–15
hygiene 66, 196, 230

identity 143, 147, 155, 189, 207–8
illness 20, 61, 151, 202, 210, 224
image
  of disability 252–4
  self 34, 207–9
immunisation 198–9
impairment 36–7, 151
income support 22–3, 78, 267
Independent Living Fund 93
injury 5, 157–61, 167, 211
inspection 5, 45
instructions 248
insurance 65, 78, 230
integration 40, 91, 93
interpreting 89
interview 111, 130, 167, 275, 276–82

job applications 231, 276–83

key worker 58, 101, 128–30, 194

language 31, 251
  in books 208